THE JEWISH
BOOK OF LISTS

THE JEWISH BOOK OF LISTS

Joel Samberg

A CITADEL PRESS BOOK

Published by Carol Publishing Group

A Citadel Press Book
Published by Carol Publishing Group
Citadel Press is a registered trademark of Carol Communications, Inc.

Editorial, sales and distribution, rights and permissions inquiries should be addressed
to Carol Publishing Group, 120 Enterprise Avenue, Secaucus, N.J. 07094.

In Canada: Canadian Manda Group, One Atlantic Avenue, Suite 105, Toronto, Ontario
M6K 3E7

Carol Publishing Group books may be purchased in bulk at special discounts for sales
promotion, fund-raising, or educational purposes. Special editions can be created to
specifications. For details, contact Special Sales Department, Carol Publishing Group,
120 Enterprise Avenue, Secaucus, N.J. 07094.

Manufactured in the United States of America

10 9 8 7 6 5 4 3 2 1

Library of Congress Cataloging-in-Publication Data

Samberg, Joel.
    The Jewish book of lists / by Joel Samberg
        p.   cm.
    "A Citadel Press book."
    Includes bibliographical references.
    ISBN 0-8065-2034-5 (pbk.)
    1. Jewish—United States—Biography—Miscellanea.   I. Title.
E184.37.S36A5   1999
973'.04924—dc21   98–33831
                                                           CIP

For Bonnie, the tov of my mazel

CONTENTS

ACKNOWLEDGMENTS

Although most new journeys take people to places they've never been before and across the paths of people they've never met before, my initial journey barely took me out of Northern New Jersey. Still, I *did* see places I've never seen before, met people I never met before, learned things I never knew before, and wrestled with ideas I had never confronted before. With telephones, fax machines, libraries, bookstores, and the Internet, anything is possible these days—but only as long as there are knowledgeable and cooperative people on the other end of the line or, as the case may be, the other side of the desk.

There were dozens of such people throughout my journey. Unfortunately, several crossed my path much too quickly, or anonymously, for proper mention—but I thank them all anyway.

I have the pleasure of thanking the others here. The journey would not have been possible without them.

First I would like to thank fellow Verona kvetcher Mike Rose for the business card that got the whole thing started, and Mike Lewis at Carol Publishing for the actual business.

The following people provided invaluable assistance, leads, resources, feedback, ideas, and many other kinds of support: Gary Alt, Bob and Ira Andelman, Wendy Barrows, Harvey Berk of the B'nai B'rith communications office, Bob Buono, Murray and Nicholas Burns, Stacey Fine of the Society for Humanistic Judaism, Joanna Fisch of the Skirball Cultural Center, Suzen Relleg, Greg at the Sherwood Forest Club, Gretchen Shapiro Haas, Lyle Halvoran of the Greater North Dakota Association, Donald Hollanger of *Newsview*, Julie Kleeman of the Museum of Jewish Heritage, Dr. Julius Kelp, Virginia Liberatore, Rabbi Jack Moline of Congregation Agudas Achim, John McDonald and Roslyn Newman of W. T. Clarke for early inspiration, the staff at Rascals in West Orange, Renee and Jerry Samberg, Norman Sandfield of the International Jewish AIDS Network, Tom Truit, Lenora Ucko of the Museum of the Jewish Family and Rosenzweig Gallery, Mel Wacks of the Jewish-American Hall of Fame,

Barbara Ward of Toys "R" Us, J. Alan Winter of the Department of Sociology at Connecticut College, and Dr. Tzvee Zahavy of the Jewish Communications Network.

Finally, a tremendous thanks to that gentile pessel of nachas, Bill Freytag, whose valued collaboration on the unsold *Jerusalem: A Prophet Center* also led to an association with this publisher.

INTRODUCTION:
NOT ANOTHER BOOK
ABOUT JEWS!

When my mother first heard I had been asked to write this book, she said, "You? My son, who says many rabbis have less maturity than Howie Mandel? You, who will order a glass of milk with your hamburger just to see someone who keeps kosher get upset? You, the anti-Moses? You of all people are going to write a book about Jews?"

Well, those may not have been her *exact* words, but the sentiment was the same. If I recall correctly, what she said was, "Really, dear? A Jewish book? But I didn't even think you liked going to temple."

I don't. And that is part of why I wrote this book. My devotion to Judaism—the inner faith, if not quite the outward expression of it—has never been my problem; my problem has been an inability to share my feelings with others. I have inquired of one too many congregations (at least in the suburban Conservative and Reform Jewish circles of which I'm familiar) where it seems as if having an ornate temple is just as important as living a faithful life. I have spoken with one too many rabbis who seem to be rabbis only because they were able to pass the written and oral exams—with no measure of spirituality in the grading curve. I have met too many parents who try to make their homes Jewish by doing Jewish things (sending their kids to Hebrew school, giving them elaborate confirmations), without necessarily discussing or even trying to understand what it all means.

I know I'm Jewish and I like it. I feel part of something special: an age-old family with members in every corner of the globe. It is a faith much more interested in life than any other alternative. Our traditions, customs, and beliefs endeavor to help us get the most out of the limited resources we have in lives far too short on a planet far too troubled. It is a religion that has survived bigotry, jealousy, misunderstanding, wars, pogroms, attempted genocide, and more. Nothing can withstand that kind of abuse and not have something to it.

Still, whatever that *something* is has always been difficult for me to discuss with other people because the common frames of reference often concern the "organized" elements (temple memberships, for instance), and those are the elements that make me want to run to the nearest Chinese restaurant. Yet, not discussing it has been a burden as well. Too many people (my mother, for one) think I don't care all that much and I want people to know that I *do* care. More than that, not discussing it has robbed me of the intellectual growth enjoyed by those who do engage in such discussions and debates.

So, when the opportunity to write this book came along, I grabbed it. First, I knew it would enable me to share my admiration for, and appreciation of, the faith that got me here in the first place. Second, I knew it would give me the time and tools to do more research, interviews, and introspection than I've ever done on the subject. After all, Judaism is learning.

One might get the impression from these two self-directed requisites for writing this book that it is a book "about faith," or about "being a good Jew." It is actually a book about pride and nothing more. As far as I'm concerned, if you live a life of goodness and hope and charity, and you at least accept the fact that it is Judaism that has created one of the finest and most resilient trees of life in the history of mankind, then you already *are* a good Jew. The best, in fact.

This book (or any book) won't make anyone live a life of goodness and hope and charity—but it might convince a few that Judaism is and always has been something very special, something of which they can be proud. I wrote it for them. And for my children.

Others might get the impression that as a book about pride it is simply another book of lists. It is not. How interesting could that possibly be? Besides, there already are books of lists aplenty. I wanted to do something different. I wanted to write something fun. If Judaism is about life, and if life is as much about having fun as having meaning (as I believe it is), then Judaism should be fun, too. In planning this book I held forth that giving myself a little room for levity and adding a little sauce to the meat of the matter would enjoin many a reader to pick it up and share some of the pride. This book, I hope, will give its readers a brand new license to *kvel*.

Another objective of this book was to keep it strictly American. This I've done for two reasons. First, to do otherwise would create a book the size of Goliath, and ultimately as lame. What would ten thousand international names prove (most of whom would be unfamiliar anyway) that wouldn't be better proven with just an intriguing few-hundred Americans? (Many of those listed, of course, were immigrants who came to American shores as children, adults, or even as old people. A few Canadians may also have slipped into the listings, particularly if their work or popularity more or less makes them American anyway.) Second, an American focus is a very neat way of bolstering pride because Jews comprise only two percent of the U.S. population, yet our role has been significant, our contributions nothing short of spectacular.

Not long ago, one of the major Jewish governing bodies issued a declaration intimating that those of us who belong to the Conservative or Reform branches of Judaism are not Jewish under Jewish law. In other words, twenty-eight years, one Jewish wedding, and three Jewish children after my bar mitzvah, I discovered I was not Jewish. (I can't even find my bar mitzvah certificate to send back.) The governing body said, in essence, that my entire religious life was a deception because of the way Judaism had been taught and presented to me. In many ways, they're right, but not for the right reasons.

The sound bites regarding this story suggested that intermarriage, acceptance of homosexuality, and the popularity of non-kosher food were among the primary culprits. My response: One, I didn't intermarry. My wife is Jewish (allegedly). Two, I am not a homosexual. I do know a few, even some who are Jewish, but I really don't concern myself with their homosexuality. Three, I do love Chinese food, some of which is extremely non-kosher, but it hasn't changed my opinion of my faith, and don't feel as if God has changed His opinion of me.

The bottom line is that there will be those who take the "rules" very seriously, and they may not like this book at all. But is it really for them? Perhaps not. First of all, they don't need a booster shot of pride. Second, they simply don't care if some of the best Mafia gangsters in the movies were played by Jews. But neither do I wish them to think I hold their brand of religiousness in low regard. I don't. As it says in Psalms, "Behold, how good and pleasant it is for brethren to dwell together in unity."

But I can't please everyone, and the decisions of who to list in this book and who not to list (who is Jewish and who isn't) were not always easy ones to make. Included are a few whose mothers were Jewish but whose fathers were not, and a few whose fathers were Jewish but whose mothers were not, but who nonetheless grew up with a Jewish heritage and consider themselves Jewish. (Herman Wouk in *This Is My God* says history ascribes that blood is not decisive in the kinship between God and his chosen people—faith is.) I've included a few converts and a few crooks. I've even included Howard Stern (although he claims to be only half-Jewish).

Time, space, and the unavailability of certain key sources kept me from making this book the undisputed king of accuracy and comprehensiveness.

But it's darn close. I wish I had the luxury of covering lesser-known but no less important people in the fields of education, medicine and community leadership, regional artists and media people, and others, and I wish I could have covered more of the non-people categories such as schools, camps, community centers, divergent views on ancient and modern Jewry, historical personalities and more.

Alas, I've done what I could do, and it was enough, for the moment, to confirm that the pride I already felt was justified. Indeed, *more* than justified. I particularly enjoyed discovering quotes like Harold Kushner's in his book *To Life*: "God wants us to choose goodness, to exercise our uniquely human power to sanctify the world. He doesn't expect us to be perfect, but He expects us to be serious about our lives."

Which is not to say that I *still* don't have a problem with a few temples, a handful of rabbis, and a couple of Jewish laws. I'm just glad I am able to get it off my chest.

So what should I do with some of my criticism, now that I am deeper into the history and heritage thing than ever before? For everyone who criticizes me for some of the simplistic statements and broad generalizations I make in this book and in other discussions that hopefully will follow, there will be several more people who will tell me to put up or shut up: to practice what I preach and start my own little congregation in my living room, where dues would be low and anonymous, and plaques honoring big donors would be forbidden.

Maybe that's not such a bad idea. I might like that. My fellow congregants and I would discuss the Bible stories, how they came to be and what they mean for us today; we would debate the need to bring some of the old traditions up to speed with twenty-first-century realities. We would share what's in our hearts and minds instead of what's in our refrigerators and wallets. My little congregation would strive to make Judaism less of a business and even more of a celebration of life than it already is. Perhaps we'd even look for a wise old rabbi (over fifty, who has lived a little before taking his rabbinical exam) and maybe we'd purchase used Torah scrolls to keep the costs down. Unless we *really* wanted to bend tradition and do without a rabbi and Torah scrolls altogether. That, of course, would make us even more heathen in some eyes. But that's okay, because those eyes would never want to see one of our services anyway. First of all, to them we wouldn't even be Jewish. Second of all, after the service, we would probably order Chinese.

Just don't tell my mother.

How Many

- How many commandments are there throughout the Torah? **613**
- How old was Moses when he died? **120**
- How many wives and concubines did King Solomon Have? **1,000**
  (300 wives, 700 concubines)
- How many Jewish zealots took their own lives at Masada? **953**
- How many days are there in the Jewish year? **354**
  (It's based on the lunar cycle instead of the solar cycle.)
- How many days in the Jewish year are devoted to holidays and festivals? **53**
- How many letters are there in the Hebrew alphabet? **26**
  (Not including vowels, which are symbols and include about a dozen variations.)
- How may Jews are there in the world? **14 million**
- How many Jews are there in Israel? **5.8 million**
- How many Jews are there in the United States? **6 million**

THE JEWISH
BOOK OF LISTS

1

Oy Vey, Can You See

60 Jewish Events in American History, 1492 to 1790

*The twentieth-century ideals of Americans have been the ideals of
the Jews for more than twenty centuries.*
—Louis D. Brandeis

By 1492 Jews had already been expelled from many lands over the course
of many centuries.

It was the year of Christopher Columbus's first journey that Spain
ordered its Jews to convert to Christianity or leave the country. Many did
convert—at least ceremonially. Others left. Still others were killed.

And several signed on with Columbus.

When the explorer set sail from Spain with three ships and ninety
crewmen to find a new sea route to India, those few Jews on board could not
have known they were en route to a new world that would become home to
half of all the Jews on Earth, a nation that would nurture Jewish individuals
who would make momentous contributions to mankind. On the other hand,
neither could they have known that, even in that new nation, there would
still be significant challenges to their religious freedom and social equality.

Freedom and equality were not necessarily easy to come by, even in
America. But in the words of some of the greatest Jewish philosophers the
world over, so what else is new?

The first Jews on American soil, then, were the Conversos or Marranos
of Columbus's crew, so called because they had converted to Christianity
(although many continued to practice Judaism in secret) or because they
were labeled "pigs" (*marranos*) by their hostile and ignorant countrymen

back home. But it wasn't until 1740 that the story of American Jewry took a populous turn, when the first large group of Jewish Portuguese merchants arrived in Newport, Rhode Island, and created a thriving industry.

Thirty years later, with the seeds of revolution sown, Jews participated in the struggle for freedom in every way possible—in finance, medicine, advisory positions, even in battle. Like most colonists, Jews despised having their liberties limited by the British economic and political powers. By the time the War for Independence began, there were a thousand Jews in the colonies, many in a growing middle class of active and quite vocal shipping and merchant tradesmen and their families, and they wanted the freedom to *keep* on growing. The only way for that to happen, they knew, was if the American Colonies were an independent nation.

A Polish Jewish immigrant named Haym Salomon arrived in New Amsterdam in 1772. He learned of British tyranny quickly and quite personally, for he was arrested as a spy during the British occupation of the city. He then fled to Philadelphia, where he founded a brokerage firm and raised an estimated $200,000 for the revolutionary effort.

Salomon wasn't the only Jew to help finance the war, but he certainly was the most vigorously promotional about it, having turned it into a lucrative enterprise through advertising and highly competitive policies. He may, in fact, have been America's first entrepreneur-financier, consultant, and publicist all rolled into one. And while he may not have gone down in history as one of the Founding Fathers, it is partially due to the efforts of that early American Jew, and the efforts of many others during and since, that we now live in the greatest and freest nation on the planet.

1492

In Spain, **Luis de Santangel**, grandson of a Converso and comptroller of Aragon, talks Queen Isabella into giving Columbus permission to sail across the sea in search of a new trade route to the Indies. De Santangel thinks Spanish rule in the Indies will be financially beneficial to him.

The Niña, Pinta, and Santa Maria land in the Bahamas. Crew members include Jewish Conversos or Marranos such as voyage comptroller **Rodrigo Sanchez de Segovia** and interpreter **Luis de Torres**, both of whom are among the first Europeans to set foot in the New World.

1654

Jacob Barsimson, one of the first Jewish Europeans to settle on the continent of North America, arrives in New Amsterdam on a Dutch West India Company ship.

Twenty-three Portuguese Jews are expelled from Recife (part of what is now Brazil), and set sail for New Amsterdam on a Dutch schooner.

1655

New Amsterdam Governor Peter Stuyvesant forbids Jews in his city to trade with Indians, buy homes, open shops for retail trade, vote, hold office, or serve in the militia.

The Dutch Reformed Church in New Amsterdam sends an urgent note to the church's governing board back home asking them to convince the Dutch West India Company to expel the Jews from New Amsterdam. One of the complaints is that the Jews need too much money from them to survive.

The Dutch West India Company orders Stuyvesent to allow the Jews to remain, trade, and travel, as long as they provide for their own poor.

Jewish taxpayers in New Amsterdam pay 8 percent of the cost of the Waal (later Wall Street).

Harvard College requires its Christian students to study Hebrew, which the Puritans regard as a sacred language.

Abraham de Lucena arrives in New Amsterdam from Holland with a Torah which is used for the first organized Passover in the city.

Asser Levy, a Jewish butcher, and the aforementioned Jacob Barsimson determine to join the local militia to protect the city but are refused and even told to pay a special militia tax. They fight the ruling.

1656

A law is passed in New Amsterdam forbidding any religious denomination but the Dutch Reformed Church to worship in public. Four months later, the Dutch West India Company forces Stuyvesant to let Jews worship in their own homes.

After years of persistence and seeking loopholes in the law, New Amsterdam's Jews win the right to own real estate, trade freely, and avoid discriminatory taxes.

Jews win the right to own their own cemetery, and one is founded on the tip of Manhattan.

1659

For the first time, Jews in New Amsterdam begin to conduct regular services in rented homes.

1660

Asser Levy purchases property in Bruecklen (Brooklyn) and also becomes the first kosher butcher in the colonies.

1662

A group of Mennonites plan a colony in Pennsylvania and put on record their determination to exclude Catholics, Quakers, Puritans, and "usurious Jews."

1663

The Torah that New Amsterdam's Jews borrowed from a synagogue in Amsterdam is sent back home after many of them determine there will never be a prosperous community for them in the New World.

1667

Three years after taking possession of the Dutch colony of New Amsterdam, and renaming it New York, Britain bestows full rights of worship, trade, property ownership, and inheritance on all inhabitants. Jews are still forbidden to build synagogues and must pay a tax to support the Anglican Church.

1669

The Carolina Charter permits Jews in the colony to become merchants, traders, and landowners.

1671

Asser Levy loans money to the Lutheran Church to build their first house of worship in New York.

1684

The General Assembly in Rhode Island rules that Jews may live and do business in the colony, even though they are "strangers."

1688

A Jew known only as **Solomon** is prosecuted in Essex County, Massachusetts, for traveling on a Sunday.

Two Jewish merchants, **Isaac Abraham** and **Solomon Franco**, viewed by some in New Hampshire as undesirable strangers, are given strong warnings to leave the colony.

1718

In three of New York's seven wards, Jews begin serving as constables.

1727

The General Assembly in New York votes that Jews no longer have to include the words "on the true faith of a Christian" in any oaths they take.

1730

The Jews of New York establish their first synagogue, Shearith Israel, meaning Remnant of Israel.

1731

The first Jewish education initiative controlled by a congregation is undertaken in New York.

1733

Sixty-seven poverty-stricken German and Polish Jews arrive in Savannah, Georgia, from London, where wealthy Jews had raised funds to finance their emigration to the colonies.

1734

Georgia Governor James Oglethorpe lets his colony's Jews, several dozen of whom had just arrived, settle on the fringes of his own land, rent a house for religious services, and use a plot of land for a Jewish cemetery.

1737

The election of a candidate to the New York colonial assembly is successfully challenged on the grounds that some votes were cast by Jews.

1740

Britain's Uniform Naturalization Act qualifies all alien residents in the colonies to become citizens if they were born in the colonies or had resided in a British colony for seven years, and if they swear loyalty to the Crown.

1745

Pennsylvania's first Jewish congregation is founded.

1752

Duarte Lopez arrives in Newport, Rhode Island, assumes his original first name, Aaron, remarries his wife in a traditional Jewish ceremony, and lays plans for a whaling business that will soon become one of the most successful nautical enterprises in Newport's colonial history.

1754

Two thousand pound Liberty Bell arrives in Philadelphia from England aboard a ship owned by Jewish merchants **Nathan Levy** and **David Frank**.

1759

In Newport, ground is broken for the second synagogue to be built in America.

1761

The first Jewish holiday prayer book created in America is printed and published in New York.

1763

The Jews of Newport celebrate the dedication of the Yeshuat Israel temple, meaning Salvation of Israel (today called the Touro Synagogue).

A Jewish indigo expert from London, **Moses Londo,** is appointed South Carolina's inspector general for indigo, the colony's second most important crop after rice.

Jewish traders **Levy Solomon** of New York and **Levey A. Levey** of Pennsylvania are killed near Fort Pitt during Pontiac's Rebellion.

1765

Two Jews are elected postal officials in Savannah, Georgia.

1768

Jewish businessman **Isaac Moses** cofounds the New York Chamber of Commerce.

Gershom Mendes Seixas, the first native-born rabbi, is appointed spiritual leader of Congregation Shearith Israel in New York.

1769

General Don Alejandro O'Reilly becomes governor of the Louisiana Territory under Spain and institutes a local inquisition, stripping all prosperous New Orleans Jews of their wealth and expelling them from the city. The Monsanto Company, a successful retail and wholesale firm owned by Jewish businessman **Isaac Monsanto,** is put out of business.

1772

Haym Salomon arrives in New York from Poland. One of his first jobs is to feed American prisoners of war.

1775

At the onset of rebellion against British rule, the Americans invade Canada. **David Franks,** a Jewish businessman in Montreal, lends the Americans money, joins their cause, and becomes a major in the Continental Army.

Look closely at a dollar bill and you'll see that the thirteen stars above the bald eagle's head form a Star of David. They represent the original thirteen colonies, but some historians say the star was a gesture of gratitude to Haym Salomon, the Jewish businessman who helped finance the Revolutionary effort.
Author's Collection

1774

Isaac Abraham becomes the first Jew in America to become a doctor through training received in the colonies.

Jewish merchant Joseph Simon donates funds to Boston to help fight against the British blockade.

1776

A Jewish patriot named Francis Salvador, who had joined South Carolina's provincial congress two years earlier, becomes the first Jew to hold state legislative office when the congress declares itself to be the state general assembly.

Francis Salvador becomes the first American Jew to die in the struggle for independence when he is killed by Indians incited by the British.

1777

New York adopts a constitution that declares "the free exercise and enjoyment of religious profession and worship, without discrimination or preference, shall forever be allowed within this state to all mankind."

A Jewish military man named Mordecai Sheftall is given the rank of colonel in the militia of Georgia and becomes commissary general of purchases and issues.

Joseph Simon donates money to start a messenger service between Lancaster, Pennsylvania, and Washington's army.

1778

Moses Levy becomes the first American Jew to qualify as a lawyer in the United States. He is admitted to the Pennsylvania bar.

1779

A Jewish soldier, **Benjamin Nones**, is cited by his captain for exceptional gallantry at the siege of Savannah.

1787

Merchant **Jonas Phillips** of Philadelphia and New York sends a passionately worded note to the Constitutional Convention to remind everyone involved that all rights guaranteed by the Constitution, such as the right to hold public office and the right of worship, must be afforded to *all* citizens, including Jews.

1788

Ancient Jewish history is included in a sermon given before both houses of the New Hampshire legislature. It is titled "The Republic of the Israelites as Example to the American States."

1789

Congress submits to the states for ratification twelve amendments to the Constitution. Ten are ratified and become known as the Bill of Rights. The first says, in part, "Congress shall make no law respecting an establishment of religion or prohibiting the free exercise thereof."

Rabbi Seixas of Shearith Israel in New York is one of fourteen clergymen to participate in the inauguration of George Washington as president of the United States.

1790

Jacob Cohen, president of Beth Elohim synagogue in Charleston, South Carolina, writes a letter to George Washington that says the government's commitment to liberty had raised Jews from a "state of political degradation and grievous oppression" which they faced in almost every other part of the world. "Peculiar and extraordinary reason have we...to be attached to the free and generous constitutions of our respective states, and indebted to you and your heroic deeds for making it possible."

There have been many Jewish-American successes, defeats, accomplishments, failures, dreams, and nightmares ever since. While there are far too many to present in a single list, it is quite clear indeed that Jews and Jewish ideals have helped make this nation great, and that's a fact that has been cast in stone many times. Or metal, as the case may be: The Liberty Bell in Philadelphia is inscribed with a passage from Leviticus, the Third Book of Moses: "Proclaim liberty throughout all the land unto all the inhabitants

Commodore Uriah Phillips Levy. Courtesy the U.S. Naval Academy Museum

Zionist, lawyer, reformer, crusader, and U.S. Supreme Court justice; in 1916 Louis Brandeis became the first Jew on the high bench. Courtesy The American Jewish Archives, Hebrew Union College, Cincinnati

thereof." A statue in Chicago shows George Washington clasping hands with Haym Salomon. Many other statues, monuments, edifices, and documents offer proof of Jewish contributions to our nation's growth.

Since the days of David Franks, a major in the Continental Army in 1775, many American Jewish soldiers, sailors, and military strategists have helped to defend the nation. In the mid-1800s, **Uriah Phillips Levy** commanded the U.S. fleet in the Mediterranean and later spent much time trying to eradicate corporal punishment. **Claude Bloch** became commander in chief of the U.S. fleet in 1938. The U.S. Navy entered the atomic age in 1954 with the nuclear-powered submarine, USS *Nautilus,* developed by Admiral **Hyman Rickover**, a skilled engineer. In the Vietnam era **Herbert Schandler** became one of the most highly decorated soldiers, with three Bronze Stars and three Vietnam Crosses of Gallantry.

And since the days of Francis Salvador, who was the first Jew to hold a legislative office in 1776, Jews have played a major role in American politics. The first Jew to serve on the Supreme Court was **Louis D. Brandeis**, an associate justice from 1916 to 1939. Brandeis opposed big business abuses, distrusted big government, and represented groups like laborers, who traditionally were powerless.

Other Jewish Supreme Court justices include **Arthur Goldberg** (1962–1965), **Benjamin Nathan Cardoza** (1932–1938), **Abe Fortas**

(1965–1969), **Felix Frankfurter** (1939–1962), **Ruth Bader Ginsberg,** the first Jewish woman on the High Court (1993–   ), and **Stephen G. Breyer** (1994–   ).

Oscar Solomon Straus was the first Jewish presidential cabinet member, serving as secretary of commerce and labor under Theodore Roosevelt from 1906 to 1909.

Jacob Javits was a four-term United States senator who introduced the War Powers Act of 1973, limiting a president's ability to wage war without full congressional approval.

Henry Kissinger was President Richard Nixon's national security advisor and, beginning in 1973, secretary of state, a position he held throughout the Ford administration. In 1973, he was awarded the Nobel Peace Prize for his role in the negotiations to end the war in Vietnam.

Bella Abzug was the first Jewish woman elected to the U.S. Congress, serving in the House of Representatives from 1971 to 1977.

Edward I. Koch served as mayor of the world's international city, New York, from 1978 to 1989. He presided with inimitable style and boundless energy ("How'm I doing?"), and kept us up to date on his achievements in such books as *Citizen Koch* and *Ed Koch on Everything.*

Jews have made an indelible impression on American politics despite the relative small number of Jewish politicians. Today, 35 of the 535 members of Congress are Jewish, representing sixteen states and including ten United States senators and twenty-five state representatives. (Twenty-four of them are split almost evenly between New York and California.)

While Jews comprise just 2 percent of the American population, they make up more than 6 percent of the Congress. That fact alone may not guarantee all Jews in America and abroad the best lives, grandest liberties, or easiest pursuits of happiness, but in the words of some the greatest Jewish philosophers, it can't hurt, either.

More Notable Events in Jewish-American History

• *1819* English watchmaker Joseph Jonas, who had earlier traveled to the Ohio wilderness from New York, is joined by enough Jewish "pioneers" to be able to hold the first official Jewish religious ceremony (on Rosh Hashanah) beyond the East Coast.

• *1860* Morris Raphael is the first rabbi to lead the opening prayer for a session of the U.S. congress.

• *1890* Women's rights activist Hannaii Greenbaum Solomon organizes the Jewish Women's Congress as part of the World's Fair, and the organization later becomes the National Council of Jewish Women.

• *1905* A mammoth four-year undertaking for the benefit of Jewish scholarship is successfully completed by the publication of the first Jewish Encyclopedia, overseen by Dr. Isidor Singer.

• *1909* Artist Victor David Brenner designs the Lincoln penny, a design that is used to this day.

• *1917* The recently founded Jewish Publication Society of America completes an English translation of the Bible. It becomes the most widely accepted version among English-speaking Jews.

• *1924* The Hillel foundation is established to help Jewish college students. A Christian professor in Illinois, Edward Chauncey Baldwin, suggests its need to rabbinical student Benjamin Frankel, who then persuades the B'nai B'rith to sponsor its creation at the University of Illinois. The Hillel foundation soon becomes a national organization.

• *1935* The Central Conference of American Rabbis repeals a long-standing policy against Zionism.

• *1943* The United States Navy launches the USS *Levy*, an escort-destroyer, named after famed navy commodore Uriah Phillips Levy.

• *1970* The Jewish population in the United States reaches six million, giving this country the largest Jewish community in the world.

2

Jewish Precedents

A List of 19 "Firsts"

*My search has brought me to Judaism. I believe it offers the best
answers to the terrible problem of how to achieve goodness among
a race of beings not strongly predisposed to its achievement.*
—Dennis Prager, *The Nine Questions People Ask About Judaism*

The debate rages on: Were the Jews the first to introduce God to the
world? If so, that gift was only the first in an impressive list of Jewish
firsts. If not, we've more than made up for it in the last two hundred years in
America alone.

Jewish-American firsts effectively highlight the vast social and commercial
interests for which American Jews have shared their skills and fortitude. It also
gives us more specific evidence of where to place our pride. After all, while we
may never know for certain whether Abraham was really the first person to
figure out there was something more powerful than a stone statue, we know
for darn sure that Levi Strauss came out with the first real pair of blue jeans.

Many Jewish-American firsts can be attributed to age-old Judaic
traditions of charity, education, self-improvement, enterprise, even
chutzpah. All told, they may not compare with the introduction of God, but
then again, after that almost everything looks like a footnote.

The first department store was opened in Vincennes, Indiana, in 1842 by
Adam Gimbel.

The first drugstore was opened in Charleston, South Carolina, in 1864 by **Dr.
David De Leon.**

The first professional baseball player, **Lipman Pike,** was paid $20 a week in
1866 by the Philadelphia Athletics.

Americans are forever in blue jeans thanks to visionary businessman Levi Strauss. Courtesy Levi Strauss & Co.

The first doctor to perform an appendectomy in the United States was **Simon Baruch,** in the 1870s.

The first denim jeans to be made and sold in America were the product of a company founded by **Levi Strauss.** Strauss and a partner in the venture, Jacob Davis, received a patent for the "riveted-waist overalls" in 1873.

The first free kindergarten class was established in 1877 by **Felix Adler.**

The first doctor to use cocaine as an anesthetic was eye surgeon **Carl Koeller,** in 1884.

The first person to form a collegiate woman's basketball team, ushering in a new era in sports in 1901, was **Senda Berenson,** physical education director at Smith College in Northhampton, Mass.

The first American to win the Nobel Prize in physics was **Albert A. Michelson,** who, in 1907, received the honor for his discovery of accurate methods of measuring the speed of light.

The first national mail-order catalog was developed and put into use in 1908 by **Julius Rosenwald,** cofounder of the Sears, Roebuck Company.

The first shopping cart was developed by **Murray Candib**'s Canco Enterprises in the 1940s. As founder and president of King's Department Stores, Candib also pioneered self-service discount stores and centralized checkout.

The first American musician to perform in the Soviet Union after World War II was violinist **Yehudi Menuhin,** in 1945.

The Philadelphia Orchestra presented the first symphonic concert shown on American TV in 1948 under the direction of conductor **Eugene Ormandy.**

The ballot of David Wolf: Not much time to think about his choice, but lots of space in which to cast it. Courtesy NASA

The first practical birth control pill was developed in the 1950s by **Dr. Gregory Goodwin Pincus**, with his collaborator, Dr. M. C. Chiang.

The first American TV news correspondent to have official Soviet permission to work in the USSR was **Irving R. Levine** of NBC, who, in the late 1950s, personally appealed to Nikita Khrushchev after covering a visit by American agriculturists.

The first commissioner of cultural affairs for New York City was film producer and writer **Dore Schary**, appointed in 1970.

The first American symphony orchestra to perform in China, the Philadelphia Orchestra, did so in 1973 under the direction of **Eugene Ormandy**.

The first American woman to win a Nobel Prize in science was **Roselyn S. Yalow**, who in 1977 received the honor for her development of radioimmunoassays of peptide hormones (having to do with procedures to measure substances in blood and other body fluids).

The first American to cast a vote from outer space was Jewish astronaut **David Wolf**, aboard the Russian space station *Mir*, in November 1997.

3

The Wanderers

Jewish Population Statistics

Let me not wander from thy commandments.
—Psalms

More Jews work in the Empire State Building than live in the states of North Dakota and South Dakota combined. Oddly enough, the Dakotas have a richer Jewish history than most of the states west of the Mississippi.

A vast majority of turn-of-the-century Jews who attempted life and livelihood in America's heartland did so in North Dakota and South Dakota between 1880 and 1910. There were several organized settlements of Jewish families and groups willing to develop government and railroad lands in exchange for a piece of frontier land to work and call their own. The first major effort, called Painted Woods, was a project conceived by Rabbi Judah Wechsler of St. Paul, Minnesota. Weschler had arranged a land grant on a spread beside the Missouri River. A group of Russian immigrant families settled there in 1882.

There were articles about Painted Woods in the Jewish press at the time, and dozens of other families, mostly Russian and Romanian immigrants, read about it and traveled to the Dakotas to take part in the enterprise. (There is a wonderful account of one family's Dakota experience in a book called *Rachel Calof's Story: Jewish Homesteader on the Northern Plains,* published in 1995 by Indiana University Press.)

Today, there are about six hundred Jews in North Dakota, four hundred in South Dakota, and five hundred in Idaho. (Another irony is that the first Jewish governor in the United States was Idaho's Moses Alexander, elected on

January 4, 1915.) Generally speaking, Jews settle where there are other Jews and where there are good opportunities in their chosen fields. There are at least four states that fit the bill better than the other forty-six, but there are Jews in every state of the union. Perhaps travelers and relocators trust the old maxim that no matter where you are, if you find another Jew, you're home.

There are almost six million Jews in the United States, which is only 2 percent of the population. In light of the enormous contributions Jews have made to American society and culture, 2 percent sounds impossibly low, but it's true.

Jewish Populations by State (1990)

State	Jewish Population	State Population
Alabama	9,000	4,253,000
Alaska	3,000	604,000
Arizona	72,000	4,218,000
Arkansas	1,700	2,484,000
California	921,000	31,589,000
Colorado	51,500	31,589,000
Connecticut	97,000	3,275,000
Delaware	13,500	717,000
Washington D.C.	25,500	554,000
Florida	644,000	14,166,000
Georgia	84,000	7,201,000
Hawaii	7,000	1,187,000
Idaho	500	1,163,000
Illinois	268,000	11,830,000
Indiana	18,000	5,803,000
Iowa	6,000	2,842,000
Kansas	14,500	2,565,000
Kentucky	11,000	3,869,000
Louisiana	16,500	4,342,000
Maine	7,500	1,241,000
Maryland	212,000	5,042,000
Massachusetts	268,000	6,074,000
Michigan	107,000	9,549,000
Minnesota	42,000	4,610,000
Mississippi	1,400	2,697,000
Missouri	62,000	5,324,000
Montana	800	870,000
Nebraska	7,000	1,637,000

Nevada	21,000	1,530,000
New Hampshire	9,500	1,148,000
New Jersey	435,000	7,945,000
New Mexico	9,000	1,685,000
New York	1,652,000	18,136,000
North Carolina	21,500	7,195,000
North Dakota	600	641,000
Ohio	129,000	11,151,000
Oklahoma	5,400	3,278,000
Oregon	19,500	3,141,000
Pennsylvania	325,000	12,072,000
Rhode Island	16,000	990,000
South Carolina	9,000	3,673,000
South Dakota	400	729,000
Tennessee	18,000	5,256,000
Texas	112,500	18,724,000
Utah	4,300	1,951,000
Vermont	5,700	585,000
Virginia	74,500	6,618,000
Washington	34,000	5,431,000
West Virginia	2,200	1,828,000
Wisconsin	28,500	5,123,000
Wyoming	500	480,000

SOURCE: *The American Jewish Yearbook,* 1997

Number of Jewish synagogues (all branches) in the four states with the largest, and the four with the smallest, Jewish populations:

California	292
Florida	218
Idaho	2
New Jersey	260
New York	1,277
North Dakota	4
South Dakota	5
Wyoming	2

SOURCE: *The National Directory of Churches, Synagogues and Other Houses of Worship,* Gale Research, 1994

Approximate number of major Jewish courses of study offered at the university level:

California	245 at 24 campuses
Florida	86 at 11 campuses
Idaho	0
New Jersey	65 at 11 campuses
New York	1,160 at 40 campuses
North Dakota	0
South Dakota	0
Wyoming	0

SOURCE: *The Hillel Guide to Jewish Life on Campus,* Random House, 1998

Approximate number of delicatessens where you can get a hot pastrami on rye:

California	3,320
Florida	1,090
Idaho	40
New Jersey	2,759
New York	4,440
North Dakota	21
South Dakota	4
Wyoming	27

SOURCE: *GTE SuperPages Interactive Services,* 1998

4

The Book of Numbers

77 Jewish-American Novelists, Storytellers, and Columnists Who Had an Impact on America...Literally

I met a Jew who had grown up in a yeshiva and knew large sections of the Talmud by heart. I met a Jew who was an atheist. I met a Jew who owned a clothing store with hundreds of employees, and I met a Jew who was an ardent communist....It was all the same man.

—Isaac Bashevis Singer

Isaac Asimov loved cemeteries as a child. He thought of them as parks without all the annoying *living* people getting in the way. They were his own personal playgrounds, where his imagination ran faster than his legs could navigate around the mysterious and silent tombstones.

A bit bizarre, perhaps, but whatever the internal and environmental influences on his life and career, they must be endorsed, for Asimov has been one of the most prolific Jewish-American writers in history, with more than 200 books to his credit. He wrote fact and fiction, for teenagers and adults, on history, astronomy, the Bible, humor, mythology and, of course, science fiction. His was an imagination and passion (if not necessarily output) consistent with many of the greatest Jewish-American writers throughout the century.

There have been Jews in America as long as there has been an America—and a few Jewish writers, as well. But Jewish-American writing is primarily a twentieth-century story.

More important than the number of American novelists, essayists, and historians of Jewish descent are the enduring novels, essays, and histories they have given us. To be sure, not all the works of these talented people are about Jews, Judaism, or the Jewish-American experience. Indeed, their words concern everything from reincarnation (Stanley Elkin's *George Mills*), to baseball (Bernard Malamud's *The Natural*), to military madness (Joseph Heller's *Catch-22*). And so on.

Still, these writers may, in fact, bring something special to their work that comes from being Jewish—or at least from having a Jewish heritage. Just what that something special is, and what it means, has been open to some the most spirited debates in literary and critical circles for decades. We may never know the answer—but we'll have a grand ol' time looking for it as we visit the Jewish landmarks along a literary road.

Beginning with the immigrant experience at the turn of the nineteenth-century, Jewish writers in America have had intriguing and troubling topics and issues to write about. Later, when estrangement, alienation, assimilation, and the struggle between the traditional and the modern became issues, Jewish writers had entirely new stories, notions, ideas, events, people, problems, challenges, needs, anxieties, larks, loves, and losses to write about. Some contemporary Jewish-American writers are dealing with the feminist-Jewish experience, the gay-Jewish experience—and interestingly enough, the experience of dealing with their own children who have adopted many of the traditions and customs of their ancestors, traditions that they themselves have often overlooked.

Some of the writers feel their driving forces stem from the sting their inner worlds experience when they get slapped in the face by reality. "I couldn't be the sort of Jew that my pious parents wanted to make of me," the great storyteller Isaac Bashevis Singer has said. "I aspired to the big, free world, but I understood already early on that the world was nowhere near as big and as free as I had envisioned. Ideas attacked me like locusts, emotions stormed within me when I was awake and while I slept. I had only one way to express all of that: with my pen, and my Yiddish language."

Then there are those who place greater value on religion as a motivational force for their work. "But for the Torah we are the most insignificant of nations," wrote Herman Wouk, author of *This Is My God, Marjorie Morningstar,* and *The Winds of War,* among other novels and plays. "Our place in the world, I believe, depends on what we contribute to mankind. We have contributed the Torah, the Mosaic vision of right conduct and of first and last things."

On the other hand, there are a few who steadfastly refuse to attribute their creativity and success to being Jewish. Saul Bellow, Pulitzer Prize-winning author of *Humboldt's Gift,* has said that pain is fundamentally the same for everyone. Never had he consciously written as a Jew, he said, but only as Saul Bellow. Never did he attempt to make himself Jewish or to write for Jews exclusively: "This whole Jewish writer business is sheer invention— by the media, by critics and by 'scholars.' I'm well aware of being Jewish and also of being an American and of being a writer. But I'm also a hockey fan, a fact which nobody ever mentions."

Many of the writers on this list are winners of Nobel and Pulitzer prizes and other awards. More significantly, they represent thousands of great stories and ideas. And even beyond their own works of literature, there are hundreds of fabulous stories about the writers themselves, well worth reading. For example, Paul Cowen grew up with no knowledge of his Jewish heritage and ended up marrying a Protestant woman who eventually converted to Judaism and became a rabbi; novelist Tillie Olsen worked as a domestic servant and raised four daughters before making time to write after reaching her forties; essayist Calvin Trillin began his career at *Time* magazine, where he wrote a religion column that he little enjoyed, so he started to prefix everything he wrote with the word "alleged," as in "the alleged parting of the Red Sea" and "the alleged Crucifixion." That promptly got him fired.

So here, for your reading pleasure, is a list of the Jewish-American writers who have made the biggest impact on American culture.

Allegedly.

David Adler (1947–) One of the top children's authors, he takes experiences from his own childhood and from his own children and turns them into bestsellers, including the successful *Cam Jansen* series. Other series include the *Fourth Floor Twins* and *Jeffrey's Ghost,* and he has written many picture books on Chanukah, Passover, the Bible, and Chasidic tales.

Shalom Aleichem (1859–1916) Shalom Rabinovich began his career in 1883 by writing satirical essays about local politics for a newspaper and signing them Shalom Aleichem, meaning Hello There. He used other pseudonyms, too, such as Baron Ogre and Robber Jew, but Shalom Aleichem is what he used on his most famous stories about Tevye the Dairyman and other tales, which became the inspiration for the stage play and subsequent film *Fiddler on the Roof.* In the United States he was called a Yiddish Mark Twain.

Shalom Asch (1880–1957) Wrote about the Jewish underbelly. Some Jews disliked him because of his negative portrayals. Works include *The War Goes On, Uncle Moses, Three Cities.*

Isaac Asimov (1920–1992) Perhaps best known in fiction for his *I, Robot*

Saul Bellow. Courtesy The National Foundation for Jewish Culture; photo by Fay Godwin

and Foundation trilogy: *Foundation, Foundation Empire, Second Foundation.* But his nonfiction is even more impressive, including *The Genetic Code, The Human Body, The Human Brain,* and more.

Saul Bellow   His bestselling *Herzog,* published in 1964 and generally considered a masterpiece, is about a Jewish Everyman seeking self-understanding. He won a Pulitzer in 1975 for *Humboldt's Gift* and a Nobel Prize for Literature in 1976.

David Berg (1920–   )   *Mad* magazine humorist who covered just about every subject under the sun in such books as *Mad's Dave Berg Looks at People, Mad's Dave Berg Looks at Living, Mad's Dave Berg Looks at Things.* An artist as well, his illustrated *My Friend G-D* was received enthusiastically nationwide.

Anne Bernays (1930–   )   Even if she hadn't been the great-niece of Sigmund Freud, she might have written *Providence Indeed, Short Pleasures, Growing Up Rich, The School Book,* and other interesting books, but maybe being Sigmund Freud's niece added a little spice.

Judy Blume (1938–   )   Called controversial for tackling tough subjects for kids like divorce and sexual awareness with remarkable openness and honesty. The controversy hasn't stopped her from becoming one of the most successful juvenile authors in history. Her books include *Are You There God, It's Me Margaret, Tales of a Fourth Grade Nothing,* and *Starring Sally J. Friedman as Herself.* She has won zillions of awards.

Daniel Boorstin   One of the top author–historians of the 1950s and 1960s, whose books include *The Americans: The Colonial Experience* and *The Decline of Radicalism, From Appomattox to the Moon*. In 1983 he wrote *The Discoverers*, an educational book for children that was fun to read, and in a genre he found he enjoyed very much.

Art Buchwald (1925–   )   Humorist whose columns spoofing politics and modern life in general have appeared in the *Washington Post* and more than five hundred other newspapers. His books, equally irreverent and opinionated, include *The Buchwald Stops Here, I Am Not a Crook, While Reagan Slept, Have I Ever Lied to You?*

Abraham Cahan (1860–1951)   *The Rise of David Levinsky* is generally considered to be the first important Jewish-American novel, written in 1917. Cahan was a long-time editor of the *Jewish Daily Forward,* and he also worked as a teacher and labor organizer. His works describe the experiences of Jewish immigrants in the melting pot, such as *Yekl: A Tale of the New York Ghetto.* He wrote in English and Yiddish.

Roger Caras (1928–   )   As popular on TV and radio as he is in the book stores, with over fifty books on animals that are both entertaining and in-formative, including *Mammals, Vanishing Wildlife,* and *Skunk for a Day.*

Robert Cohen (1957–   )   Sometimes cited as a likely heir to Saul Bellow and Philip Roth with his pointedly humorous writing. His novels include *The Organ Builder* and *The Here and Now;* his short fiction has appeared in *Harper's, Gentleman's Quarterly,* and *Paris Review.* He also teaches at Harvard.

Norman Cousins (1912–1990)   Writer, editor, lecturer, peace advocate. He's been on staff at the *New York Evening Post* and *Saturday Review,* lectured in India and Pakistan, and wrote *Who Speaks for Man* and *The Religious Beliefs of the Founding Fathers.*

Paul Cowan (1940–1988)   *An Orphan in History* is a fascinating account of his personal odyssey of rediscovering his heritage and faith in Judaism when he was already a grown man. He was a longtime *Village Voice* reporter and antiwar activist, and he also wrote *The Tribes of America* and *The Making of an Unamerican.*

Frederic Danny (1905–1982) and **Manfred B. Lee** (1905–1971)   Cousins who created the detective character Ellery Queen and founded *Ellery Queen's Mystery Magazine.*

E. L. Doctorow   Won a National Book Critics Circle Award in 1975 for *Ragtime.* He also wrote *The Book of Daniel* and *World's Fair* and is one of the best at "fictive biography," in which real people make appearances in fiction (such as Henry Ford, Scott Joplin, Emma Goldman).

Stanley Elkin (1930–1995)   Known for satire, symbolism, and black humor, his works include *The Living End* and *George Mills*. The former is about the death of an ordinary man and how God judges him, the latter covers a thousand years of a man's continual reincarnations.

Nora Ephron (1941–   )   Author of the novel *Heartburn*. Proudly wearing the critical tag of an acerbic, she has written for *Esquire* and *New York* magazine and published several collections of her articles, including *Wallflower at the Orgy* and *Scribble, Scribble: Notes on the Media*. She also directed the movie *This Is My Life*, which she wrote (based on someone else's book) with her sister Delia, and directed and cowrote *Sleepless in Seattle*.

Leslie Epstein (1938–   )   His recent *Pandemonium* has been called "a lunatic comedy" with "moral seriousness." Other works are *P. D. Kimerakov, The Steinway Quintet Plus Four, King of the Jews*, and *Goldkorn Tales*, a novella. Some of the reviews describing his highly stylized work talk of "unbreakable moral dilemmas" and "mysteries of humanity and mortality."

Howard Fast (1914–   )   From penetrating character studies to sweeping generational sagas—and everything in-between. His novels include *Citizen Tom Paine, Spartacus, The Immigrants, The Outsider, The Crossing*, and *Freedom Road*.

Edna Ferber (1884–1968)   Frequent topic was romance and longing in places as diverse as Wisconsin and Alaska. Polish immigrants were another favorite. Her novels include *Fanny Herself, Show Boat, American Beauty*, and *So Big*, for which she won the Pulitzer Prize in 1924.

Bruce Jay Friedman (1930–   )   Dark–humor novelist, short story writer, playwright, and screenwriter whose work has been called a Twilight Zone with Charlie Chaplin in it. His books include *A Mother's Kisses, Stern, Tokyo Woes*, and *The Current Climate*, and his screenplays include *Stir Crazy* and *Dr. Detroit*.

Herbert Gold (1924–   )   One of the best at making emotional drama out of ordinary life. A prolific chronicler of modern America, his fiction includes *The Great American Jackpot, True Love, A Girl of Forty, Mister White Eyes*, and the nonfiction *My Last Two Thousand Years*, an exploration of how Jewish history relates to his own personal history.

Gloria Goldreich (1934–   )   Won the National Jewish Book Award for the enormously popular *Leah's Journey*, which was followed by *Leah's Children, Four Days, This Burning Harvest, This Promised Land*, and *Season of Discovery*.

Lois Gould   Popular contemporary fiction writer whose words and stories critics have called "gorgeous," "lyric," "audacious," "fascinating," "crisp," and "enchanting." Her novels include *Subject to Change, la Presidenta, A Sea-Change, Final Analysis, Necessary Objects, Such Good Friends,* and *Medusa's Gift.* Her first book was *Sensible Childbirth: The Case Against Natural Childbirth* (1962).

Gerald Green (1922–   )   Evocatively recreated people and places in *To Brooklyn With Love, The Heartless Light, The Last Angry Man, The Lotus Eaters, The Sword and the Sun,* and then he chillingly recreated the horrors of the Hitler era for TV with the miniseries *Holocaust.* He had many positions earlier in his career with NBC News.

Joanne Greenberg (1932–   )   Mushroomed onto the scene overnight with *I Never Promised You a Rose Garden.* Her fiction, highly praised, can hardly be classified into one specific genre, which has added to the praise. She's written on farm life, deafness, academia, doctors, and more. "Astonishingly varied" is how one critic put it. Her books include *The Monday Voices, Rites of Passage,* and *Seasons of Delight.*

Dan Greenburg (1936–   )   Hugely popular children's book author–The Zack Files series–who began that part of his career only after years of writing funny, sexy thrillers, wry books of observation, and satirical magazine articles. His books include *Love Kills, Kiss My Firm but Pliant Lips, Chewsday,* and *How to Avoid Love and Marriage.* His first book was *How to Be a Jewish Mother,* which his mother loved, with reservations.

Bette Greene (1934–   )   Winner of the New York Times Outstanding Book Award for *The Summer of My German Soldier,* which was made into a highly rated TV movie in 1978. Other juvenile works include *Morning Is a Long Time Coming, Philip Hall Likes Me, I Reckon Maybe;* and *Them That Glitter and Them That Don't.* She has received the Parents' Choice Award.

Robert Greenfield   His *Temple* was a critical yet admiring look at the sometimes claustrophobic world of Orthodox American Jewry in the 1970s. Other books include *S.T.P.: A Journey Through America With the Rolling Stones, The Spiritual Supermarket,* and *Haymon's Crowd.* He had worked for a time as the London bureau chief of *Rolling Stone* magazine, and music plays a big part in all his writing.

Joseph Heller (1923–   )   Has the distinction of creating one of the world's most famous phrases, from the book of the same name: *Catch-22.* Other distinctions are a shelf of engrossing stories in such novels as *Something Happened, Good As Gold,* and *God Knows,* a first-person account of the biblical David.

Nat Hentoff (1925–   )   Through his *Village Voice* and *New Yorker* pieces he constantly reminded us of our rights and liberties under the U.S.

Constitution. His novels include *This School Is Driving Me Crazy, The Man From Internal Affairs, The Day They Came to Arrest the Book,* and *Jazz Country.*

Irving Howe (1920–1993)   Brilliant educator, literary critic, and nonfiction author. He taught at Brandeis and Stanford and has lectured on Judaism all over the country. His books include *The Critical Point, Steady Work, Thomas Hardy, World of Our Fathers: The Journey of the Eastern European Jews to America and the Life They Made and Found,* and *Favorite Jewish Stories.*

Erica Jong (1942–   )   *How to Save Your Own Life, Parachutes and Kisses,* but most famously, *Fear of Flying,* about a neurotic woman in New York who embarks on an energetic two-week sexual experience with a Brit.

Sue Kaufman (1926–1977)   She turned big-city neurotics into poetic heroines. Many of her fictional characters are described as living on the edge of insanity. *Falling Bodies, Diary of a Mad Housewife,* and *The Headshrinker's Tale* are among her novels.

Alfred Kazin   (1915–1998)   A novelist, social observer, and critic who brought a lyrical and anecdotal quality to everything he wrote. His works include *On Native Grounds, The Inmost Leaf, Contemporaries, Starting Out in the Thirties,* and *A Walker in the City,* which is an autobiography.

Jerzy Kosinski (1933–1991)   The Holocaust wiped out most of his family and a traumatic experience afterward made him lose the ability to speak. He finally arrived in the United States, cured, and eager to work, learn and study. He obtained a Ford Foundation scholarship to Columbia University, then wrote *The Future Is Ours, Comrade,* a collection of essays that was a bestseller. Novels followed, including *Steps, Being There, The Devil Tree, Cockpit, Blind Date, The Painted Bird,* and *Passion Play,* all haunting in one way or another, as they explore aspects of his own life. *Steps* won a National Book Award,.

Julius Lester (1939–   )   African-American convert to Judaism. Works include *Black Folktales; This Strange New Feeling,* and *Do Lord Remember Me. Lovesong: Becoming a Jew* is about his conversion and his personal life before and since, and *How Many Spots Does a Leopard Have?* combines folktales from African and Jewish culture. He has also been a professor, music festival director, radio producer, talk-show host, and civil rights photographer.

Ira Levin (1929–   )   Sophisticated and successful frightener, ranging from *Rosemary's Baby* to *The Stepford Wives* to *The Boys From Brazil.*

Meyer Levin (1905–1981)   Acclaimed author of the Jewish experience in the first half of the century. *The Old Bunch* is widely considered one of the all-time classic stories of Jewish-American life. His other works include *The Golden Mountain, Citizens, My Father's House, Compulsion,* and *If I Forget Thee.* Several of his books are based on actual news stories of his day. He was also associate editor of *Esquire* and a war correspondent and spent several years in Israel and Europe writing about Jewish survivors.

Walter Lippman   One of the first journalistic superstars. His "Today and Tomorrow" column was syndicated to 250 newspapers in the 1930s and 1940s, his books include *The Phantom Public* and *The Cold War,* his commentaries appeared in the *Washington Post* and *Newsweek,* and his Pulitzers were awarded in 1958 and 1962.

Norman Mailer   Novelist, journalist, almost a character in one of his own stories. Books include *The Naked and the Dead, An American Dream; The Armies of the Night* (1968 Pulitzer); *Miami and the Siege of Chicago,* about the 1968 presidential conventions; and *The Executioner's Song,* another Pulitzer winner in 1979, about convicted murderer Gary Gilmore.

Bernard Malamud (1914–1986)   Tremendously powerful storyteller who writes, among other things, about relationships between Jews and non-Jews, and the uselessness of hate. Works include *The Fixer, The Assistant,* and *Dublin's Lives.* He was the recipient of several National Book Awards and a Pulitzer for *The Fixer* (1967).

Tillie Olsen (1913–   )   Lived a full life as a working mother before giving us *Tell Me a Riddle, Silences,* and many short stories. Much of her writing deals poetically with opportunities lost. While a young woman she was arrested twice for political activities involving strikes.

Cynthia Ozick (1928–   )   Mixing fantasy with reality, satire with scholarship, she produced a large portfolio of novels, short stories, essays, criticism, poems, and translations. She even dealt with Jewish law and history, including the subject of idolatry, always with language one critic said had "stylistic vitality." *Levitation: Five Fictions, The Messiah of Stockholm, Fame and Folly: Essays,* and *Portrait of the Artist as a Bad Character* are among her works.

Grace Paley (1922–   )   A short story writer of vivid recollections, whose works reveal enormous qualities of memory, inspiration, humor, and passion. An activist and teacher, she has written manifestos, opinion pieces, and poems in addition to her stories. Her latest collection is called *Just as I Thought,* and that's just what it is.

Gail Parent   She was funny writing for TV in the 1960s and 1970s, and funny in print. She won an Emmy for writing *The Carol Burnett Show* and also wrote for *The Mary Tyler Moore Show* and *Mary Hartman,*

Grace Paley. Courtesy The National Foundation for Jewish Culture; photo by Gentil & Heyers

Mary Hartman, but her books enabled her to be *more* than funny. *Sheila Levine Is Dead and Living in New York, David Meyer Is a Mother,* and *The Best Laid Plans* are also romantic, ironic, sardonic, hopeful, philosophic…

Dorothy Parker (1893–1967)   A member of the Algonquin Round Table, her stinging essays and sardonic prose for *Vanity Fair* and the *New Yorker* made her one of the most famous writers of her day. She also wrote short stories and screenplays.

S. J. Perelman (1904–1971)   Humorist, screenwriter, dramatist, cartoonist, and one of the preeminent *New Yorker* humorists. His collections of short pieces include *Baby, It's Cold Inside; Rising George;* and *Eastward Ha!* He also wrote *Monkey Business* and *Horse Feathers* for the Marx Brothers.

Letty Cottin Pogrebin (1939–   )   Her titles give it away: *How to Succeed in Business Without Really Typing, How to Make It in a Man's World.* But there's a lot more, and it's actually all very scholarly, serious, and convincing. She was also an editor and columnist for *Ladies' Home Journal.*

Chaim Potok (1929–   )   The hasidic psyche and the struggle between tradition and modern American society has never been handled as tenderly, emotionally, and evocatively as it is in *My Name Is Asher Lev, In The Beginning, The Book of Lights, Davida's Harp,* and others.

Philip Roth. Courtesy The National Foundation for Jewish Culture; photo by Nancy Crampton

Harold Robbins (1916–) Sex, violence, power, and corruption were never used so lucratively by a writer until he hit the scene. *The Carpetbaggers, Dreams Die First, 79 Park Avenue, Never Love a Stranger,* and others are sold in more than sixty countries and forty languages.

Anne Roiphe (1935–) Critics almost always talked about the power and richness of the core "story" of Roiphe's works. Her family sagas, by turns tragic and hilarious, include *Up the Sandbox, Lovingkindness, The Pursuit of Happiness,* and *If You Knew Me.*

Tina Rosenberg Won a Pulitzer for nonfiction in 1996 with *The Haunted Land: Facing Europe's Ghost After Communism.* She also wrote *Children of Cain: Violence and the Violent in Latin America* after living there for six years. Her grandfather Phillip Sandler was editor of the *Jewish Daily Forward* in the 1970s.

Judith Rossner (1935–) Wrote her first book while being bored as an employee in a real estate office. Childbirth, love, friendship, sex, and women's roles in life and modern society are her topics, and *Looking for Mr. Goodbar, Any Minute I Can Split, Emmeline,* and *His Little Women* are some of her books. *Goodbar* was inspired by a real-life event.

Leo Rosten (1908–1997) The world's foremost teacher of Yinglish 101 with his groundbreaking *The Joys of Yiddish.* He also wrote *Captain Newman, M.D.* and *The Education of H.Y.M.A.N. K.A.P.L.A.N.*

Henry Roth *Call It Sleep,* written in 1934, is often considered one of the finest novels by an American. Broad public recognition didn't come for three decades after it was published. He claimed writer's block got him until 1979, when he began the first draft of *Mercy of a Rude Stream.*

Philip Roth   Riotously and decisively proved that decent, honest Jewish intellectuals can have tons of guilt and sex on their fertile minds. His works include *Goodbye, Columbus; Letting Go, Zuckerman Unbound;* and *Portnoy's Complaint. Goodbye, Columbus* in 1959 and *Sabbath's Theatre* in 1995 won National Book Awards.

Maurice Samuel (1895–1972)   Known for his tough, provocative, often satiric books and lectures on America's Jewish-gentile relationship. Titles include *I, the Jew, You Gentiles, Jews on Approval,* and *The Great Hatred.* He also wrote about shtetl life and kibbutz life in Palestine, where he lived for a decade.

Budd Schulberg (1914–   )   Gritty, dynamic words, stories, and characters, with such works as *What Makes Sammy Run, The Harder They Fall,* and the screenplays for *On the Waterfront* and *A Face in the Crowd.*

Delmore Schwartz   A writer of poetry, stories, lyrics, and plays, he suffered twenty years of mental illness. His books of esoteric prose and poetry include *Genesis, Book One, Summer Knowledge: New and Selected Poems, 1938–1959,* and *In Dreams Begin Responsibilities and Other Stories.* He also edited *Partisan Review* from 1943 to 1947.

Irwin Shaw (1913–1984)   With a dozen plays, a dozen screenplays, and countless books to his credit, he's been called an old-time storyteller in the best sense of the phrase. His fifty-year writing career began with radio scripts for Dick Tracy and proceeded through such blockbuster novels as *The Young Lions; Rich Man, Poor Man; Beggarman, Thief;* and *Bread Upon the Waters.* Many of his books were critically acclaimed.

Isaac Bashevis Singer   Won the Nobel Prize in 1978. He started in the United States with the *Jewish Daily Forward,* which published many of his stories. His novels, translated from Yiddish, include *The Manor, The Estate, Shosha,* and *The Magician of Lublin.* Subjects include mysticism, relationships, sexuality. He also wrote several books for children, including the National Book Award winner *A Day of Pleasure.* The films *Yentl* and *Enemies: A Love Story* were based on his stories.

Susan Sontag (1935–   )   Called by turns an intellectual, argumentative, outrageous, unpredictable, and controversial essayist, she herself is as studied by media critics as what she writes. Her works include *The Benefactor, The Volcano Lover: A Romance, Death Kit, Styles of Radical Will,* and *Trip to Hanoi.*

Gertrude Stein (1874–1946)   Experimented with composition, time, and structure in some of her works. She also lectured and wrote autobiographically. Her books include *Making of Americans, The Autobiography of Alice B. Toklas, Yes Is for a Very Young Man.*

Irving Stone   One of the best at fictional biography, such as *Lust for Life* , about Vincent Van Gogh; *Sailor on Horseback,* about Jack London; *Love Is Eternal,* about Mary Todd Lincoln; *The Agony and the Ecstasy,* about Michelangelo; and *The Origin,* about Darwin.

Jacqueline Susann (1904–1978)   Influential? Debatable. But with *Valley of the Dolls* and *Once Is Not Enough,* how can she be left out?

Sydney Taylor (1904–1978)   Another juvenile fiction champ. She began writing for her daughter when her daughter asked why there weren't any good books for Jewish kids. The results include *The Holiday Story Book, Now That You Are Eight, The Boy Who Came to Dinner,* and *All-of-a-Kind Family.* She also wrote, directed, and choreographed several of her own plays.

Studs Terkel (1912–   )   Some of the most revealing portraits of the real America came from his tape recorder, which he used to write first-person narratives of startling power. Topics include the Great Depression, World War II, and the American Dream. Perhaps his most famous book is *Working: People Talk About What They Do All Day and How They Feel About What They Do.*

Calvin Trillin (1935–   )   Journalist, critic, novelist, observer, humorist. He wrote "Uncivil Liberties," a popular column for The *Nation,* and his books include *Alice, Let's Eat: Further Adventures of a Happy Eater,* and *Third Helpings.* He has been called a modern Mark Twain.

Barbara Tuchman   One of our most respected historian journalists. *The Guns of August* won a Pulitzer in 1962; *Stilwell and the American Experience in China 1911–45* won it in 1972.

Leon Uris (1924–   )   Serious and educational entertainment, from the creation of Israel in *Exodus* to the British trial of American novelists in *QBVII* to the conflict in Northern Ireland in *Trinity.*

Irving Wallace (1916–1990)   Complicated plots seductively spun. Wrote well over fifty novels, nonfiction books, screenplays, and plays. The novels include *The Chapman Report* and *The Seven Minutes,* and the nonfiction includes *The People's Almanac* and *The Intimate Sex Lives of Famous People.* His daughter is writer Amy Wallace and his son is writer David Wallechinsky.

Nathaniel West (1903–1940)   His fiction, bitter at best, was not widely appreciated during his lifetime. After his death *The Day of the Locust, A Cool Million, Miss Lonelyhearts,* and others became famous.

Elie Wiesel   Among his honors are the Jewish Heritage Award in 1966, the Congressional Gold Medal in 1984, and the Nobel Peace Prize in 1986.

The Top Ten Topics of "Jewish Books" in the 1990s

1. Anti-Semitism
2. Biblical explorations
3. The future or demise of Judaism
4. Holidays and traditions
5. The Holocaust
6. Jewish history
7. Jewish mysticism
8. Jewish wisdom, truth, and fulfillment
9. Jews in business, society, and culture
10. Raising Jewish children in America

As a Talmud student at the age of fifteen, he was sent by the Nazis to the death camps at Auschwitz, Buchenwald, and others (his parents and younger sister were killed). His fiction and nonfiction address the themes and issues a survivor must address. *Night* is a novel about a teenager who is consumed with guilt for surviving the Nazi death camps. *Twilight* is about a man's discovery that the universe is immersed in madness.

Herman Wouk (1915–   ) International bestselling author with, among others, *The Winds of War* and *War and Remembrance*. He also wrote *Marjorie Morningstar* and *Inside, Outside. This Is My God*, nonfiction, is a must read about Judaism.

5

Reasonable Opportunities

44 Jews Who Made It Their Business to Keep America in Business

I wish there were some award for the myriad nameless Jewish immigrants—our parents and grandparents—who never attained celebrity but who have provided a substantial part of the bone and flesh and robust spirit of our community.

—David Sarnoff

One of the myriad of Jewish immigrants who, in some ways, helped build this country was Abraham Sarnoff, a dirt poor house painter from Russia who immigrated to America with his family in the late 1890s. Abraham was of ill health and minor skills, and he died young. But his son David, who was fifteen when his father passed away, would build two of the most important, successful, and influential companies in United States history: RCA and NBC. Abraham would have been proud—even though he never knew what radio or television was.

There are many such stories of young American Jews who made good on the promise of the American dream. Some of the most interesting from yesterday and today are listed below.

If we were to round up the founders and guiding geniuses of a vast and diverse number of top U.S. firms since the beginning of the century we would find dapper Jewish immigrants and sons of immigrants who just a few years before were anything but dapper, being poor and, in many cases, hungry young men from the tenements or the old country.

There have been many suggestions that the religious and family ties (which often were one and the same) that these early business moguls enjoyed were at least partially responsible for the inspiration, aspiration, and skills that contributed to their success. David Sarnoff was careful to thank his immigrant parents, as he did in a speech to the Hebrew Immigrant Aid Society in 1959, but he also gave credit to life on the street. "As an immigrant boy," he said, "I was tossed into the bewildering whirlpool of a metropolitan slum area, to sink or swim. I started my business career, at once, by selling newspapers on the sidewalks of New York. I learned the hard way what a helping hand, a sympathetic word, a reasonable opportunity can mean in giving hope to a new arrival in this wonderful land."

Still, some of the Jewish business barons of the late 1800s were anything but princes. According to Stephen Birmingham, author of *The Rest of Us: The Rise of America's Eastern European Jews,* they shared many of the character traits of the Fricks, Carnegies, Vanderbilts, Harrimans, and Rockefellers, proving that "new money and bad manners did not rule each other out." Among the shared characteristics, says Birmingham, were "brashness, energy, vast egotism, a certain rapacity, and an almost touching absence of humor. All viewed 'business' as a deadly, fascinating, zero-sum game with only one winner in any field, and a joyful opportunity to outmaneuver the federal government...."

The author spins a far nicer tale about twentieth-century Jewish entrepreneurs. "Almost without exception...they believed in giving good weight. They were exceptionally careful about customer opinion.... The Talmud itself enjoins against sharp practice, and cautions against, say, a Jewish cobbler's placing his shop in too close proximity to the shop of another cobbler."

Indeed, there are several business directives in biblical literature. Talmudic scholars have long held that Jewish law requires employers to pay their employees fairly and on time and to lend a sympathetic ear when conflicts arise. In return, all employees must put in a full and productive day's work. Workers are allowed to recite important daily prayers on scaffolding because leaving the workplace to go elsewhere to do it would waste their employers' time. In Deuteronomy, it says that workers in a vineyard are allowed to pick as many grapes as they wish to eat, for it would be unfair to them to have to work in a luscious vineyard and not eat at all. But they must not stow any grapes to take home because that would also be unfair.

While it is unlikely that most of the Jewish-American business giants actually used biblical precepts to light their path from shtetl to board room, there were a handful who did cite religious convictions as part of their makeup and thus as influences on their business decisions. Many of the more recent ones have taken such initiatives as equal opportunity, workplace

The Home Depot's Arthur Blank (left) *and Bernard Marcus.* Courtesy Home Depot

diversity, and community support as seriously as any other corporate project. Some, like Howard Jonas, founder of International Discount Telecommunications, even try to create new molds of executive leadership by never wearing a tie to the office.

But what about Birmingham's brash and humorless bunch from a century ago? Why were they so different? Maybe they wanted to accomplish too much in too short a time.

Or maybe their ties were just too tight.

Arthur Blank and **Bernard Marcus**   Cofounders of Home Depot in 1978, which was a pioneer in the consumer warehouse concept. Prior to creating what has become America's largest home-improvement retailer, Blank worked for the somewhat smaller Handy Dan Home Centers in various financial positions. He served as president and CEO of Home Depot from its inception until 1997. Marcus had been president and chairman of Handy Dan's and also ran a few other manufacturing and hard goods operations. Home Depot was named America's most admired retailer by *Fortune* magazine five years in a row.

Louis Blaustein   started as a kerosene peddler and devised a way to transport fuel in steel drums with a spigot. This was the forerunner of the modern tank truck. In 1910 he founded the American Oil Company—Amoco—which at one point was earning $400 million a year.

August Brentano   Arrived in New York in 1853 at age twenty-two, from Austria, penniless, and began to sell newspapers. By the time he was forty years old, he owned the largest bookstore in New York, Brentano's, which doubled as a meeting place for writers. Three nephews helped expand it into what was once the largest bookselling establishment in the world.

John Brunswick   Billiards and bowling may not necessarily be considered sports with a huge Jewish presence, but if it weren't for this Jewish manufacturer, who immigrated to the United States from Switzerland in 1934, billiards and bowling may not have become popular American pastimes at all. Brunswick apprenticed to a carriage maker in Philadelphia and then founded his own carriage firm in Cincinnati in 1845, to which he later added billiard table manufacturing. His family took over the business upon his death and added bowling equipment.

Ben Cohen and **Jerry Greenfield**   Friends since their junior high school days in Merrick, Long Island, Ben and Jerry went into the ice cream business together in 1978 in Burlington, Vermont, in a renovated gas station. Ben was a scooper, taste-tester, truck driver, marketing director, salesman, president, CEO, and chairman. Jerry made the ice cream and has been vice chairman and director of mobile promotions. Known for its innovative flavors, Ben & Jerry's Ice Cream is distributed nationwide and has franchised shops in thirty states. The company is very active in philanthropy and foundation support.

Harry Cohn   Founder of Columbia Pictures in 1924. Cohn, like many of the other early studio men, took an abiding interest not only in financial but also artistic matters. Story lines were as important to him as bottom lines. Under his leadership, Columbia made such commercial and artistic successes as *Born Yesterday, Bridge Over the River Kwai, From Here to Eternity, It Happened One Night, Mr. Smith Goes to Washington,* and *On the Waterfront.*

Max Factor   Arrived in the United States from Poland in 1904 at age twenty-seven and built one of the leading cosmetics firms in the nation, Max Factor and Company. He worked closely with stars like Jean Harlow and dozens of other top performers and members of society.

Isaac and **Jacob Gimbel**   Founded Gimbel's department store—in Milwaukee in 1889, and in New York in 1910. Their father, **Adam**, was a traveling peddler who, with his own brothers and sisters, opened a store in Vincennes, Indiana, in 1842. The sons built it into a multimillion dollar commercial enterprise that also included Saks Fifth Avenue.

Samuel Goldwyn (1879–1974)   Through various partnerships (and name changes, including his own), he was responsible for creating both Paramount Pictures and MGM. He personally involved himself in most aspects of each film made by his studios, which included *The Best Years of Our Lives, Guys and Dolls,* and *Wuthering Heights.*

Andrew Grove Founder, chairman, and chief executive officer of Intel, which makes 90 percent of all the personal computer microprocessors in the world. Grove, who was *Time* magazine's Man of the Year for 1997, is proud of many of his firm's accomplishments, just one of which is the fact that the Mars Sojouner, which walked around the Red Planet a bit in 1997, used a solar shield controlled by an Intel chip.

Ruth Handler In 1939, her husband, Elliot, and she began selling trinkets that Elliot made in his small shop. He handled design and production while she handled the marketing. Then she decided it might be lucrative to team up with Elliot's former partner, Harold Matson, who was able to produce picture frames, doll furniture, and other items. The company that resulted was Mattel (the name is a combination of Matson and Elliot). In 1959, Ruth came up with the idea for the Barbie doll after seeing a much more risqué doll for adults being sold in Germany.

Howard Jonas (1959–   ) Founder and president of International Discount Telecommunications, a hundred million dollar-a-year Internet provider. A thirty nine-year-old, New Age businessman who doesn't wear a tie, Jonas, who is Orthodox, puts an emphasis on doing all things morally, in and out of company headquarters. The Torah, he states, is a libertarian document that supports his opposition to any form of censorship on the Internet.

Donna Karan Founded her namesake apparel firm in 1984 after several years of working for Anne Klein, and she quickly became one of the world's most influential fashion designers. Hillary Clinton, Barbra Streisand, and Candice Bergen are among her fans and customers.

Calvin Klein In 1968, founded what soon became a world-famous apparel firm. His line was primarily informal sportswear noted both for comfort and elegant simplicity. His first big client was Bonwit Teller, to which he sold trench coats, but from there he expanded, eventually adding jeans, jackets, cosmetics—and controversial ads.

Carl Laemmle Founded in 1912 what became known as Universal Pictures. He is generally credited with creating the star system, and he was the first to use creative publicity to develop what we now take for granted as typical Hollywood glitz and glamour. Universal's films included *All Quiet on the Western Front, Dracula,* and *Frankenstein.*

Estée Lauder Her uncle was a chemist who made skin creams. Something told her skin cream could run in the family. So in 1946 she founded the

Toys "R" Us founder Charles Lazarus.
Courtesy Toys "R" Us

cosmetics firm Estée Lauder, Inc., and through creative marketing (including the use of free samples), ingenius placement (Saks Fifth Avenue and other exclusive retailers), and a good business sense (aided by her husband and, later, her sons), Estée Lauder grew to be the largest family-owned cosmetics firm in the world.

Ralph Lauren   Began as a tie designer. His designs sold well, so he went into shirts. That did well, too. His Polo menswear collection drew much favorable attention for being classy yet contemporary—and both highly original and adaptable. In 1970 Bloomingdale's opened a special shop devoted to his line, noted for the use of extremely good fabrics. Ten years later, his empire, which now included clothes for women and boys, as well as perfume and luggage, grossed about a hundred million dollars.

Charles Lazarus   Founded Toys "R" Us in 1957, nine years after opening his first discount baby furniture store near Washington, D.C. Timing was everything: toy manufacturers were just beginning to be innovative and aggressive. Two baby furniture and toy supermarket stores followed. The growing popularity of children's television with aggressive toy advertising helped the chain grow. By 1966, he had four stores. Bankruptcy threatened in the mid-1970s, but his persistence, determination, and innovations avoided it. Today there are over seven hundred Toys "R" Us stores. The company became known for its workplace diversity, equal opportunity—and featuring only kids in its advertising.

Albert Lippert   Founder of Weight Watchers. He began his career as a buyer for women's apparel. In 1963 he and his wife, both overweight, met a woman who had successfully designed a diet program based mostly on a balanced meal and personal encouragement. Lippert saw the marketing potential, talked the originator into turning it from a hobby into a business, developed it into a franchise operation, and guided its growth, which eventually included cookbooks and its own line of frozen foods. In 1968, it was sold to the H. J. Heinz Company for $72 million, although Lippert stayed on board as an executive and then a consultant.

Israel Matz   Probably helped a lot of his fellow entrepreneurs by founding the Ex-Lax Company in 1907, when he was twenty-seven-years old.

Samuel Irving Newhouse   Built a communications empire, beginning in the 1920s, that was worth about seven hundred million dollars at its peak, with twenty-one newspapers, five magazines, six television stations, and twenty cable systems. He was also a great philanthropist whose gift to Lincoln Center was the Mitzi E. Newhouse Theatre, named in honor of his wife.

William Paley   In 1927 he took a small group of radio stations collectively called the Columbia Phonographic Broadcasting System and turned it into the CBS television and radio network. Under his leadership, the network became known for news, newsmakers, and big-name entertainment. Bing Crosby, Bob Hope, Edward R. Murrow, Walter Cronkite, and Ed Sullivan were all CBS mainstays for many years.

Nicholas Pritzker   Began acquiring real estate in the early 1900s, and his investments at various times included Hyatt Hotels, the Hammond Organ Company, and Continental Airlines. By the mid-1980s, his real estate holdings amounted to at least seven hundred million dollars.

Ida Rosenthal   Cofounded Maidenform Brassieres, manufacturers of the world's first modern bra. She began as a dressmaker but regarded the styles of the 1920s as being too constrictive. So, with her husband William's guidance and support (no pun intended), she developed a cotton bra that would fit instead of constrict. At first, they gave away bras with each sale of one of their dresses, but demand prompted them to start the Maiden Form Brassiere Company in 1923. Ida took over the business entirely when her husband passed away in 1958.

Julius Rosenwald   With a successful clothing business behind him, he acquired an interest in a firm called Sears, Roebuck and Company in 1895 and guided it from humble beginnings as a watch repair company to a catalog sales innovator to one of the world's top retail chains. His Julius Rosenwald Fund supported many causes, including schools and recreation centers for low-income black children.

Helena Rubinstein   Born in Poland, she ran away to Australia, where people seemed to crave the skin cream she had gotten from a family friend who was a chemist. She opened a store in Australia, then one in

England, and then came to the United States in 1914, where she began to manufacture many different cosmetic products and run a line of salons in which to apply and sell them. A tough businesswoman, she was known for yelling insults to her employees and turning off lights in the office to save money. Still, she founded not only a successful firm but an entire industry.

David Sarnoff As a wireless operator in 1922, at age twenty-one, he received the first message that the *Titanic* was sinking. From that auspicious yet humble beginning, he built up RCA and founded NBC, putting a visionary emphasis on research and development of communications technology throughout his industry stewardship.

Max Schuster Cofounder (with **Richard Simon**) of Simon & Schuster in 1924, as well as Pocket Books and the venerable Little Golden Books.

Max (1898–1982) and **Leonard Stern (1938–   )** Father and son who built the Hartz Mountain Company into one of the preeminent pet products firms in the world. Max founded it, and Leonard turned it into an empire.

Isidor and **Nathan Straus** Brothers who built Macy's into the biggest department store in the world. They didn't found the company but became partners as early as 1888 and owners in 1896. Isidor perished on the *Titanic*. Nathan became a great philanthropist with a strong interest in public health. He also successfully campaigned for pasteurization of milk in New York.

Levi Strauss Born in Bavaria, arriving in San Francisco in 1853, he accumulated a large fortune in the mercantile business and founded Levi Strauss & Co., which was singularly responsible for making blue jeans the American symbol they became. He also established twenty-eight scholarships at the University of California.

Diane von Furstenberg Waltzed onto the fashion scene in 1970 with a distinctive collection of clothes, then opened a Seventh Avenue showroom in New York in 1972. Five years later, her line of simple, elegant, cost-conscious dresses was earning over $142 million. She left the business in 1983 but soon grew dissatisfied with the products that were using her name, so she returned in 1990.

Julia Waldbaum She married a man who owned a small butter-and-egg store and turned it into a 140-store supermarket giant that grossed over a billion dollars in 1986. When her husband died in 1947, there were seven Waldbaums stores that carried 400 products, many of which featured the Waldbaum brand label. Julia took a personal interest in every aspect of the chain, from testing the recipes to counseling the sales clerks. Eventually, it was bought out by the Great Atlantic and Pacific Tea

Company, but Julia still made surprise visits to the stores to check on quality, cleanliness, and service.

Albert, Harry, Jack, and **Samuel Warner**   Founders of Warner Brothers Pictures in 1923. This was the studio that produced *The Jazz Singer,* the first motion picture to have synchronized sound. The four Warners, each with a different responsibility at the firm, made some key decisions that gave Hollywood one marketing or technical advance after another such as the first full-length all-talking motion picture and the extremely popular Busby Berkeley series of musicals. Among the Warner pictures were *Little Caesar, The Maltese Falcon, My Fair Lady,* and *A Streetcar Named Desire.*

Harvey and **Bob Weinstein**   Founders and cochairmen of the little movie company that could, Miramax Films. From meager and barely connected beginnings in the mid 1980s, the Weinstein boys, who named their firm after their parents, Miriam and Max, built a production and distribution firm that can claim some of the biggest movies of the 1990s to its credit, including *The English Patient, Pulp Fiction, Reservoir Dogs,* and *Good Will Hunting.*

6

Chutzpah, Inc.

12 Businesses With Names of Moxie

You are not to charge interest to your brother.
—Deuteronomy 23:20

They're the proud, the few, the gutsy. They are business owners who don't mind wearing their heritage on their sleeves—or at least on their trucks. Some would think that naming a business with words or phrases of strong ethnic identity would automatically slash the potential customer base by perhaps two-thirds, if not more.

Not this bunch. They found out that pride and moxie are two ingredients that can make a business rise. There are, of course, no guarantees; businesses can fail just as easily with atypical names. But for many of the few, the proud, and the gutsy, failure just isn't kosher.

Boychiks Deli is a full-service delicatessen in Glen Allen, Virginia. A longtime counter worker named Joe says that while Boychiks doesn't have a particularly strong Jewish clientele, the name, chosen by the deli's Jewish owner (from the Yiddish phrase meaning "nice little boy") prompts many conversations, and that often translates to friendly and long-lasting relationships between the store and its customers. "When I first started here I thought Boychik was someone's last name," Joe says. Some customers *do* know what it means—usually Jewish mothers and grandmothers—and they start conversations just as easily as anyone. Phone Boychiks Deli at 804-747-1030.

Exodus Relocation Services based in Raleigh, North Carolina, helps people find the perfect home through "a network of handpicked realtors in over 1,000 cities" at no cost to the customer. The name, according to a company spokesperson, was chosen in 1994 as an attempt to establish immediate name recognition, retention, and uniqueness. It worked. The relationship to the biblical phrase is obvious to most—as in a hasty exodus from New Jersey to just about anywhere—but little if any religious significance is attached to it by clients (although in its ads placed in Jewish publications there are references to relocation guidance provided on such things as available congregations and kosher butchers). They can be reached at 1-800-233-4853.

Gelt Financial Corporation   provides home equity loans, problem credit mortgages, refinancing, and other financial services for homeowners in Alaska, Indiana, Louisiana, Mississippi, Pennsylvania, Texas, Washington, West Virginia, and about ten other states. The Jewish founder of Gelt Financial picked the name *gelt* for its bullseye association with the word *money*, a Yiddish word known even to many non-Jews. "About 30 percent of our clientele knows what *gelt* means," says a company spokesman, although he couldn't speculate on whether or not the name attracts more attention than another more anglicized name would have attracted. Still, he says in the best tradition of Jewish wisdom, it hasn't hurt, either. Gelt can be reached at 1-800-355-GELT.

Mazel Tov Gifts   is a store in a strongly Jewish community outside of San Francisco. The store sells Judaica items to locals who range from Reform to Orthodox, items that include everything from yarmulkes and menorahs to tallises and mezuzahs. The store, which opened in 1996, is very successful not only because of its mostly Jewish clientele, but also because of its small but appreciative group of non-Jewish customers who need a store just like it to buy gifts for friends, relatives—or even themselves if they are thinking about or in the process of converting. Mazel Tov Gifts is, in fact, the only store of its kind in the area, and its name leaves little doubt as to what kind of good luck one is likely to find there. The company is at 415-668-7876

Mensch Films   is the company founded by filmmakers Marc Ostrick and Ezra Soiferman to distribute their controversial comedy short *Pressure Drop* and to produce the feature-length version. As students at the Tisch School of the Arts at New York University, Ostrick and Soiferman produced a film about elderly individuals suffering from glaucoma who decide to use marijuana as treatment instead of having operations. It was their senior thesis film. According to the filmmakers, mensch, a Yiddish word for someone who is very honorable and decent, describes the brave and resilient men and women in the film. Because of the difficulty in breaking into the motion picture industry even with conventional stories, mensch may also describe Ostrick and Soiferman: Because of their belief in the project and their boundless energy, *Pressure Drop* has been featured at fourteen film festivals and at thousands of screenings. Mensch Films is at 213-882-6210

Mitzvah Man   is a company formed by Ira Andelman, who, thirteen years ago, decided to put his deejay talents to the test. His party entertainment firm actually has two names: Mitzvah Man and 1-800-DIAL-DJS. Both cleverly tap into marketing savvy. When Mitzvah Man is advertised in Jewish-oriented newspapers, it instantly alerts people who are planning bar mitzvah and bat mitzvah parties (in addition to weddings and anniversaries) that this is one outfit that means Jewish party business. But when Andelman advertises in more mainstream papers as 1-800-DIAL-DJS, which obviously is also a telephone number, it tells people that a disk jockey service is one free call away. The Jewish to non-Jewish clientele is about 50-50, according to the owner. Serving New York, New Jersey, and Connecticut, Andelman's company also provides videotaping services, party lights, and more.

A Nice Jewish Boy Moving Company   is a commercial and residential moving and storage outfit in New Orleans. According to a company spokesman, although the city has a sizable Jewish population, it is by no means only Jews who contract the company's services. The name—different, catchy, a calculated investment in irreverence—attracts attention out of a New Orleans universe of nearly one hundred moving and storage companies, and then it becomes the job of customer service and price to recoup on the investment. A Nice Jewish Boy's success proves the risk paid off. They can be reached at 504-243-2040.

Renta Yenta   is a total party planning outfit founded and owned by Deanna Susskind, who says that most of her non-Jewish clients think of a yenta as simply a busy person. That, she points out, can be a good thing, for it denotes both a successful and an energetic operation. The company, based in Long Island, New York, *is* busy and successful, and it has a healthy share of Jewish and non-Jewish customers throughout the New York metropolitan area. Oddly enough (or maybe not), the name Susskind picked for her firm goes over a little more favorably with the non-Jews than the Jews (who have a more negative view of the word *Yenta*). Renta Yenta is at 516-367-8282.

Shalom Home   a national real estate relocation service, assists homeowners in everything from the search for and purchase of a new home to information on inspections, schools, financing, community centers, kosher merchants, local congregations, and more. They operate under the philosophy that if people feel connected with their communities even before they get there, their affiliations will be established quicker and their eventual ties will be stronger. The company points out, as well, that it gratefully serves the needs of all interested persons, regardless of race, religion, color, sex, or national origin. They can be reached at 1-800-8-SHALOM.

Shalom 2000, Inc. is a nonfranchised moving and storage company. With local and nationwide capabilities, Shalom 2000 promotes the fact that they use no agents or brokers, and therefore their customer service is high while their prices are low. "Each move is planned and coordinated according to each individual's needs," they say. "We are licensed, bonded and insured for your peace of mind." Shalom 2000, of course, means peace, which is what you need when you move, as well as hello and goodbye, which are also appropriate words for a moving company. They can be reached at 1-800-SHALOM-1.

Shleppers is a residential and commercial moving company for local or long distance hauls. Louisa Benjamin Bohm founded it twenty years ago, and for twenty years it has been getting laughs—and business. The company's trucks and advertisements feature various dictionary definitions and tag lines, such as "Shlep: slang, rhymes with pep, verb meaning to carry or lug"; "20 years and shlepping"; "Don't Shlep, call Shleppers and let us shlep for you." How can anyone resist? The New York City–based company is at 1-800-84-SHLEP.

Zaftig Boutique enjoys a growing clientele even though customers and potential customers throughout its Nashville home base typically do not know what *zaftig* means (Yiddish for full-bodied or buxom). But Lisa Riback, who started the plus-size consignment store three years ago, took a chance on the quality of her operation over the mystery of its name to generate effective word-of-mouth. "Most customers like the name when they find out what it means," she reports. "Some initially think it's my last name, so I have the definition blown up to poster size and hanging in the store." Most of the shop's Nashville customers are not Jewish, but when Riback's friendly atmosphere mixes with a successful shopping trip, many Zaftig clients walk away with a little bit of that old-time religion. Zaftig is at 615-463-8770.

7

Thinking at the Speed of Light

46 Esteemed Jewish-American Scientists

*Cast your bread upon the waters, for after
many days you will find it.*
—Ecclesiastes 11:1

Thirty years before Jurassic mammals began stomping on lawyers and chasing Jeff Goldblum, there was Arthur Kornberg. In 1959, Kornberg won the Nobel Prize for physics and medicine for creating biologically active DNA in a test tube. Less than twenty years later, a fellow Jewish scientist, Daniel Nathans, won the presitigious prize for mapping the genetic components of a DNA molecule.

It should come as no surprise that a large number of American Jews have excelled, and continue to excel, in biology, physics, chemistry, mathematics, medicine, astronomy, and other scientific endeavors. As has been discussed in countless books and articles, inquisitiveness and resourcefulness seem to endure as "traits" that have been passed down through the generations. So it was in Europe throughout much of the early part of the century, and so it is in America, yesterday and today.

Many who choose the sciences as a profession, or even a hobby, often seem to do so both with an altruistic motive—to do some good for the world—and a superior work ethic that sees many of their goals come to fruition. Here is an honor roll of some of the greatest and most significant Jewish-American scientists; many emigrated here from Europe, and many are Nobel laureates. While their bonds to Judaism may have been little scrutinized and even less reported, perhaps Einstein's theory of motivation holds true for more of his Jewish colleagues than we know: "The cosmic religious experience," Einstein said, "is the strongest and the noblest driving force behind scientific research."

While it has never been anyone's intention to re-create dinosaurs (as far as we know), it is indeed intriguing to see how varied, unique, important, or even problematic their endeavors have been. Some of these scientists took a shine to light—its speed and relation to other matter. Others were concerned with the effects of cholesterol on our health, or with hepatitis, polio, and tuberculosis. Einstein's own concern, on the eve of the splitting of the atom, was that nuclear power be used for peaceful means, and many other Jewish scientists who pioneered nuclear energy echoed his desires. They have only partially succeeded. Now we could use another Einstein, Jewish or otherwise, to make nuclear energy completely safe in the right hands and utterly useless in the wrong. Maybe she's just around the corner.

Ralph Alpher (1921–   )   Brilliant physicist at the General Electric Research and Development Center, Applied Physics Labs, Johns Hopkins University and elsewhere at a time when serious space science was first getting underway. He developed one of the first models of the universe in which the Big Bang played an important role, and he also predicted cosmic microwave background radiation that was observed by others seventeen years later.

David Atlas (1924–   )   One of the preeminent radar meteorologists in the field, he developed storm detection devices that have significantly improved aircraft safety.

Emile Berliner   Perfected as much as invented: In 1877 he improved upon Alexander Graham Bell's telephone with a better transmitter. In 1887 he improved upon Thomas Edison's phonograph system with a flat disc instead of a cylinder. He also improved airline engines and perfected the helicopter.

Felix Block   Nobel Prize winner for physics in 1952, he discovered nuclear induction, which led to the development of a medical diagnostic device called nuclear magnetic resonance, used in hospitals around the world. He also worked on the Manhattan Project.

Konrad Block   Nobel Prize winner in 1964 in physiology and medicine, he discovered that cholesterol is an integral component of body cells, and his work in the field led to even more discoveries for fighting cholesterol-related ailments and diseases.

Baruch Blumberg   His Nobel Prize in 1976 for physiology and medicine was awarded in recognition of his work in discovering the Hepatitis B antigen capable of stimulating an immune response. He devotedconsiderable energy to vaccination research and to determine methods

The sound of genius: It's impossible to imagine life without Emile Berliner's contributions, which include the microphone and the first working recording studio. Courtesy The American Jewish Archives, Hebrew Union College, Cincinnati

of screening blood donors with hepatitis.

Franz Boas (1858–1942)   He helped develop anthropology into a serious and exciting field through his teaching and his books. He studied and described cultures and languages of previously unknown societies, and preached that understanding cultures is the way to understanding the world.

Michael Brown   His 1985 Nobel Prize for physiology and medicine was based on research and discoveries about cholesterol metabolism and regulation and for his work on behalf of the treatment of diseases caused by elevated cholesterol levels.

Edwin J. Cohn (1892–1953)   Discovered elements of blood plasma which proved invaluable in the treatment of surgical shock.

George Dantzig   Mathematician, educator, and computer researcher who won the National Medal of Science in 1975 for his discoveries. He is credited with inventing linear programming and other methods that led to widespread applications in computer programming. Portions of his career were spent at the Rand Corporation and United States Air Force Headquarters.

Albert Einstein   Physicist who, through theoretical analysis, helped us understand some of the characteristics of light, time, mass, and energy. He received a Nobel Prize in 1921.

Gertrude B. Elion   She and other biochemists developed the first drugs to fight viruses, childhood leukemia, and transplant rejection. A Nobel

Prize winner in 1988, she also was instrumental in developing more effective ways to produce drugs.

Donald Glaser Invented the bubble chamber, a device necessary for discovering new particles and researching known ones. For his work he received a Nobel Prize in 1960.

Leo Goldberg (1913–1987) Working at the McMath-Hulbert Observatory in Michigan, he made spectacular films of solar flares and other solar features, greatly aiding in the study of our sun.

Peter Carl Goldmark Between 1936 and 1971, he held various top spots at CBS Laboratories and developed some of the most important devices in modern communications history—including color TV and the long-playing record.

Stanley Goldrich (1937–   ) Invented medical instruments for the treatment of eye movement disorders. One is called the Orthotone Biofeedback Coordinator and another is the Goldrich Contour Rotator. A psychologist and optometrist, he conducted extensive research on vision, perception, and all manner of eye disorders and treatments.

Stephen Jay Gould (1941–   ) Leading paleontologist who proposed the theory of punctuated equilibrium, which says that the evolution of a species does not occur at a steady rate but can suddenly accelerate with rapid change over a few hundred thousand years.

Jesse Leonard Greenstein (1902–1959) His work at various scientific institutions led to the discovery and interpretation of quasars in outer space. He worked with NASA and the National Academy of Sciences in future planning and is a world authority on the evolution and chemical composition of stars. He predicted that in 7 billion years, our sun will be a blue-white dwarf so small that the temperature of the earth will be 300 degrees below zero.

Jeffrey Hoffman Astronaut who flew on the space shuttles *Discovery* and *Columbia* five times between 1985 and 1996, including on a Hubble mission in 1993. He took Judaic objects with him each time, including bringing the Torah on *Columbia*.

Arthur Kantrowitz (1913–   ) The space program is indebted to him for his development of high-temperature shock tubes for a rocket's safe reentry into the earth's atmosphere. A physicist and educator who crossed disciplines easily, he also developed an intra-aortic balloon pump, which is an important heart-assist device. Kantrowitz served on many science education advisory groups.

Arthur Kornberg Synthesized artificial DNA. Received the Nobel Prize in 1959.

Space Shuttle astronaut Jeffrey A. Hoffman. Courtesy NASA

Edwin Land   Inventor (and college dropout) whose lifelong fascination with the properties of light led to several advances in the fields of photography and human optics, the most famous of which was the instant camera—the Polaroid Land camera—in 1947. Other contributions from Land and his lab improved such products as camera filters and sunglasses. He also researched and proved new theories of color perception.

Karl Landsteiner (1868–1943), **Philip Levine** (1900–1987), and **Albert Weiner**   Three pioneering scientists who helped identify and classify the human blood groups. Levine and Weiner developed the concept of diseases being caused by autoimmunization, which concerns the reaction of the body to its own normal tissue. Weiner went on to discover the Rh blood factor.

Joshua Lederberg (1925–)   A leading biochemical geneticist who pioneered the usefulness of bacteria in genetic research.

Leon M. Lederman   A Nobel Prize winner in 1989 who discovered a neutrino that advanced the study of particle physics. He also designed and built machines that physicists use regularly for advanced research.

Harold Masursky (1922–1990)   A senior member of the NASA team that chose landing sites on the moon. He worked on the Ranger, Apollo, Viking, and Voyager programs and greatly contributed to important research about the surface of the moon and planets.

Edwin Land demonstrating his landmark peel-off photo developing process with a serious self-portrait. Courtesy Polaroid Corporate Archives

Albert Abraham Michelson   Physicist who discovered an accurate method for measuring the speed of light. Awarded a Nobel Prize in 1907.

Herman Joseph Muller   Nobel science laureate in 1946 for his studies on the effect of X rays in producing congenital defects and mutations.

Daniel Nathans   Developed the first genetic map of DNA and won the Nobel Prize in 1978.

John Von Neumann   Internationally recognized leader in designing high-speed "computing machines" in the 1940s and 1950s, and one of the key developers of the central processing unit, or CPU. He directed the Electronic Computer Project at the Institute for Advanced Studies.

Robert Oppenheimer (1904–1967)   Director and chief architect of the nuclear project at the Los Alamos laboratory near Santa Fe, New Mexico. His leadership led to the development of the atomic bomb. He later championed against the use of nuclear weapons.

Gregory Goodwin Pincus (1903–1967)   With collaborator M. C. Chiang, he developed the first practical birth control pill.

Stanley Prusiner   Nobel Prize winner in 1982 for his research into several rare brain diseases. A professor of neurology, biochemistry, and biophysics, he proposed that many such diseases are caused by microscopic life forms that self-replicate without traces of RNA or DNA.

Isidore Isaac Rabi   Physicist who discovered how to measure the magnetic characteristics of atoms. He was a science advisor in the Eisenhower administration and did work at Brookhaven National Laboratory on atomic research. A Nobel Prize winner in 1944, his work also led to the invention of the laser.

Astronaut Judith A. Resnick, who died in the Challenger *explosion.* Courtesy NASA

Lias E. Reiss Scientist who in 1923 invented the device that made it possible to add sound to film. He also developed the first practical converter for alternating current, which made it possible to electrify many of the nation's railroads.

Judith Resnick (1949–1986) Mission specialist on the ill-fated space shuttle *Challenger.* She had previously worked as an electrical engineer, design engineeer, and biochemical engineer at Xerox, RCA, and the National Institutes of Health.

Albert Sabin (1906–1993) Virologist who claimed the Salk polio vaccine needed refinement and succeeded in developing a vaccine that could be taken orally and last much longer. He also developed vaccines against encephalitis and dengue fever.

Bernard Sachs (1858–1944) Neurologist who identified what came to be known as Tay-Sachs disease, a genetic disorder characterized by arrested cerebral development.

Jonas Salk (1906–1995) Most noted for developing the first effective vaccine against polio, he also helped develop vaccines for influenza, ran his own Institute for Biological Studies, and, at the time of his death, had been working on an AIDS vaccine.

Julian Schwinger Helped develop quantum electrodynamics, which led to a wider general understanding of the interaction between light and matter. A 1965 Nobel Prize winner.

Selman A. Waksman Microbiologist who coined the term *antibiotics* after discovering streptomycin, a microbe found to cure tuberculosis and other diseases. He won the Nobel Prize in 1952.

David Wolf (1956–   )   Astronaut who lived on the Russian space station *Mir* for four months. He's also a doctor and an acrobatic pilot.

Roselyn Yalow   For her work in developing methods of accurately measuring substances in blood, she received a Nobel Prize in 1977. Her work was also of great importance to the treatment of hormonal disorders such as diabetes.

Jerrold R. Zacharias (1905–1986)   Physicist who worked at the Los Alamos nuclear lab in New Mexico and whose work led to the creation of the atomic clock.

Microbiologists, quantum physicists, and other such scientists, by the very nature of their fields, tend often not to be media darlings, and that's just the way most of them like it. Many of them don't even make it into school textbooks. Unfortunately, most students lack the time to learn about more than a select few anyway; besides, it is not every textbook writer and science teacher who can turn those who think at the speed of light into engaging, intriguing personalities—even though most of them are.

Oddly enough, America's love affair with the estimable and courageous Christa McAullife more or less kept Judith Resnick out of the news before, during, and after the explosion of *Challenger*. Resnick was not only the second American woman in space but also the first Jew.

After the tragedy, then Ohio Governor Richard Celeste appeared at Temple Israel in Resnick's native Akron and said, "She knew she would be home in space. And she was. And she is."

She is also at home in Jewish-American history.

8

Headline Jews

40 Who Made News Making News

*People often ask me why I returned to Judaism. 'I saw
the rest of the world,' I tell them.*
—Dennis Prager

Add up their frequent flyer miles and you can go to Pluto and back and still have some miles left over for a first-class upgrade.

Jews have played a significant role in the American news game for over a century. In 1917, a Hungarian-born Jew named Joseph Pulitzer, who had immigrated to the United States, established an annual awards program to recognize literary and journalistic excellence. Pulitzer was a lawyer, businessman (at one time owning the *New York World*), philanthropist, and political activist. The Pulitzer Prize became a symbol of uncompromised talent and dedication—and sometimes courage—in the worlds of newspaper and magazine writing and reporting. The first winner, Herbert Bayard Swope, also Jewish, was cited for his prodigious reporting from Germany during the First World War, thereby proving that newspeople can be as newsworthy as the news they report.

There are literally thousands of Jewish newspaper and magazine reporters, editors, and publishers and local TV and radio anchors and correspondents coast to coast, and the vast majority do a fine job of bringing continued honor to the profession. But there are a few dozen over the last century who have elevated the news business to even higher levels because of their contributions, investigations, courage, and dignity. They are not *all* Pulitzer Prize winners, but each has won something that often is even more valuable: respect.

Elie Abel   All-around, highly skilled journalist who won a Pulitzer Prize in 1958, worked for the *New York Times* and NBC News, was dean of journalism at Columbia University from 1970 to 1979, and wrote several acclaimed volumes on current events, including *Roots of Involvement: The U.S. in Asia, 1784–1971* (with Marvin Kalb).

Shana Alexander (1925–   )   Prolific writer for *Life* and *Newsweek* and biographer of Jean Harris and Patty Hearst.

Meyer Berger (1898–1959)   One of the best-ever personality journalists. He wrote about people with unique or peculiar professions, and about the exotic, bizarre, and pathetic. His stories were collected in a book called *The Eight Million: Journal of a New York Correspondent.* As a feature reporter for the *New York Times*, he won a Pulitzer.

Carl Bernstein (1944–   )   Investigative journalist on the *Washington Post* who, with Bob Woodward, helped expose the Watergate cover-up.

Wolf Blitzer   Became famous for his coverage of the Gulf War on CNN. Before that he covered the Israeli–Egyptian peace conference in Egypt in 1977, accompanied President Jimmy Carter to Egypt and Israel, wrote for the *New York Times, Wall Street Journal, Washington Post,* and *New Republic* and authored *Between Washington and Jerusalem* in 1985 and *Anatoly and Avital Shcharansky: The Journey Home* in 1986.

Robert Capa   Combat news photographer who covered the 1948 Israeli War for Independence. He was killed in 1954 when he stepped on a landmine in Indochina.

Alfred Eisenstaedt (1898–1995)   Photojournalist who developed his craft into an artform. He took the famous photo of the sailor kissing the nurse in Times Square on V-J Day.

Max Frankel   Career-long *New York Times* man who began there as a college student in the 1950s. At various times he was a foreign correspondent, chief Washington correspondent, Washington bureau chief, Sunday editor, and editorial page editor. He was the one who pushed the *Times* to publish the Pentagon Papers. In 1972 he accompanied President Nixon to China, filing twenty-four stories that won the 1973 Pulitzer Prize for international reporting.

Leslie Howard Gelb (1937–   )   Excelled in newspaper news, TV news, and journalistic books. Gelb was a diplomatic correspondent for the *New York Times*, a senior correspondent on the *ABC Nightline* special "The Crisis Game" (for which he won an Emmy), and was the author of *The Irony of Vietnam: The System Worked; Our Own Worst Enemy: The Unmaking of American Foreign Policy;* and others.

Jeff Greenfield (1943–   )   Worked for Robert Kennedy and New York City mayor John Lindsay before becoming a political news correspondent for CBS and CNN. A favorite of radio personality Don Imus.

Bettina Gregory   Started out as a local reporter and anchorwoman on a Long Island radio station and went on to cover the White House, Congress, and the Vietnam War for ABC News on TV and radio. She also freelanced for the *New York Times* and the Associated Press in 1973 and 1974 and was named one of the top ten TV investigative reporters by *TV Guide* in 1983.

David Halberstam   Investigative reporter for the *New York Times* who won a Pulitzer in 1964 for international reporting. He covered Vietnam in detail, writing what he saw—which many politicians and other Americans didn't want to believe was true. He also wrote for *Harper's, Esquire,* and *Atlantic Monthly* and authored biographical studies of Dean Rusk, Gen. William Westmoreland, President John Kennedy, and President Lyndon Johnson.

Seymour Hersh (1937–   )   Investigative reporter who exposed the My Lai massacres and the CIA's domestic spying activity and recently authored a new book on President John F. Kennedy called *The Dark Side of Camelot.* He also wrote *Gulf War Syndrome: The War Between America's Ailing Veterans and Their Government.*

Marvin Kalb   A top diplomatic correspondent for CBS and NBC News for thirty years with more than six Overseas Press Club Awards to his credit. He also moderated *Meet the Press* from 1984 to 1987, coauthored *Kissinger; Roots of Involvement: The U.S. and Asia;* and *The Nixon Memo;* he is currently the director of the Joan Shorenstein Center on the Press, Politics and Public Policy at Harvard University.

Henry Kamm   *New York Times* reporter who spent a dozen years overseas for the paper in Athens, Rome, Moscow, Paris, Eastern Europe, and Asia. He's won many awards, including the 1978 Pulitzer for international reporting.

Ronald Kessler (1943–   )   Investigative reporter for the *Washington Post* who exposed FBI wiretapping activities.

Larry King (1933–   )   Popular CNN talk-show host.

Ted Koppel (1940–   )   Longtime host of ABC'S Nightline.

Irving R. Levine (1922–   )   Correspondent and economics specialist for NBC News for over forty-five years. Starting out as a general reporter, he became the first network newsman to cover economics full-time. He accompanied presidents Carter, Reagan, Bush, and Clinton to their annual economic summits around the world.

Walter Lippmann (1889–1974)   Political journalist who founded the *New Republic.* He won several Pulitzers.

Lester Markel (1894–1977)   *New York Times* Pulitzer winner who was the innovative editor of the Sunday section. He developed Sunday's Week in Review and began the trend for large Sunday papers across the nation to have multiple sections.

Edwin Newman   Venerable, popular television and radio news commentator. He worked with Eric Sevareid in the late 1940s, was a London reporter for NBC in the 1950s, reviewed theatre on TV in the 1960s with a new level of seriousness (producer David Merrick barred him from all Merrick productions after Newman panned a play), narrated many documentaries, moderated the 1976 Ford–Carter debate, and wrote a few books about the English language.

Adolph Ochs   Bought the *New York Times* in 1896 and turned it into the most important newspaper in the country, staying on as publisher for forty years. He was the one who coined the phrase "All the news that's fit to print."

Miriam Ottenberg (1914–1982)   Investigative reporter for the *Washington Star,* and a Pulitzer Prize winnner.

Sylvia Porter (1913–1991)   Nationally syndicated economic reporter whose columns appeared in over four hundred newspapers. Her much-needed skill was in turning financial and economic concepts and phrases into those the average person can understand. She also wrote over twenty books on the subject.

Geraldo Rivera (1943–   )   Former investigative TV reporter (mother, Jewish; father, Puerto Rican) who exposed the Willowbrook psychiatric home atrocities. Now a popular TV talk-show host.

Dan Riviv   CBS foreign correspondent for twenty years. He worked in over thirty countries, covered the Persian Gulf War, and wrote *The Complete History of Israel's Intelligence Community.*

A. M. Rosenthal (1922–   )   Pulitzer Prize-winning editor of the *New York Times.*

Morley Safer (1931–   )   A *60 Minutes* correspondent for more than twenty-five years. Despite being a gentler, kinder investigator than some of his colleagues, he still covers topics such as organized crime and business fraud.

William Safire (1921–   )   Conservative, influential, highly respected *New York Times* columnist who earlier had been a speechwriter for President Nixon.

Sidney Schanberg (1934–   )   Investigative reporter whose experiences in Cambodia inspired the film, *The Killing Fields.*

Daniel Schorr (1916–   )   CBS Washington correspondent for ten years, known for bringing techniques of print journalism to television broadcasting and for the publication of the Pentagon Papers.

Mike Wallace has been one of TV's most prominent investigative reporters, appearing on 60 Minutes *since its debut in 1968.* Courtesy *The Jewish Week,* New York

Bob Simon   Veteran TV news correspondent who was held captive in Iraq during the Gulf War in 1991. He wrote about his ordeal in a book titled *Forty Days.*

Louis Stark (1888–1954)   *New York Times* Pulitzer winner who covered the Washington beat for twenty years.

I. F. Stone   Unique and independent reporter and editor whose *I. F. Stone's Weekly* was famous for covering American foreign and domestic issues. In 1973 a documentary called *I. F. Stone's Weekly* showed why he was considered a maverick journalist.

Herbert Bayard Swope   (1882–1958)   The first recipient of the Pulitzer Prize, he was a longtime staff correspondent for the *New York World* and showed courage in chasing such news as the Ku Klux Klan, organized crime, and labor conditions in the South.

Mike Wallace   A *60 Minutes* correspondent since the show's inception in 1968. Made television news investigations a thing of high drama with his take-no-prisoners approach.

Barbara Walters (1931–   )   The first female news anchor on network TV who also cohosted *The Today Show* and *20/20.* One of the most popular interviewers in TV history.

Theodore White   Political journalist who detailed presidential campaigns in 1960, 1964, 1968, and 1972 in books and articles. He won a Pulitzer for general nonfiction.

Walter Winchell   Father of the gossip column. His column "On Broadway" in the *New York Evening Graphic* started it all in 1924. He went on to the *New York Daily Mirror,* which syndicated his column to a readership of over thirty million. Before long, he was using his unique, opinionated style to discuss politics, crime, and other topics.

9

The Chosen

41 Jewish-Americans Who Have Been Noted and Noticed—and Needed

The Jews are the yeast in the bread of civilization
which causes it to grow.
—Ben Hecht

We teach modesty and then shower accolades. Hypocritical? Not when we're dealing with those who have made the kinds of contributions to American society and culture that these American Jews have made. Such accolades are unavoidable.

Whether based on a person's skill, philanthropy, or celebrity, these honors, bestowed by a variety of entities, show once again how from a population lilliputian in size, giants have arisen.

Or at least *mensches* and *menscheles* of tall order.

The Emma Lazarus/Statue of Liberty Awards

This award is presented by the American Jewish Historical Society to individuals who have made contributions to improving the human condition. It has been awarded only a few times in the society's 107-year history.

Edgar M. Bronfman (1929–   )   Son of the founder of Distillers-Seagram's Limited (Samuel Bronfman) and a multimillionaire businessman in his own right who gives generously to many charitable causes.

Aaron Feuerstein   is the chief executive officer of Malden Mills. The company made headlines in the mid-1990s when his upholstery-fabrics factory in Methuen, Massachusetts, burned down after a massive boiler explosion and he continued to pay his 2,500 workers for a full year until the plant was rebuilt.

Armand Hammer (1898–1990) Industrialist who for forty years was instrumental in initiating and spearheading positive, humanitarian, cultural, and commercial relations between the United States and the Soviet Union. His causes included the plight of Soviet Jews and the welfare of the victims of the Chernobyl nuclear power accident.

Sylvia Hassenfeld From 1988–1992 served as the first female president of the American Jewish Joint Distribution Committee.

Abraham L. Sachar First national director of Hillel Foundation, a founding president of Brandeis University, lecturer, news analyst, and author of *History of the Jews*. During his presidency, Brandeis went from a student population of one hundred and seven to over eight hundred students in just four years.

The National Women's Hall of Fame Honorees

The National Women's Hall of Fame, founded in 1969, is located in Seneca Falls, New York, home of the first Woman's Rights Convention in 1848. The Hall includes on its honor roll women of every ethnic and racial classification. Here are the Jewish inductees:

Bella Abzug First Jewish woman elected to the United States Congress, and served from 1971 to 1977. She was also a civil rights lawyer and a writer.

Betty Friedan Wrote *The Feminine Mystique* in 1963, which is frequently credited with starting the modern feminist movement. Three years later she became the founding president of the National Organization for Women, which also champions political change, equal rights, and other causes.

Francis Wisebart-Jacobs (1843–1892) Founder of what became the National Jewish Hospital for Immunology and Respiratory Medicine. She was instrumental in organizing groups and causes that eventually led to the creation of the United Way.

Hannah Greenbaum Solomon (1858–1942) A skilled organizer whose influential Jewish Women's Congress, the first group of its kind, later became the National Council of Jewish Women.

Rosalyn Yalow (1921–) First American woman to win a Nobel Prize in science. A medical physicist, she investigated the possibility of using radiological substances to diagnose and treat diseases.

Jewish Cultural Achievement Awards in the Arts

This award is presented by the National Foundation for Jewish Culture, a group that works to enhance the quality of Jewish life in America through the arts and humanities.

Naomi Cohen (1927–) Prominent historian, author, and educator. A member of many scholarly organizations, she conducted extensive research on U.S. history and American-Jewish history and wrote and edited *American Jews and the Zionist Idea; Essential Papers on Jewish-Christian Relations in the United States: Imagery and Reality; After the Riots: American Responses to the Palestine Crisis of 1929–1930;* and others.

Geoffrey H. Hartman (1929–) Preeminent educator in languages. A Guggenheim fellow and a visiting professor at Yale, Cornell, the University of Iowa, the University of Chicago, and others, he wrote *The Unmediated Vision; Beyond Formalism; Selected Poetry and Prose of William Wordsworth; Holocaust Remembrance: The Shapes of Memory; The Fate of Reading;* and other titles.

Yochanan Muffs (1927–) Organizer, educator, and consultant. She worked to modify dozens of textbooks and reference books to more accurately portray Jews and Judaism and founded and participated in many organizations, seminars, and institutes for Jewish learning. She worked with the Anti-Defamation League for twenty-five years, as well as with the National Conference on Catholic Bishops to provide an accurate depiction of Jews and Judaism in Catholic schoolbooks. She also acted as a consultant for many books and films.

Roberta Peters (1930–) Opera singer and musician. A soprano with the New York Metropolitan Opera, she brought style and grace—and new popularity—to opera performance in America.

Chaim Potok (1929–) Novelist and Rabbi. Potok wrote the novels *The Book of Lights, The Chosen, Davida's Harp, In The Beginning, My Name Is Asher Lev,* and the nonfiction *Wanderings: Chaim Potok's History of the Jews.* He also served as an army chaplain in the Korean War. Potok has won many awards for his work.

Elizabeth Swados (1951–) Innovative experimental musical theatre composer. Her works include *Jerusalem, Job, Jonah,* and *Bible Women.* Her most popular musical-theater piece was the long-running Broadway show *Runaways.*

Chaim Potok. Courtesy The National Foundation for Jewish Culture

Elizabeth Swados. Courtesy The National Foundation for Jewish Culture; photo by Chuck Pulin

Great Americans

Those in this list have been chosen by the esteemed *Marquis Who's Who* organization. The original *Who's Who in America* was founded and published by Albert Nelson Marquis in 1899. The standard of admission for the regularly scheduled volumes is based on demonstrated achievement, but its Great Americans series holds even higher standards. In 1995, fifty individuals were honored at a Library of Congress Office of Scholarly Programs exhibit as part of the special Marquis program. Among them were the following Jewish-Americans:

Walter H. Annenberg (1908–   )   Publisher who added some of the most successful magazines in history, including *Seventeen* and *TV Guide,* to the empire founded by his father. He was also a great philanthropist and was appointed by President Richard Nixon as U.S. ambassador to the United Kingdom.

Avram Noam Chomsky (1928–   )   Writer, political activist, and professor of linguistics. He spent considerable time studying man's language capabilities. He served on several committees devoted to antiwar activities, disarmament, and peace.

Lincoln Kirstein (1907–1996)   Director of the School of American Ballet in

Theodore Bikel: Finding international acclaim on stage, screen, and in song.
Courtesy The National Foundation for Jewish Culture

the 1940s, director of the New York City Center of Music and Drama in the 1950s, and author of many books on ballet.

Arthur Miller (1915–   )   One of America's most important, innovative, studied, and performed playwrights, whose works include *Death of a Salesman, All My Sons, A View From The Bridge,* and *The Crucible.*

Beverly Sills (1929–   )   Soprano and musical director of the New York City Opera who brought style, grace, intelligence, thoughtfulness, humor, and warmth to opera in New York and around the world.

Susan Sontag (1933–   )   Essayist, author, and social critic who holds high standards for American art and culture in all her writings. Works include *AIDS and its Metaphors* and *Under the Sign of Saturn.*

Steven Spielberg (1947–   )   One of the most successful film directors in the history of American cinema. His movies include *Jaws, Raiders of the Lost Ark, Jurassic Park, E.T., the Extra Terrestrial, Schindler's List,* and *Saving Private Ryan.*

Elie Wiesel (1928–   )   Nobel Peace Prize–winning author whose works often reflect the horrors of the Holocaust. His works include *Night, The Fifth Son,* and *The Gates of the Forest.*

The Dor l'dor Award

This award is presented by B'nai B'rith to "individuals whose contributions to the Jewish world have transcended generations." (Note: Roberta Peters and Chaim Potok—who were noted earlier—are also Dor l'dor recipients.)

Shari Lewis: Hand-in-hand with several generations of adoring fans. Courtesy Diane Fradin

Theodore Bikel (1928–   )   Brought tons of class to the showbiz world as a multitalented gentleman of song, screen, and stage. He was the first Captain Von Trapp in *The Sound of Music* on Broadway, starred in the movies *The Defiant Ones* and *The African Queen,* and was a folksinger of note and performed in several languages.

Sid Caesar (1922–   )   Kept the country in stitches for an entire decade with his intelligent comedy and schtick on TV's *Your Show of Shows, Caesar's Hour,* and other TV and movie appearances.

Marvin Kalb (1930–   )   Veteran diplomatic correspondent for CBS and NBC News, former *Meet the Press* moderator, political author, and visiting professor at George Washington University.

Shari Lewis (1934–1998)   Television best friend to countless children over several generations through her TV shows. Her personable (and educational) routines with her puppet characters Lamb Chop, Charlie Horse, and others were truly her creations—from the voices to the skits and everything in between. She also made records and a series of fun and educational videos.

Robert Merrill (1919–   )   One of the most popular baritones of all time, he sang primarily with the New York Metropolitan Opera. Merrill was able to share his gift with an international audience.

Edwin Newman (1919–   )   Popular reporter, TV anchor, critic, author, and social commentator—particularly on America's abuse of the English language. He has won several awards for his television work, and his books, including *Strictly Speaking* and *A Civil Tongue,* were bestsellers.

Albert Sabin   Virologist who, in the late 1950s, developed an oral vaccine for polio. He also developed vaccines against encephalitis and other viral diseases, and was a tireless researcher and dedicated teacher.

The Jewish-American Hall of Fame

Inaugurated in 1969 at the Magnes Museum in Berkeley, California, the Jewish-American Hall of Fame was designed to encourage the creation of Judaic art and to educate the general public on the important contributions made by the inductees. (Note: Many other members not mentioned here are listed elsewhere in categories directly related to their areas of endeavor.)

Louis D. Brandeis The first Jew to serve on the Supreme Court as associate justice, beginning in 1916. As a private attorney, he specialized in representing people or groups that would otherwise have had a weak or nonexistent voice in their legal defenses. Brandeis University in Waltham, Massachusetts, is named after him.

Benjamin Cardoza Associate justice of the U.S. Supreme Court from 1932–1938. During President Franklin Roosevelt's administration, he upheld the constitutionality of Roosevelt's New Deal programs. He also served on the New York Supreme Court as associate justice and chief judge.

Rebecca Gratz Founded the Hebrew Sunday School Society of Philadelphia in 1838, the first Jewish Sunday school in the United States. She was also involved in other organizations devoted to the welfare of foster children.

Harry Houdini The most famous magician and escape artist of all time. He entertained millions all over the world in the early 1900s with tricks involving handcuffs, padlocks, and water tanks, setting a standard for his profession that lasts until this day.

Emma Lazarus Poet whose "New Colossus," written in 1883, was chosen to be inscribed on the base of the Statue of Liberty.

Uriah P. Levy Commodore of the U.S. Naval fleet in the Mediterranean in the early 1800s who strived to eliminate corporal punishment in the navy.

Judah L. Magnes Charismatic, intellectual, and opinionated religious leader in the first half of the twentieth century who, in addition to leading several congregations in New York, publicly demonstrated against pogroms and was very active in the peace movement. He helped establish the American Jewish Committee and devoted his life to Jewish public service. His pacifist activity, however, prompted his removal from Jewish community leadership, so he left for Palestine, where he helped found Hebrew University in Jerusalem.

Bela Schick   Noted pediatrician and pioneer for universal immunization. Throughout the 1920s, 1930s, and 1940s she worked at hospitals such as Mt. Sinai and Beth Israel in New York City, taught about disease at the Columbia University College of Physicians, and invented a test to determine susceptibility to diptheria.

Gershom Seixas   Served for fifty years as the cantor of Congregation Shearith Israel in New York. He fled during the British occupation of the city during the Revolutionary War and helped establish a synagogue in Philadelphia. After he returned to New York, he was chosen as one of thirteen clergymen to attend the inauguration of President George Washington in 1789.

Henrietta Szold   Primary organizer of Hadassah, which she and a group of others founded in 1912. Hadassah soon became the largest Zionist group and Jewish woman's organization in the world.

The Daughter of Zion, depicted in this 1910 Jewish New Year's card, was an early symbol of the organization founded by Henrietta Szold, later known as Hadassah. Courtesy The Jewish Historical Society of Greater Washington

10

The Promise

22 American Jews Who Have Championed Important Causes

*So teach us how to number our days that
we get us a heart of wisdom.*
—Book of Psalms 90:12

Why do so many Jews accomplish so much? Is it, as has been suggested by some scholars, because we want to thank God for seeing us through so many hard times? Is it because so many of us believe that God measures our deeds more than He does our faith? Is it because as members of a family- and charity-centered faith we try to provide well for everyone before our time is up?

American Jews have always had visions for the betterment of people, or groups of people, and through hard work, dedication, and skill we have consistently turned those visions into reality. Not all wish to credit their Jewishness for any measure of their success; they cannot, however, stop *us* from doing that.

Cyrus Adler   Public servant and community leader of incomparable ability and output. Between the 1890s and 1930s he helped found, develop, or lead, among other institutions, the Jewish Publication Society, American Jewish Historical Society, American Jewish Committee, and United Synagogues of America. He also served as president of the Dropsie College for Hebrew and Cognate Learning in Philadelphia and the Jewish Theological Seminary, and as editor of the *American Jewish Year Book* and the *Jewish Quarterly Review*. For fifty years, he was involved in virtually every aspect of American Jewish society and was highly respected by a vast number of dignitaries, religious leaders, and government officials for his efforts, dedication, and knowledge.

Samuel Belkin   Educator and organizer who was responsible for helping to create some of the most important institutions of higher learning in the 1950s, 1960s, and 1970s. A rabbi and scholar, Belkin began his work on the faculties of the Rabbinical College of New Haven and Yeshiva College, of which he eventually became president. After a stellar career there—having turned it into a large, respected, and internationally acclaimed institution with many graduate schools—Belkin helped establish New York's Albert Einstein College of Medicine, the Wurzweiler School of Social Work, the Benjamin Cardozo School of Law, and Stern College for women. He was also a prolific writer and persuasive exponent of cooperation between Orthodox and non-Orthodox Jewish groups and ideologies.

Peggy Charen   Founder of Action for Children's Television (ACT). Her interest came from glancing at the tube whenever her children were watching. She saw a pressing need for more quality television programming for young people and started ACT, a nonprofit organization, in 1968 to lobby for more diversity in children's TV. The organization closed shop in 1992, but Charen continued to work for the cause, and in 1996, FCC rules were strengthened to require stations to schedule more children's programming before their licenses would be renewed. In 1995 she was honored with the Presidential Medal of Freedom.

Suzanne Fineman Cohen   Professional volunteer who, throughout the 1970s and 1980s, worked tirelessly for such Baltimore-area organizations as the Board of Associated Jewish Charities, the Welfare Fund for Human Resource Development, the Health and Welfare Council, the Council for Jewish Federations, and several hospitals and colleges.

Robert J. Desnick (1943–   )   Established the International Center for Jewish Genetic Diseases at Mt. Sinai Medical School. A geneticist, pediatrician, and educator, he conducted some of the most important research on Jewish genetic diseases while working for the Genetics Society of America, the American Federation of Clinical Research, the New York Academy of Science, and other medical venues.

Samuel Gompers   One of the most important leaders in U.S. labor history. In 1882, he founded the American Federation of Labor and was its president for thirty-seven years, working diligently to use nonpolitical power and influence to improve wages and working conditions for its members.

Isaac Hays   Physician who, in 1846, developed the American Medical

Association's first Code of Ethics. Hays, an eye specialist, passionately promoted the idea that medicine was more a moral enterprise than a business during the meetings of physicians that eventually became the AMA.

Herbert Lehman   Politician and philanthropist whose social conscience and aversion to discrimination appealed to millions. He was the U.S. director general of the U.N. Relief and Rehabilitation Adminstration and then became New York's forty-seventh governor in 1932, a post to which he was reelected three times. He worked against racial and religious descrimination, averted potentially damaging strikes, and advanced the cause of old-age security.

Abraham (1880–1962), **William** (1907–1994), and **Alfred Levitt**   Father and two sons who visualized affordable and progressive communities for young families just after World War II and, through their Levitt & Sons construction firm, built successful Levittowns in New York, New Jersey, and Pennsylvania.

Annie Nathan Meyer   Champion for women's rights to higher education in the late nineteenth century. Meyer, a writer, was displeased with most colleges and universities, whose policies did not allow women to be admitted. An article she wrote for *The Nation* impressed many, and, in 1889, she founded Barnard College. Later she spent much of her time convincing women that they could go to college without compromising their desirability or marriageability, as was commonly thought. Meyer also wrote two novels, twenty plays, and a dozen short stories. Her autobiography is titled *It's Been Fun.*

Robert Moses   One of the most successful urban-suburban planners in U.S. history. He was responsible, in the 1940s, 1950s, and 1960s, for developing many of New York's most important bridges, highways, and public areas, including Long Island's famed Jones Beach (officially known as Robert Moses State Park). He was also New York State's Parks Commissioner from 1924–1964, New York City's Parks Commissioner from 1934–1960, and president of the 1964–1965 New York World's Fair.

Ernestine Louise Rose   One of the earliest and most eloquent feminists whose skilled and impassioned writings, debates, and orations also extended to the subjects of slavery and anti-Semitism. Born in Poland, where she received a Jewish education much finer than that of most women of the time, as a young woman she rebelled against her family's old-fashioned ways, traveled around Europe, married in England, and came to the United States in the 1840s. She then met Susan B. Anthony and became a vocal feminist. She wrote stirring rebuttals to works defending slavery and brilliantly debated the editor of a Boston newspaper who claimed that Judaism was inferior to Christianity. About slavery she said that even the most well-treated slaves could never truly be happy because they were robbed of belonging to themselves. About Judaism she said that while American Jews may be no better or worse than other groups, perhaps they were better citizens because of their appreciation of the United States.

Jacob Schiff Philanthropist and founding member of the American Jewish Committee and the American Jewish Relief Committee (later called the Joint Distribution Committee). He made his fortune with the railroad. In 1897, he joined E. H. Harriman to purchase the Union Pacific, which proved to be enormously lucrative. He also led one of America's largest investment banks in the early part of the twentieth century to support increased industrialization, especially the railroads.

Rose Schneiderman Labor leader who became deeply involved in women's labor problems in the early 1900s. Her observations, ideas, and organizational skills came together to help her found and preside over the National Women's Trade Union League in 1928. She was also secretary of the New York State Labor Department from 1937 to 1944.

Alan Sherman Businessman from Bethesda, Maryland, who conceived and cofounded the North American Maccabi Youth Games in 1982, based on the renowned Maccabiah Games in Israel. The Maccabi Youth Games are geared toward youngsters sixteen years of age and younger and give many youths the opportunities they might not otherwise have to develop their physical skills and to compete. He has also been very involved in U.S.–Israeli sports relations and was chairman of the International Jewish Sports Hall of Fame.

Adolphus Solomon Printer and publisher who helped found the American Red Cross. Solomon, a patriot and a very well respected man in Washington, D.C., organized the first training school for nurses in the city, was an officer in the Provident Aid Society and the Emergency Hospital of the Society for the Prevention of Cruelty to Animals, and was a founder of Mount Sinai Hospital, the Montefiore Home for Chronic Invalids, the Jewish Protectory and Aid Society, and the Russian Jews Immigration Aid Society. The key meetings in 1881 to form the American Red Cross were held and run by him in his home.

Joel Springarn Literary critic, professor, poet, publisher, and reformer who, in 1905, helped found the National Association for the Advancement of Colored People (NAACP), over which he presided for a decade. He regularly invited the black people with whom he dealt to his home during a time when separatism of the races was the norm. During World War II, he promoted the establishment of a training program for black officers. In 1913, he developed the Springarn Medal for blacks who provided immeasurable service to other blacks nationwide.

Edith Rosenwald Stern   Philanthropist who used her wealth for innumerable good causes, culturally and socially. The daughter of Julius Rosenwald (of Sears, Roebuck fame), Stern supported educational initiatives throughout New Orleans, where she and her husband, Edgar Bloom Stern, lived, including initiatives for educational opportunities for blacks. She saved the New Orleans Symphony in 1957 with financial support, endowed the New Orleans Museum of Art, and set up the Stern Fund to contribute more than $10 million to various causes—including some of Ralph Nader's efforts, studies on the side effects of nuclear energy, and the establishment of the Fund of Investigative Journalism. Voter registration was another of her favorite causes. In 1961, she was appointed by President Kennedy to serve on the National Cultural Center Advisory Committee on the Arts.

Lillian Wald   In 1890 she helped establish the first nonsectarian visiting nurse program in the United States, in New York's lower east side. Having noticed the deplorable health conditions of tenements and their inhabitants, she resolved to create a system by which skilled nurses visited infirm residents and sometimes had the patients visit the nurses at other locations. In time, her program became the famed Henry Street Settlement, the model for many other such lifesaving programs in cities around the world.

Felix Warburg   Financier and philanthropist who was an enormously positive influence on many less fortunate New Yorkers in the early 1900s. Among his activities were continued support of the Henry Street Settlement and the establishment of a babies' and children's tuberculosis prevention center. He was a major force behind the Federation for the Support of Jewish Philanthropic Societies, raised money to help Jews in Nazi Germany, and was one of the biggest patrons of the Juilliard School of Music and the New York Philharmonic Orchestra. He also served as commissioner of the New York City Board of Education.

11

The Wise Bunch

11 Rabbis Who Go Beyond the Call

*The best way to understand a story in the Bible
is to make up another story about it.*
—Rabbi Marc Gellman

Rabbi means teacher, and sometimes master. The best ones, then, are those who go beyond conducting services, officiating at ceremonies, and appealing for funds and instead teach us a little about humanity, humility, resilience, and common sense. Listed here are a select few who, through their consequential ideas, special accomplishments, persuasive writings, influential organizations, and noble deeds, reach those ideals and more.

Paula Ackerman   Not *really* a rabbi—but she played one in temple. She was the wife of Rabbi William Ackerman, who presided over the Temple Beth Israel congregation in Meridian, Massachusetts. Ackerman was a very spiritual woman and was very passionate about her involvement. At Beth Israel, she taught preconfirmation classes and led services when the rabbi was away. When William died in 1950, the congregation asked her to succeed him. She was skeptical but received informal permission from the head of the Union of Hebrew Congregations. She viewed it as a divine call—and a way to increase the role of women in religious life. The Union rescinded its permission, but it was too late. The congregation wanted her, and for a few years she was the "rabbi" of Temple Beth Israel. In 1962, she took on the role of spiritual leader of a temple in Florida until they were able to find a rabbi.

Marc Gellman   Rabbi, author, lecturer, and frequent guest on *Imus in the*

Rabbi Mark Gellman: Spiritual leader and advisor; author of books on Bible stories, faith, and religious tolerance; and a popular radio and TV guest with Monsignor Tom Hartman—they are known together as the God Squad. Courtesy HarperCollins

Morning as half of the God Squad, with Monsignor Tom Hartman. Together, Gellman and Hartman show how different faiths can peacefully coexist. Friendship, admiration, humility, humor, and open-mindedness are the ingredients of a peaceful religious society, as evidenced on Imus's radio show and in books such as *How Do You Spell GOD?* (written with Hartman) and *Does God Have a Big Toe?* Gellman also has a Ph.D. in philosophy and officiates at a temple on Long Island.

Morris Gordon   Rabbi in Virginia who cofounded eight Conservative congregations in the Washington, D.C., area and also started a successful business on the side so that he could serve those congregations without collecting a salary. During World War II, Gordon served as a chaplain in the U.S. Air Corps.

Mordecai Kaplan   Founder of Judaism's Reconstructionist Movement. In the 1940s, his Reconstructionist Foundation claimed more than three hundred Conservative and Reform rabbis as members, along with several hundred Jews from other fields, clearly establishing his ideals as those being seriously considered by a growing number of American Jews. His reforms were many, including the establishment of the bat mitzvah as a legitimate Jewish ceremony. His Judaism was the Judaism of an evolving civilization where the needs of people are the most important needs.

Isaac Leeser   A Conservative religious leader in America before there was a Conservative movement. Leeser was appointed *chazan* (cantor) of the

Tradition on the march: Sally Priesand, the first woman to be ordained as a rabbi (Reform) in the United States by a theological seminary. Courtesy The American Jewish Archives, Hebrew Union College, Cincinnati; photo by Garrett Cope

Sephardic community in Philadelphia in the mid-1800s. Throughout his life he had a string of impressive "firsts" that made him one of the most important religious public servants of the day, including establishing the first Hebrew school and rabbinical college and publishing the first English prayer book and American-Jewish translation of the Bible.

Sally Priesand   The first female rabbi ordained in the United States by a theological seminary. Her first love was teaching—and what she wanted to teach was Judaism. Ordained in 1972, her success as a dedicated teacher–rabbi prompted the rule makers to change the rules and, within a few years, female rabbis were being ordained regularly. Her first congregation was in Elizabeth, New Jersey.

Solomon Schechter   His greatest contribution was the concept that the whole of the observant Jewish community should decide on Jewish law. He presided over the Jewish Theological Seminary of America and established the United Synagogues of America, bringing Conservative Judaism into the mainstream in the early 1900s.

Menachem Schneerson   Charismatic and influential rabbi who helped turn the Lubavitcher hasidic sect into the fastest-growing and singularly dynamic wing of Orthodox Judaism. He was the first Lubavitcher rebbe to receive a secular education (he studied engineering), and when he arrived in the United States in 1942, as the movement's seventh leader, he devoted much attention to preparing effective information on Orthodox Judaism for American Jews. He also wrote many volumes of

The Ten Most Popular Temple Names in the United States

1. Beth Israel
2. Beth Shalom
3. Beth El
4. Beth Torah
5. Beth Am
6. Beth Hillel
7. Temple Emanuel
8. Young Israel
9. Temple Israel
10. B'nai Israel

Note: *Beth* means *House of,* thus Beth Israel means House of Israel, Beth Shalom means House of Peace, and so forth.

Torah commentary and helped establish many Hebrew day schools, synagogues, and counseling centers across the United States and Canada. Schneerson, who died in 1994, is still considered by the sect to be the Messiah.

Joseph Telushkin   Rabbi, scholar, lecturer, and bestselling author noted for his warm, inviting writing and speaking style. His books include *The Nine Questions People Ask About Judaism* (written with Dennis Prager); *Jewish Literacy*; *Jewish Wisdom*; and *Jewish Humor: What the Best Jewish Jokes Say About the Jews.* Topics in *Jewish Wisdom* include when, if ever, lying should be permitted, and how as an adult one can carry out the commandment to honor one's parents, even when they make unreasonable demands. Telushkin has also been the spiritual leader of the Synagogue for the Performing Arts in Los Angeles.

Isaac Mayer Wise   His Union of American Hebrew Congregations, organized in 1875, made enormously positive contributions to American Judaism by synergizing conventional customs and traditions with modern sensibilities, needs, and directions. The Central Conference of American Rabbis, which he founded in 1889, further helped establish Reform Judaism as a major and dynamic movement in the United States. Wise felt that the liberation enjoyed by all Americans should reflect the liberation to be enjoyed by all Jews. He also founded Hebrew Union College in Cincinnati.

Stephen Wise (1874–1949)   Zionist rabbi whose views on free speech, the rights of rabbis to speak out, and the need to open synagogue doors to all made him one of the most esteemed religious leaders in the first half of the twentieth century. He was a founder of the American Jewish Congress, created the Free Synagogue and Jewish Institute of Religion in New York, worked with many Zionist leaders including Chaim Weizman and David Ben-Gurion, and helped establish the NAACP and the American Civil Liberties Union. He also spoke out on civil rights and child welfare.

12

Good Sense Happens

8 Advice and Self-Help Superstars

So [said the doctor]. *Now vee may perhaps to begin. Yes?*
—closing line in *Portnoy's Complaint,* by Philip Roth

Philip Roth called the last line of his 1967 seminal novel, *Portnoy's Complaint,* a punchline, but there is obviously some seriousness to the sentiment. We all need a little help and advice from time to time. Some more than others. Actually, it's the *next* to last line of *Portnoy's Complaint* that really captures the focus: "A aaaaaaaaaaaaaaaaaaaaaaaaaaaaaaaaaaaaaaaaaaaaa aaaaaaaaaaaaaaaaaaaaaaaaaaaaaaaaaaaaaaaaaaaaaaaaaaaaaaaaaahhhh!!!!"

Typically, people in the help and advice business consider environmental issues much more than ancestral ones, scientific objectivity much more than racial explanations. Perhaps that is why, despite quite a healthy number of American Jews in the psychiatric, counseling, self-help, and advice fields, Judaism as an issue of topic of its own really has not been part of the equation or, in the case of those with books or TV and radio programs, Jewishness has rarely been part of the publicity machine.

That has been changing, however. Dr. Ruth Westheimer discusses Judaism's attitude toward sex in some of her published material. Rabbi Harold Kushner has used his success as a life-advice author to spread his thoughts on the values and wonders of Judaism. Popular radio talk-show host Dr. Laura Schlessinger was recently seen on posters all over the New York metropolitan area and in several magazine features proudly wearing a Star of David around her neck, and every once in a while speaks on the air about her faith. (Schlessinger, who was raised without religion by a Jewish father and a Catholic mother, embraced Judaism fully in the early 1990s.)

Obviously, many of the problems we face today simply aren't funny, but what is amusing (in a serious sort of way) is how the advice and self-help field, which was once so private, has turned into one of the most popular genres of mass communication.

Joyce Brothers (1928–)   For over forty years she has appeared in various media as a psychologist with the highest credibility. With a doctorate in psychology (her dissertation was on anxiety avoidance) underneath her belt, she made her first media appearance as a contestant on TV's *$64,000 Question,* and that exposure led to a TV show of her own, as well as radio spots and syndicated columns. One of the major themes of her counseling is that people with problems aren't alone.

Harold Kushner   A rabbi for over thirty years, Kushner wrote a book in 1981 to help himself and those around him cope with a family tragedy, but the public response to the book was so overwhelming that a new career was born out of it. *When Bad Things Happen To Good People* became a best seller, and it was followed by *When All You've Ever Wanted Isn't Enough, How Good Do We Have To Be, Who Needs God,* and others. *Who Needs God* discusses how religious commitment can make a difference in our lives. People appreciate his wise, gentle, sensible manner with words, and his reputation as a counselor helped earn him six honorary doctorates. He also wrote *When Children Ask About God* and *To Life! A Celebration of Being Jewish and Thinking Jewish.*

Ann Landers and **Abigail Van Buren**   Esther Pauline Friedman and her twin sister Pauline Esther Friedman have been among the most widely read and discussed newspaper advice columnists in America over the last forty years. As Ann Landers and Dear Abby, they have given pointed, caring, common-sense answers to every personal question imaginable. Esther, who had a background in political activism and volunteerism when she was asked to take over the "Ann Landers" column in the *Chicago Sun-Times* in 1955, provided more useful referrals to her readers than the previous writer of the column. Pauline, who took the name Abigail Van Buren, began her own column (Dear Abby) in the *San Francisco Chronicle* at about the same time, with a similar tough-love approach. Today, their syndicated columns reach millions of readers daily. In 1975, Landers openly shared with her readers the news of her divorce.

Dennis Prager   Lecturer, theologian, teacher, author, and radio talk-show host. Common sense, morals, and wisdom, along with the skills of a personal storyteller are the instruments he uses in his shows, his essays,

Dr. Ruth Westheimer: TV, radio, and hardcover good-sex guru. Courtesy Dr. Ruth Westheimer

his lectures, and his books to make his point. His writings include *Happiness Is a Serious Problem* and *Think a Second Time.* He also wrote *The Nine Questions People Ask About Judaism* with Joseph Telushkin.

Dr. Laura Schlessinger Famous radio talk show therapist. Dr. Laura, as she is known to the eighteen million listeners of her nationally syndicated radio show, has strong convictions about relationships and parenthood. She tells people not to blame anyone but themselves for their unhappiness—and then she'll cheer them on by making them feel encouraged, self-respected, and morally sound. Dr. Laura has a Ph.D. in physiology, is a licensed marriage and family therapist, and has taught at the University Medical School in New York and Pepperdine University in California. Her books include *Ten Stupid Things Women Do to Mess Up Their Lives, Ten Stupid Things Men Do to Mess Up Their Lives, How Can You Do That?* and *The Ten Commandments.*

Martin Seligman (1942–) One of his primary themes is not to waste time on trying to make impossible changes in your life: recognize what can be changed, and then make the changes with realistic expectations. His books include *The Biological Boundaries of Learning; Helplessness: On Depression, Development, and Death; Learned Optimism;* and others. Seligman has done extensive research on mental health and depression with grants from the National Institute of Mental Health, the National Institute on Aging, the National Science Foundation, the Guggenheim Foundation, and the MacArthur Foundation.

Ruth Westheimer (1928–   )   Born Karola Ruth Siegel in Germany, she lived for a while in Poland, then Switzerland, then Palestine, where she taught kindergarten, and then Paris, where she received a psychology degree. Once in New York, she went to the New School for Social Research on a scholarship for Holocaust victims, worked for a planned parenthood clinic, and earned a degree in family counseling in 1970. Shortly thereafter, she became radio's most famous sex counselor as Dr. Ruth, known for her exuberance and her smile. Her TV shows include *Good Sex With Dr. Ruth* and *Sexually Speaking,* and her books include *Dr. Ruth's Guide to Good Sex* and *Sex for Dummies.*   She also has a CD-ROM. Her teachings include sexuality with joy and responsibility.

13

Double Minority

The Facts on Black Judaism

I've got to be me, I've got to be me...
—from the song popularized by Sammy Davis Jr.

According to most of the estimates available from various sources, there are between 135,000 and 260,000 black Jews in America today.* Many descend from the vigorous Ethiopian Jewish community. Others are born of white Jewish mothers and black fathers. Some are descendants of black converts to Judaism dating back to American and West Indian slavery. A segment are more modern converts.

It is often not easy being black in America and sometimes it's not that easy being Jewish. Being a black Jew has got to be positively frightening.

But it's not, apparently. By and large, they are a proud people, optimistic and deeply spiritual. Many black Jewish congregations trace their origins to the teaching and philosophy of the late Rabbi Wentworth A. Matthew, who had presided over Harlem's Ethiopian Hebrew Congregation. Matthew credited the collective strength of his community to what he termed collectively towering father figures and tenacious mothers who set the tone and mood of family life.

According to a spokesman for Beth Elohim Hebrew Congregation in New York, most black Jews follow customs closely resembling those of the modern Orthodox, with definite Conservative and African-American influences. At Beth Elohim, for example, they follow kosher dietary laws but do not require the separation of milk and meat products. They allow travel

---

*The *Reference Library of Black Americans,* vol. V, estimates only about 44,000 black Jews in the United States.

Reuben Greenberg, Chief of Police,
Charleston, South Carolina. Courtesy
Charleston Police Department

on the Sabbath. They observe and celebrate Passover, Rosh Hashanah, Yom
Kippur, Chanukah, and Purim, among others, but also have special Sabbath
services in memory of Rabbi Matthew and Dr. Martin Luther King.

The Alliance of Black Jews was recently formed to "unite people of
African-American descent who believe in the Torah and/or the practice of
Judaism." It was co-founded by Robin Washington, a black Jew who is
managing editor of the *Bay State Banner,* a black community newspaper in
the Boston area. Washington was brought up in Chicago in the 1950s and
1960s as a Reform Jew by his black father and white Jewish mother and says
he is "one hundred percent of both." For him, religion was just another civil
rights issue.

Black Jews put an emphasis on family and education, not divisiveness
and controversy, which may be why black Judaism is not as hot a media topic
as it might otherwise be. And yet, the Beth Elohim spokesman says his group
is in constant contact with minister Louis Farrakhan of the Nation of Islam
on various issues and that "the dialogue has been good." The controversial
Rev. Al Sharpton has also been a visitor to their synagogue.

From time to time we come across references to the positive dialogues,
events, and actions concerning the black-Jewish relationship. These actions
may not be weighty enough or numerous enough to truly make that much of
a difference, but they are real, and they are genuine: in 1940, for example,
the NAACP was founded by (among others) literary critic, publisher and
professor Arthur B. Springarn, who served as president of the organization,

and many Jews marched with Martin Luther King. So there is some synergy, and if the black Jewish population estimates are correct, that synergy still has a chance to turn into a true bond.

Among the notable black Jews in America yesterday and today are actor and comedian Godfrey Cambridge, actor Yaphet Kotto, author Julius Lester, and Reuben Greenberg, Chief of Police in Charleston, South Carolina.

Greenberg was appointed Chief of Police in 1982 and has had a distinguished career in law enforcement from California to Florida. (He has also taught sociology and political science on the university level.) His paternal grandfather was white and Jewish and died before Reuben was born. The family's Jewish identity died with him. His parents shortened their surname to Green and raised their children as Methodists. Reuben began to reidentify with his Jewish roots while in college. He has stated that the knowledge of his Jewish heritage, combined with his secular experiences with Jews, made him feel that Judaism could offer him a religious path with the kind of dignity and reverence he demanded of life.

14

The Tummlers

The 116 Funniest Jews in the World

The Jews are members of the human race—
worse I can say of no man.
—Mark Twain

A poor, sickly old Jewish man looks up to the heavens and says, "Why, God, why? Why do you make me suffer so?" And God answers him, "Because you're always nudging me."

Milton Berle once commented that if you need proof that humor can insulate almost an entire people against everything life can dump on it, don't look any further than the Jews.

Why are Jews so funny? Is it because so much of life is sad? One interpretation rests squarely on the cramped shoulders of ghetto life and the difficult assimilation many immigrant families suffered. Young men from the ghetto quickly discovered they had a gift for discussing their tough childhoods with humor and a bit of introspection. And after they exhausted that topic, they turned to other crazy things, like sex, wives, mothers-in-law, and brothers-in-law.

Jewish comics through the years have helped us put life and its disappointments into perspective. Just as often, they let us set aside our psychological baggage and feel good about ourselves for a moment or two (unless you happen to be seeing Don Rickles).

There's one theory that places the genesis of modern Jewish humor in Czarist Russia. Jewish foreign students were allowed to attend talmudic schools there, and in doing so they spent virtually every hour of every day in their little groups to study, dine, and pass the time. Winter nights were long and tedious. The students would gather around the stove for warmth and talk about many subjects, including sex; then they shared old folk tales from back home. They discussed their visions of the past and their hopes for the future. They took all these collected stories and jokes and tales with them when they finally returned to their hometowns, and eventually to America, where the stories were Americanized, revised, embellished, and sometimes immortalized.

> *"Mrs. Finklestein, there's just one little problem. You have a floating kidney. But if you want to know the truth, if it was my kidney I really wouldn't worry about it."*
> *"Dr. Nudelman, if it was your kidney I wouldn't worry about it either."*

> *"Close the window, Sam. It's cold outside."*
> *"You mean if I close the window it will get warm outside?"*

Many of the great vaudeville and burlesque comics actually began as showbiz kids. Georgie Jessel was nine when he sang for the first time at the Imperial Theatre in New York while his mother sold tickets at the box office. Meanwhile, across town, Sandra Berlinger became obsessed with the dream of having one of her children become a star, so she poured all her dreams and energy into little Milton after deciding her older three boys didn't stand a chance. "Milton," she said to him when he was just a toddler, "be funny."

Milton Berle listened to his mom.

The Marx Brothers proved that motion pictures could be an even greater medium for laughter because of the ability for audiences to get a close look at the boys' classic sight gags and facial expressions, much of which did not have the same effect on stage. Meanwhile, behind the microphone, Jack Benny's famous bouts with Fred Allen forever changed the course of radio humor.

The Catskill inns, where even the radio and early TV people came to polish up their acts from time to time, were originally owned by Eastern European Jews who made their comics work hard for a few dollars a week. The comics were paid to be funny all day, and if that meant jumping into the pool wearing tuxedo, so be it.

At one point there were over a thousand Catskill resorts. It was the Jewish Alps, the Borscht Belt, the place to be seen. For many comics, working the mountains was *the* way to build a carrer.

> *Two Jewish ladies are having lunch together at a restaurant in Miami Beach. The waiter comes over to them and asks, "Ladies, is anything all right?"*

Eve: Adam, do you really love me?
Adam: You're the only one!

In 1948, there were thirty television stations in fifteen states, and about four hundred thousand households had TV sets. By the following year, the number had more than quadrupled to two million television families, and many of them got in the habit of watching Milton Berle on *Texaco Star Theater,* Sid Caesar on *The Admiral Broadway Revue,* and Jerry Lester and Morey Amsterdam on *Broadway Open House.* Eddie Cantor and Jack Benny moved swiftly and effortlessly from radio to TV. Steve Allen and Jack Paar were soon on the air introducing the likes of Joey Bishop, Shelley Berman, Phil Ford, and Buddy Hackett, and soon after Steve Allen introduced a new breed including Mort Sahl and Lenny Bruce. For over twenty years it was a career-making move to get on the *Ed Sullivan Show.* For over forty years the same has been true of *The Tonight Show.*

In the late 1950s, both Mort and Lenny led a parade of intellectual tummlers through the comedy club scene, from clubs like "the hungry i" in San Francisco to The Comedy Store in Los Angeles a few years later, followed by The Improv and Catch a Rising Star. But then TV regained its power from the 1970s on, with Gabe Kaplan reining in the Sweathogs in *Welcome Back, Kotter,* Roseanne Arnold running the house on *Roseanne,* Richard Lewis kvetching on *Anything But Love,* and Paul Reiser documenting urban love in *Mad About You.* Their views on life and their nagging quandaries were not much different from those of Alan King and Joan Rivers, who nagged and philosophized in the Borscht Belt years earlier. The difference is, of course, that a comic can reach a greater audience on one night in a hit TV show than in twenty years of Catskill appearances.

Alan King and Joan Rivers represent dozens of Jewish comics with regard to the reasons they chose the paths they did. And while they may never have had hit TV shows, they bounced around with amazing skill and ease from the Catskills to the nightclubs to the TV screen and back again.

Alan King's impoverished father, who held over forty jobs while Alan was growing up, told his son that when people listen to you, you're important. "The greatest gift I've given you is that I'm nothing, so you got no footsteps to follow in," the comedian quotes his father as saying. Alan King wanted to be listened to. But it was tough. Smart alecks in the neighborhood and tough guys on the street provided unfair competition. "Clowning around was my way of standing out in the crowd," King says.

One of the happiest moments of Joan Rivers's childhood was when she played a kitten in a prekindergarten play. She wore a bunny hat which got a lot of attention. Afterwards, wanting her happiness to continue, she refused

to take the hat off. She realized that she didn't have to be herself. She could
be a beautiful princess with a little make-believe up on stage.

May a child be named after you. Soon.

A woman goes into the Kosher deli, points to two pickled herrings
  and asks the counterman, "How much for the herring?"
The man answers, "Two for $5."
"How much for just that one?" she asks.
"$3."
"Okay. I'll take the other one."

For almost a hundred years now, Jewish tummlers have made fun of Jews
while at the same time showing how much they loved and admired their own
people. Even some non-Jews did it. Eddie Murphy's old Jewish man on
Saturday Night Live had an aura of respect around him. Steve Allen, who's
not Jewish but should be and probably would be if not for the fact that he
isn't, once roasted Sammy Davis Jr. at a Variety Club luncheon with a couple
of Jewish-flavored zingers. Sammy, Allen said, would consider starring in one
of the popular TV series of the day only if the names were to changed to *Gun
Schmuck, Star Drek, The Ghost and Mrs. Meyer, The Man From Yankle,
Batman and Son,* and *Hawaii $49.95.*

Which just goes to prove that you don't *have* to be Jewish to be a Jewish
comedian. But it helps.

Joey Adams (1911–   )   Wrote the book on the Borscht Belt, literally and
figuratively (*The Borscht Belt,* Bobbs-Merrill, New York, 1966). He
specializes in one-liners, parodies, and wrote the "Strictly For Laughs"
column in the *New York Post* for years.

Marty Allen (1922–   )   "Hello dere." A hairy nut, with or without sidekick
Steve Rossi.

Woody Allen (1935–   )   From *Annie Hall* to *Zelig,* he's the schnook who
took the money and ran. Allen truly believes the universe is merely a
fleeting idea in God's mind, which is a pretty uncomfortable thought if
you've just made a downpayment on a house.

Robert Alper (1945–   )   The world's only practicing clergyman doing
stand-up comedy…intentionally.

Morey Amsterdam (1914–1996)   The human joke machine. Amsterdam
wrote for Jack Benny and Bob Hope on the radio and cohosted the first
regularly scheduled late-night program on network TV. He also played
Buddy Sorrell on *The Dick Van Dyke Show* with nagging perfection.

Rabbi-turned-comic Bob Alper.
Courtesy Bob Alper

Sandy Baron Baron played Lenny Bruce perfectly on stage in *Lenny* in Los Angeles, even though Baron himself was one of the nicest and cleanest of the comedy lounge stars.

Benny Bell (1906—) Funniest nonfamous novelty songwriter in the world. His songs include "Shaving Cream," "Everybody Loves My Fanny," "Take a Ship for Yourself," "I'm Going Home Again (Without Pants)," and more.

Richard Belzer (1944—) Has been a rising star for over twenty-five years at clubs and on TV. Reagan was his big thing. With Reagan gone, dramatic TV has been a good replacement.

Jack Benny (1894–1974) World's richest miser. His brilliant use of comic timing set the industry standard. His TV show was groundbreaking, his career prolific.

Molly Berg Molly personified. She created *Molly Goldberg* on radio in 1929, did *Me and Molly* on Broadway in 1948, *The Goldbergs* on TV from 1949 to 1955, and the movie, *Molly* in 1951.

Shelley Berman (1926—) One of the first neurotic schlemiels, a sort of benign Lenny Bruce. Berman also had roles on TV's *That's Life* and *Fernwood Tonight*.

Sandra Bernhard (1955—) Coarse, raw, and nervy, with a stare that can be as vicious as her diatribes. Bernhard was great in *The King of Comedy* as the moll who ties up Jerry Lewis.

Comedian and novelty songwriter Benny Bell, from the cover of his landmark Pincus the Peddler *(1946).* Author's Collection

Joey Bishop (1918–)   From Burlesque to Vaudeville to the Catskills, Bishop was an early fave of Frank Sinatra's, who let him become one of two Jewish Rat Packers, the second, of course, being Sammy Davis Jr. He also did lots of TV, including his own sitcom and talk show.

Ben Blue   A limber-limbed, glum-faced comic who never attained the stardom many of his peers did, although he did do several movies, including *College Rhythm* and *My Wild Irish Rose.* Mime was one of his specialties.

Elaine Boosler (1952–)   A close buddy of the late Andy Kaufman's who has appeared many times on David Letterman's and Jay Leno's shows. She does stand-up about being single, sex, worry warts, sex, growing up, sex.

Victor Borge (1909–)   When he was kicked out of Denmark, it was America's gain. A piano-based humorist whose inspired musical lunacy sort of creeps up on you and doesn't let go.

David Brenner   A documentary filmmaker before he tried stand-up. Brenner was a frequent talk show guest in the 1970s and 1980s, where he spilled more whine than a drunk Manischewitz salesman.

Fanny Brice   Baby Snooks. A funny, funny girl. Signed by Florenz Ziegfeld in 1910, she cracked up audiences on stage and on radio for many years.

Albert Brooks (1947–)   From losing his mind in *Lost in America* to winning Meryl Streep in *Defending Your Life,* Brooks is a comic filmmaker whose comedy is a very unique acquired taste.

Mel Brooks   The 2,000-year-old comic who has blazed humorous trails in the movies since *The Producers* in 1968 (for which he won an Oscar for best original screenplay).

Lenny Bruce   His album *Sick Humor* was nominated for a Grammy in 1959; four years later he was dead of a drug overdose. Bruce talked about everything from small-time operators to big ol' vibrators.

George Burns (1896–1996)   The first sitcom star to talk directly to the audience and the first comic to make millions by doing virtually nothing but standing there. He was also the first entertainer to be booked well into the twenty-first century as early as 1982.

Psychiatrist: Mrs. Stein, do you usually wake up grumpy in the morning?
Mrs. Stein: No, I usually let him sleep late.

What do you mean I don't make good money. My salary runs to four figures: my wife and three daughters.

Red Buttons (1919–   )   Strange things are happening. A little guy who finally got a dinner.

Sid Caesar (1922–   )   He used his skill with dialects and rubber facial features to find success on Broadway, in the Catskills, and on the best sketch comedy variety show in TV history.

Eddie Cantor (1892–1964)   Banjo-eyed vaudevillian and star of the Ziegfeld Follies of 1917, 1918, and 1919. He was big in movies, too, including *Roman Scandal* and *If You Knew Susie.*

Jack Carter   A sort of frenetic, nervous, classic cut-up, he did lots of TV hosting and guesting in the late 1940s and early 1950s, including *Cavalcade of Stars* on Dumont in 1949, then became a prince in Atlantic City.

Myron Cohen (1902–1986)   Classic Jewish storyteller. As a salesman, preshowbiz, he told funny stories to his customers. They laughed, so he took it to nightclubs and TV. When asked why he called a man a black bastard, he replied he didn't—the guy asked him where the drug store was and he said he was a *block past it.*

Irwin Corey (1912–   )   The real nutty professor, Corey was blacklisted for a while by the networks for a less than decent tongue.

Norm Crosby (1927–   )   Celebrity roasts were the pineapple of his career.

Billy Crystal (1947–   )   Sammy, Muhammad, Buddy Young Jr. From his early days on *Soap,* he rose to *City Slickers* and hosted the Oscars to great acclaim. Don't get me started.

Bill Dana (1924–   )   The first Jewish Latin American astronaut, as José Jiminez, which he did on *The Steve Allen Show* and on his own show. José at one time was a bullfighter who gave himself the name *El Chicken.*

Selma Diamond   had a voice like Brillo, by her own admission. Others said it was more like a chainsaw. Before she became famous for playing bailiff Selma Hacker on *Night Court,* she wrote comedy for Groucho Marx, Sid Caesar, Perry Como, and was a regular on *The Jack Paar Show.* She also did some stage work and appeared in the movies *My Favorite Year* and *All of Me.*

Jack Eagle   Catskill plunk and Xerox monk.

Herb Edelman (1933–   )   Played the stage and movie versions of the telephone repairman in *Barefoot in the Park,* Murray the cop in the film *The Odd Couple,* and dozens of other memorable character parts on the big and small screen.

Harry Einstein   Parkyakarkas.

Bennie Fields   With his partner, wife Blossom Seeley, he was a regular on the Vaudeville, nightclub, and hotel circuits for many years. Mostly she sang and he did the comic relief, although he had a pretty good voice himself.

Totie Fields (1930–1978)   The ultimate talk-show guest, like a funny old aunt who visits and stays longer than your mother wants her to. She was big and bumptious.

Phil Foster (1914–1985)   Catskills, clubs, Caesar, Paar, Sullivan, *Laverne and Shirley.*

David Frye (1934–   )   Scathing political humor, much of it on TV, with Nixon his biggest butt. He also did JFK, Nelson A. Rockefeller, and Hubert H. Humphrey.

Jackie Gayle   Lounge Star of the Year, 1973.

Jack Gilford (1907–1990)   Shuffled amiably between Broadway, TV and films for over fifty years. *Soap, The Duck Factory, Save the Tiger,* and *Catch-22* among the many.

Gilbert Gottfried   Lent his voice to a parrot in *Aladdin,* but thank God no one parrots that voice, which is a cross between Broderick Crawford and Joe Pesci.

Sheckey Greene (1926–   )   Mr. Las Vegas. Nice with clothes, nimble with words, naughty with innuendo. His daughter went to SMU. She could have gone to UCLA but it was one more letter she'd have to remember.

My doctor told me I had low blood pressure, so he gave me the bill. That raised it.

> *A resourceful mohel created a little leather pouch in which he kept the tools of his trade. Upon entering the Greenberg's house where he was to perform a circumcision, Mrs. Greenberg asked about his leather pouch.*
>
> *That's my bris kit, the mohel proudly replied.*
>
> *"Oh, that's not necessary," she said instantly. "I have a roast in the oven."*

Morty Gunty   A solid loop on the Borscht Belt. He was Woody Allen's choice to play Catskill pro Morty Gunty in *Broadway Danny Rose.*

Buddy Hackett (1924–   )   For a crooked-mouthed little tub, he sure made his mark in showbiz. His Catskill, nighclub, and talk show appearances and celebrity roasts would *never* have aired on TV in the old days. He was also in *The Music Man* and *The Little Mermaid.* Word is he has a sign on his intended burial plot: Coming Soon.

Stanley Myron Handleman   He looked, acted, and sounded like a Stanley Myron Handleman, which could be funny at times. A regular on TV's *The Golddiggers* in 1968, he then played the elevator operator on *Make Room For Granddaddy* in 1970. Other than that...? Maybe his name was too long.

Willie Howard (1886–1949)   Vaudeville schlump. Also a singer and mimic.

Marty Ingels (1936–   )   Hyper-vocal comic actor from *I'm Dickens, He's Fenster,* Ingels was Rob Petrie's army buddy on *The Dick Van Dyke Show.*

Lou Jacobi (1913–   )   Everything you always wanted to know about stereotypical old Jewish men but were afraid to ask. Jacobi was a riot in *My Favorite Year.*

Georgie Jessel (1898–1981)   The Toastmaster General and one of the first dais kings. He starred in the Broadway production of *The Jazz Singer.*

Milt Kamen (1924–1977)   Old reliable on game shows and Merv Griffin.

Gabe Kaplan (1947–   )   From clubs to Carson to a successful one-man show called *Groucho,* and in between, *Welcome Back, Kotter,* which gave the world Arnold Horshack and John Travolta.

Mickey Katz (1909–1985)   Musician and parodist extraordinaire, he played with Spike Jones and his City Slickers. His own comedy recordings included *Duvid Crockett* and *Shleppin' My Baby Back Home.*

Andy Kaufman (1949–1984)   Took on Elvis, Mighty Mouse, Latka, and female wrestlers.

Danny Kaye (1913–1981)   A red-headed *pessel* of *naches,* he made classic movies like *The Secret Life of Walter Mitty* and *The Kid From Brooklyn,* did encore performances at the London Palladium, and was a UNICEF ambassador, pilot, baseball team owner, and symphony conductor.

Alan King (1927–　) A cross between a Jewish college professor and a kindly uncle who made sure you stayed out of trouble, King shared pet peeves with hundreds of Catskill and TV audiences. Airlines were a particularly fertile target.

Robert Klein (1942–　) King of the college campuses in the 1970s. He began with Second City, and did Broadway, TV, movies. He showed us how we *all* grew up in the Twilight Zone. He went to Alfred University, which accepted the top 105 percent of his high school class.

Harvey Korman (1927–　) A classic second banana comic foil: Carol's guy on TV, Mel's in the movies.

Bert Lahr (1895–1967) Gnong gnong gnong. Burlesque to Vaudeville to Oz.

Steve Landesberg (1945–　) The deadpan Dietrich on *Barney Miller* got his start on the club circuit and lately has been loaning his voice to radio ads.

Pinky Lee (1916–1993) Ha Ha Hee Hee. A sight-gag song-and-dance man whose TV career ranged from variety shows like *Those Two* in 1951 to children's programs like *The Gumby Show* in 1957.

Carol Leifer After more than a decade of stand-up, she went into writing (*Seinfeld*) and producing (*The Larry Sanders Show*) and finally got a show of her own, *Alright, Already*.

Jack E. Leonard (1911–1973) Was insulting people even before Rickles. There was nothing wrong with him that reincarnation won't cure.

Father to swimming club director: "This is a restricted club? Well, my son's only half Jewish. Maybe he can go in up to his knees."

Mrs. Schmulnik came home from the doctor and was very upset. "He told me I had too big a tuchis and have to lose fifty pounds," she cried to her husband.

Mr. Schmulnik promptly went to the doctor's office to complain. "Did you tell my wife she has too big a tuchis and has to lose fifty pounds?"

"No," said the doctor, "I told her she has tuberculosis and has to lose fifty pounds."

Sam Levenson (1911–1980) A folk humorist who made frequent appearances on *To Tell the Truth* and talk shows. Children were a favorite topic of his routines. Wrote the book *In One Era and Out the Other.*

Jerry Lewis (1923–   )   A nutty guy, with or without Dean. Julius Kelp was brilliant, in more ways than one. It's Jerry's hammy, muggy billboard face many used to see on the way up to the Catskills.

Richard Lewis   A cross between Woody Allen and Columbo, with an extra dose of Seinfeld's angst thrown in. His routines covered everything *and* love.

Jon Lovitz (1957–   )   Yeah, that's it. That's the ticket! *Saturday Night Live, The Critic.* That's right. Yeah…

Howie Mandel   He's not really a doctor but he played one on TV. Good thing he's not, because if you gave him a surgical glove he'd just as soon stick it over his head and blow it up.

The Marx Brothers   Groucho (1890–1977), Chico (1887–1961), Harpo (1888–1964), and sometimes Zeppo (1901–1979) and Gummo. From Broadway to films, Minnie's boys tore up any sanity clause they had and threw lots of cocoanuts and horsefeathers off a viaduct into immortality.

Jackie Mason (1903–   )   The greatest comedian in the world—according to him. He was already an adult when he figured out what playing doctor meant. By that time, he couldn't get a game started. "Even the kids who wanted to be accountants played doctor."

Marilyn Michaels   Impressionist; does Joan Rivers sometimes better than Joan does; Streisand, too. Her mother was a cantor.

Howie Morris (19 –   )   A regular on *Your Show of Shows,* Morris also played Jerry Lewis's father in *The Nutty Professor.*

Zero Mostel (1915–1977)   A funny thing happened on the way to Anatevka. A one-of-a-kind performer.

Jan Murray (1917–   )   Imagine if all game shows had schticklers like him at the helm? Murray played the mountains—but also hosted *Sing It Again, Blind Date, Treasure Hunt, Chain Letter, Dollar a Second,* and others.

Mike Nichols (1913–   ) and **Elaine May** (1932–   )   were graduates of the cerebral era, in which they performed at cabarets and improv joints and eventually had separate movie careers behind the lens. They recently collaborated on *Primary Colors* (she wrote, he directed).

Molly Picon (1898–1992)   Yiddish theatre legend. *Shmendrick* on Broadway, as well as *Hello, Dolly* and *Hello, Molly.* Was also Yenta the Matchmaker in the film version of *Fiddler on the Roof.* Right? Of course right.

Gilda Radner (1948–1989)   It's always something. Radner was a brilliant sketch and character comic who left us far too early, taking Baba Wawa and Roseann Rosanadanna with her.

Carl Reiner (1923–   )   Alan Brady on *The Dick Van Dyke Show,* of which he was the major architect. Before that he was Sid Caesar's main support beam. He also wrote or directed dozens of films like *The Thrill of It All; The Jerk; Where's Poppa;* and *Oh, God!*

Paul Reiser (1956–   )   A stand-up guy who went back in time for *Diner,* ahead for *Aliens,* and is *Mad About You* right here and now.

Don Rickles (1926–   )   He's the merchant of venom—but how can you get mad at someone who looks like Mr. Potato Head? His movies include *Kelly's Heroes* and TV guest shots include a warm-hearted burglar on *The Dick Van Dyke Show.*

The Ritz Brothers   Al (1901–1965), Jimmy (1903–1955), and Harry (1906–1986). A comedy dance team in Vaudeville, they were three of the best second bananas in early films like *Sing, Baby, Sing* and *Life Begins in College.*

Joan Rivers (1935–   )   With a style of her own, several talk shows of her own, and a few books of her own, she can now own Larchmont if she so desires. If God wanted her to cook, he would have given her aluminum hands. Her books include *Enter Whining* and *Still Whining.*

Roseanne (1953–   )   The female Ralph Kramden. From The Comedy Store to *The Tonight Show* to the Conner family of Lanford, Illinois.

Benny Rubin (1899–1986)   Four hundred bug-eyed appearances on Jack Benny's radio and TV programs.

Mort Sahl (1927–   )   A clean-cut rebel from the "hungry i" crowd and a social and political critic who would laugh at his stuff even before we did.

Soupy Sales (1926–   )   White Fang. Black Tooth. And lots of pies. One of a kind.

Adam Sandler (1966–   )   His "Chanukah Song" listing lots of famous Jewish actors hit a popular chord a few Chanukahs ago, and now he's trying to become one of them.

Avery Schreiber (1935–   )   Huh? Yeah. Huh? Yeah. Huh? Yeah. With Jack Burns, he went from Second City to Sullivan and also did a lot of solo work as an actor.

Jerry Seinfeld (1955–   )   Multimillions from a show about nothing—and he always looks like he can't believe it.

Single white Jewish professional, 38, 5'9", not too thin, not too fat, still have most of my hair, seeking good-looking maidel who likes a good book and priceless old-fashioned jukeboxes. If interested, please send a picture of your jukebox.

"Pop, in science we're learning about vacuums. What's a vacuum?
"A void."
"I know it's a void, but what does it mean?"

Garry Shandling (1949–) With a face that is the visual equivalent of indigestion, he was brilliant as Larry Sanders. No flipping.

Dick Shawn (1924–1987) From *Arthur Godfrey's Talent Scouts* to Vegas with Marlene Dietrich and Zsa Zsa Gabor, Shawn will always be remembered as the lead in the "Springtime for Hitler" number in *The Producers.*

Allan Sherman (1924–1973) *Sarah Jackman, Sarah Jackman. Glory, Glory Harry Lewis.* Besides being a "folksinger," he also cocreated *I've Got a Secret.*

Sammy Shore (1925–) King of the warm-ups, Shore is the "preacher" who founded the Comedy Store in Los Angeles.

Phil Silvers (1911–1985) Once Silvers was a big nightclub draw, but he really struck it rich on TV's *You'll Never Get Rich.*

Smith and Dale The original Sunshine Boys. Joe Smith (1884–1981) and Charles Dale (1881–1971) were top sketch Vaudevillians as early as 1906.

Arnold Stang (1925–) A Milton Berle regular in the 1950s, he was chinless but took it on the chin better than anyone when it came to providing comic support. Appeared in *The Goldbergs, December Bride,* and was the voice of the cartoon feline Top Cat.

David Steinberg (1942–) One of the Smothers Brothers' best sermoners, despite what all the hate mail said. Anti-war, pro-sarcasm.

Jon Stewart (1953–) Unstoppable, unpredictable, unleavened, but nevertheless fast-rising comedian who has had a real talk show, took over a fake one (*The Larry Sanders Show*), an HBO special, a movie, and several writing projects. By his own admission, he'll write anything from screenplays to comments on hospitality cards in hotel rooms.

Jerry Stiller (1927–) Half of the cute, endearing, and enduring Stiller and Meara. They actually went from Sullivan to Shakespeare with ease, although in Central Park they stayed away from the Jewish—Irish–Catholic thing. Recently, Jerry has had to put up with his son, George Costanza. "You want a piece of me?!"

Harold J. Stone (1911–) There haven't been too many "Jewish" television shows over the last few decades, but he starred in two of them as the quintessential funny Jewish father. He was the second Jake Goldberg on *The Goldbergs* and Sam Steinberg in *Bridget Loves Bernie.*

The Three Stooges Moe (1897–1975), Shemp (1900–1955), and Curly

(1903–1952) (Larry was not a brother). Fine bunch of boys, if slapface comedy is your thing.

Marc Weiner (1952–)   Every once in a while, a comic comes along with an entirely new concept—and sometimes it works. His *Weinerville* schtick—human faces over puppet bodies—became a successful entry on the Nickelodeon cable channel beginning in 1993. He also regularly gets "slimed" on the Nickelodeon game show.

Gene Wilder (1935–)   Dependable comic film actor. Leo Blum in Mel Brooks's *The Producers,* the Wako Kid in Mel Brooks's *Blazing Saddles,* Dr. Frankenstein's grandson in Mel Brooks's *Young Frankenstein;* has also done a lot without Mel thank you very much.

Dennis Wolfberg   Fast-rising, wild-faced comic from the club circuit in the early 1990s who made colon exams funny. He was about to go big-time but died too young.

Robert Wuhl (1951–)   Introduced as the Jewish Jerry McGuire by Billy Crystal during *Comic Relief* because of his role as a sports promoter on HBO's *Arli$$*. He may not have Tom Cruise's looks, but Tom doesn't go from stand-up to *Batman* to TV like Wuhl does.

Ed Wynne (1886–1966)   Clownish, giggling, childlike nebbish with a lisp who started as a haberdasher but threw his hat into comedy with *The Ziegfeld Follies* of 1914 and 1915. Television and movies followed, including *The Absent-Minded Professor, Cinderfella,* and *Mary Poppins.*

Henny Youngman (1906–1997)   Take his one-liners, please. Used to do more than two hundred engagements annually in clubs, roasts, bar mitzvahs....That's about two million one-liners a year.

15

Heavyweights

35 Good Sports

*You mean they want to give you that kind of money just to go out
and play with the baseball?*

—David Greenberg to his eighteen-year-old son Hank

"**M**y Benny the boxing champ" has never been part of the classic Jewish mother's repertoire of *what-I-want-my-son-to-be-when-he-grows-up* anthems. Still, the number of Jewish-American boxing champions in the first half of the twentieth century is an eyeopener (unless you happen to be a Jewish mother, in which case it is probably something you don't want to discuss). From Abe Attell, who was the world featherweight champ from 1901 to 1912, to Barney Ross, the world lightweight champ from 1933 to 1935 and welterweight champ from 1934 to 1938, boxing for a time seemed almost a Jewish sport.

And why not? Boxing, for all its lumps, is still a sport of discipline and skill, and those are two traits rather typical of the Jewish professional, from business to Broadway to boxing. Jackie Fields, Louis Kaplan, Battlin' Levinsky, Benny Leonard, Al McCoy, Maxie Rosenblum and others joined Attell and Ross in the champion's corner through the years.

The need to knock some sense (vicariously, at least) into an otherwise senseless world might explain the attraction of boxing to young Jews from the ghetto, but it wouldn't even begin to explain baseball, football, swimming or any of the other sports in which Jewish-American heroes have excelled. Perhaps there *is* nothing specific that can explain that—other than the passion each pro had for their sport. (Passion is also a Jewish trait.) Today we can look not only to the major sports for our Jewish-American heroes and heroines but to such diverse endeavors as bowling, table tennis—even bullfighting (Sidney Franklin, born Sidney Frumkin in New York).

Unfortuately for Mr. Franklin, bullfighting has not been considered for the International Jewish Sports Hall of Fame. But nearly one hundred other Jewish American athletes have already been inducted, in twenty separate sports. The International Jewish Sports Hall of Fame honors Jewish men and women "who have accomplished extraordinary achievements in sports." Now based in Israel, it originally began as the Jewish Hall of Fame in the United States honoring American athletes only. The following—the heaviest of the Jewish-American heavyweights in sports—all are honorees of the International Jewish Sports Hall of Fame.

Sam Balter (1907–   )   Member of the gold-medal U.S. basketball team at the 1936 Berlin Olympics. Balter helped bring the sport into the limelight as an Olympic event. He was a UCLA all-American in 1929, and following the Olympics became a popular broadcaster.

Issac Berger (1936–   )   First weightlifter to lift double his bodyweight. With a gold medal at the 1956 Olympics in Melbourne and a silver four years later in Rome, he broke many world records and became very popular because of it. He retired after the 1964 Olympics in Tokyo, went into business, and did cantorial work in synagogues.

Larry Brown (1940–   )   A University of North Carolina basketball star from 1961 to 1963, he won a gold medal at the 1964 Olympics in Tokyo. He then spent five seasons with the American Basketball Association in New Orleans, Washington, Virginia, and Denver, leading the league in assists, and was an all-star game Most Valuable Player. He later coached the Carolina Cougars, Denver Nuggets, and New Jersey Nets. He brought the Indiana Pacers to the playoffs and now coaches the Philadelphia 76ers.

Benny Friedman (1905–1982)   Quarterback who played with four pro teams including the New York Giants from 1929 to 1931, after a brilliant college football career. Credited with making the forward pass—thrown with powerful, pinpoint accuracy—a regular feature of the game, he was recognized as one of the best pro quarterbacks from 1927 to 1931. In 1928, when he was playing for Detroit, the Giants purchased the entire Detroit team in order to get Friedman. At that point, he became the highest-paid pro football player in the NFL.

Mitch Gaylord   An Olympic gold medalist in the gymnastic team event at the 1984 Los Angeles games, he won a silver medal in vaulting, and won double bronze medals in rings and parallel bars. When he was twenty years old he competed in the eleventh Maccabiah Games in Israel, winning six gold medals. The only one he didn't win was the vault, which was won by his brother, Chuck.

Hank Greenberg   Voted the American League's Most Valuable Player in 1935 and again in 1940, Greenberg won the league's home-run championship four times. He had 331 homers, 1,276 RBIs, and eleven grand slams in a career that began as a first baseman and outfielder for the Detroit Tigers, and ended with the Pittsburgh Pirates. He played in four World Series contests with the Tigers. In 1956, he became the first Jew elected to the Baseball Hall of Fame.

Nat Holman (1896–1955)   City College of New York basketball coach with a 422-188 record who also played professionally on weekends in the 1920s and 1930s. Once a Boston Celtic, he is credited with inventing the center pivot play, in which a player can pass or shoot in any direction without taking a step.

Ken Holtzman (1945–   )   Left-handed pitcher for the Chicago Cubs, Oakland A's, Baltimore Orioles, and New York Yankees. He won 174 games in his thirteen-year career, from 1966 to 1979. He never pitched on Jewish holidays and kept a kosher home.

Sandy Koufax (1935–   )   Spent his entire major league pitching career with the Brooklyn and Los Angeles Dodgers, was the first to throw four no-hitters, and the first National Leaguer to retire his opponents in one inning with nine pitches. In 1972, six years after retiring, he became the youngest inductee into the Baseball Hall of Fame.

Benny Leonard (1896–1947)   Spent over seven years as the world lightweight boxing champ, from 1917 to 1924. He is known for perfecting such key moves in the sport as bobbing and weaving, as well as the well-planned and well-placed jab and uppercut. Leonard lost millions in the stock market crash of 1929.

Sid Luckman (1916–1998)   Quarterback who took the Chicago Bears to four NFL championships. An All-American in 1938, Luckman was a runner, punter, and passer and was known for his intelligence and dedication, which more than made up for his lack of power and speed. He was the NFL's Most Valuable Player in 1943 and set several records in the game. In 1965, he was the first Jew elected to the Pro Football Hall of Fame.

Ron Mix   Offensive tackle with the San Diego Chargers, he was unanimously chosen to the all-time AFL team by the Professional Football Hall of Fame. An aggressive and highly skilled player, he continued to study law at night and was inducted into the Hall of Fame in 1979.

Charles "Buddy" Myer (1904–1974)   Widely considered the greatest Jewish second baseman in the history of professional baseball, Myer won the

American League batting title in 1935, hit .300 or better for nine seasons, and had a great seventeen-year career, mostly with the Washington Senators. In 1926, the Senators sold him to the Boston Red Sox, but he did so well with the Red Sox that Washington immediately bought him back.

Lipman Pike   In 1866, he was offered twenty dollars a week to play third base for the Philadelphia Athletics, thus becoming the nation's first professional baseball player. Pike was a home run champ, and in the first year of his professional career, he hit six home runs in one game.

Myer Prinstein   Five-time Olympic track and field medalist with four golds. His first gold was won at the 1900 Paris games for the triple jump. In 1904's St. Louis games, he won a gold in the long jump and triple jump.

Al "Flip" Rosen (1924–   )   Third baseman for the Cleveland Indians who was the first-ever unanimous selection as a Most Valuable Player. He made a hundred or more runs for five consecutive seasons between 1950 and 1954.

Maxie Rosenbloom (1904–1976)   World light-heavyweight champ from 1930 to 1934. One of the busiest boxers on the circuit in his time, working the mat 196 times during his championship reign. He went into acting afterward and made over a hundred films, including *Each Dawn I Die* (1939) and *Hollywood or Bust* (1956).

Barney Ross (1909–1967)   was the world lightweight and junior welterweight champ from 1933 to 1935 and the world welterweight champ in 1934 and again from 1935 to 1938. He was the first pro boxer to hold three world titles at the same time.

Dick Savitt (1927–   )   One of the greatest backcourt tennis players of all time. In 1951, he was the Wimbledon singles champ, Australian singles champ, and number-one player on the U.S. Davis Cup team. Then, in 1952, 1958, and 1961, he was the U.S. National Indoor champ.

Adolph "Dolph" Schayes (1928–   )   Named to twelve consecutive NBA All Star games, Schayes displayed an uncommon versatility early in the game. In 1948, he was an all-American at New York University and then joined the Syracuse Nationals (which later became the Philadelphia 76ers). By the time he retired from playing, he held many career records, including most points and most free throws.

Mark Spitz (1950–   )   World-famous swimmer who, at twenty-two, won seven gold medals at the 1972 Munich Olympics. His Olympic gold was even more impressive, for they all represented new world-record times. They included the 200m butterfly, 400m freestyle, and 800m freestyle relay.

*One-time coach Arnold "Red" Auerbach
is now vice chairman of the board of the
Boston Celtics.* Courtesy the Boston
Celtics; photo by Steve Lipofsky

The world of sports would not spin nearly as majestically as it does if not for
dozens of Jewish pros who have coached and managed teams, broadcast, and
documented games, or modified and created new components of the games.
All members of the International Jewish Sports Hall of Fame, they include:

Mel Allen   Long-time voice of the New York Yankees, beginning in 1939,
until his death in 1996. Earlier in his career, he had been a disk jockey
and news broadcaster.

Arnold "Red" Auerbach (1917–   )   Coached the Boston Celtics to nine
NBA championships, from 1959 to 1966. He now works in the Celtics'
front office.

Howard Cosell (1918–1995)   Opinionated, informed, influential sportscas-
ter and journalist whose words, voice, convictions, and comic imitators
made him as much a celebrity as he was a serious sports newsman.

Dan Daniel   Famous newspaper sports reporter.

Barney Dreyfuss (1865–1932)   In 1903, as owner of the Pittsburgh Pirates,
he proposed a series of games between teams leading to a championship,
and the idea led to the creation of the World Series.

Charlotte Epstein (1885–1938)   Established women's swimming as a serious and recognized sport in the United States. She founded what later
became the New York Women's Swimming Association, and her efforts
led to women's swimming being included in the 1920 Antwerp
Olympics.

Nat Fleisher (1887–1972)   Boxing promoter and writer who worked diligently to reform and further legitimize the game.

Gladys Heldman (1922–   )   A key proponent of women's tennis and onetime editor and publisher of *World Tennis* magazine, which was the number-one magazine for the sport.

William "Red" Holtzman (1920–   )   Legendary coach of the New York Knicks who led the team to two NBA titles in 1970 and 1973 and some of the winningest seasons in the sport.

Fred Lebow   Founder and guiding spirit behind the New York City Marathon, which in time turned into one of the most popular marathons in the world.

Murray Olderman   Popular sportswriter in the 1950s and 1960s who at one time was the president of the Football Writers of America.

Abe Saperstein (1903–1966)   Manager who invented the Harlem Globetrotters when the team that he owned, the Savoy Big Five, won too many games and couldn't find another team to play against them. By 1950 the clowned-princes of basketball were known around the world.

Morris Berg is not in the International Jewish Sports Hall of Fame. A skilled catcher with the Brooklyn Dodgers, Chicago White Sox, Cleveland Indians, Washington Senators, and Boston Red Sox between 1923 and 1936, Berg had a law degree, spoke twelve languages (including Yiddish and Japanese), and worked as a spy for the U.S. State Department. But he wasn't a fast runner and broke no records.

And Bobby Fischer is absent from the list as well. In 1958, he was the youngest chess player ever to become a Grand Master, and he was the first American to be the World Chess Champion, between 1972 and 1975. But chess is rarely considered a sport. That certainly satisfies those detractors who claim that Jews are much better at analytical challenges than physical ones. Chess, they say, is just a game. Some have even said it's a Jewish game. Perhaps it is. After all, the *check* in the phrase checkmate is from the Hebrew word meaning sheik, and the *mate* is Hebrew for dead.

Regardless, when 16-year-old Bobby Fischer pronounced *dead sheik* in 1958, he joined an impressive group of Jewish-American champions—even if he didn't have to leave his chair.

16

Thou Shalt Not Dress

An Interview With 1 Jewish Nudist

They were both naked, the man and his wife,
and were not ashamed.
—Genesis 2.25

Tzvia Alexander is a Jewish nudist, and a devout one at that.

In the United States today there are more than 225 campgrounds, resorts, and clubs for nudists, or naturists, as they prefer to be called, and, according to one statistic, more than 30 million Americans are active naturists at least part of the time. Ms. Alexander founded a very active club in South Carolina and a second one in Oklahoma. While naturism typically avoids religious exclusivity, Ms. Alexander does host naturist Seders during Passover and considers Judaism a very important part of her life.

Propriety and modesty has more or less been a tradition among Jews, particularly religious Jews, but so has honesty, spirituality, and a sense of community. Here, then, is an interview with a Jewish woman, Tzvia Alexander, who is honest about the spirituality she feels within her naturist community. Those who are offended need only to turn the other cheek. So to speak.

Q: Tzvia, has anyone ever criticized you for being a Jewish naturist?

A: No one, not even my rabbi, has criticized me. While I consider myself a Reform Jew, I know of no theologic document calling naturism indecent.

Q: How did you first get into naturism?

A: I was vacationing at a resort in the Caribbean. The first two days were spent on the beach in a soggy, sandy swimsuit. I signed up for a boat trip to another island and heard that there was a nude beach there. I thought, no way will anyone get me to go nude, and, in fact, I was the last one to shed my suit. But then, I was hooked. I said to myself, Why hadn't someone told me about this before? I was the last one to get dressed and return to the resort. That was thirty years ago. Now I live by the phrase "nude when possible, clothed when practical." Until people experience it for themselves, words cannot accurately describe how naturism feels.

Q: You sound quite passionate about it.

A: It's just that naturists are no different from other people—just more comfortable. Naturism builds self-esteem. There are no perfect bodies, no ugly bodies. The body is just the vessel for the person. It is well known that there is a feeling of wholeness, honesty, and well-being among people who enjoy themselves with family and friends in a naturist environment. We are lawyers, doctors, secretaries, accountants, models, teachers, government employees, clergypeople, parents, teens, infants, taxi drivers, neighbors. Everyone!

Q: And hasn't it been called a healthy way of life by several credible sources?

A: Yes. Naturism is a way of shedding tension, aggression, and anxiety. It is medically proven. Not only that, but we have a lower divorce rate and stronger family ties. Naturism happens to be the fastest growing segment of tourism in North America.

Q: Has there ever been any trouble with the law, local ordinances, that sort of thing?

A: Not with either of my clubs, no.

Q: Have you ever known a person in some sort of community leadership role voice one opinion about naturism in public and another, more personal, opinion in private?

A: No.

Q: Are Passover Seders the only Jewish events undertaken by some members of your clubs?

A: We have a Winter Holiday party each year for everyone, Jews and non-Jews alike.

Q: Where are the Seders held?

A: Usually my home. All club members are welcome.

Q: Are they conducted in the nude?

A: Yes.

Q: Do you find the need to change any procedures of the Seder?

A: No.

Q: Can you foresee the day when an entire Jewish naturist congregation will be established?

A: No, I don't see that happening.

Q: Orthodox tradition requires modesty in dress. In your opinion, can one be Orthodox and a naturist at the same time?

A: Yes. I don't see why not.

Q: Many people you know outside the club no doubt are aware that you are Jewish and a naturist—two things that can be the source of joking. Do you ever get any of that?

A: Like what?

Q: Oh, I don't know…like "Do you have Bring Your Own Mohel parties?"

A: No.

Q: Is God naked?

A: I don't see God as a physical entity.

Q: Do you nevertheless see God as having an opinion on naturism?

A: To quote an old phrase, "If God didn't want us to be naked, he would have created us with our clothes on."

Q: There is a fair amount of sensuality and even sexual plotting in the Bible. Although naturism is considered a non-sexual pastime, does it ever turn into one?

A: Not at my club. Nor has it at any of the clubs I visit.

Q: There is at least one Christian naturist group. Would you ever consider founding a Jewish naturist group?

A: No. My religion is a private thing, as it is to most Jews I know. That's why we don't proselytize. At least about that.

17

A Tapestry of Sounds

82 From the World of Music

Send me moving to your sweetest song.
—Carly Simon, "The Right Thing to Do"

When I was eleven or twelve years old, I heard Tom Jones on an album singing "My Yiddishe Mama," and days later I learned that both "White Christmas" and "Easter Parade" were written by a Jew.

No wonder I'm still crazy after all these years.

Actually, it makes sense. Stated plainly, the music business is a crazy thing. The changing technology alone can drive anyone nuts: from transcription discs to 78s to 33s to 45s to cassettes to 8-tracks to quad to CDs to DAT. And then there are the categories, which pop up quicker than Elvis sightings: rock, rhythm-and-blues, rap, country, bluegrass, Latin jazz, contemporary blues, contemporary soul gospel, world music, small-ensemble....

Some say it's crazy, others insist it is merely enormously varied. Both are probably correct. Why, then, talk about it in Jewish-American terms? That would neither add nor delete anything to its study. "I've never heard a label put on the music industry to the effect of 'it's a Jewish business' or 'it's an Italian business,'" says Jay Lustig, music critic of the Newark [New Jersey] Star Ledger. "It's never been an issue in any way whatsoever. It's *everyone's* business."

In *Coat of Many Colors*, Israel Shenker quotes British director and performer Jonathan Miller talking about some of the great Jewish composers, such as George Gershwin and Irving Berlin. They may have been Jewish, he says, "but I think you'd find it very, very difficult to point out anything that is specifically Jewish [about their music]. They wrote music out of the full potboiling of American sounds."

Jumping ahead several decades, author Charles E. Silberman notes in *A Certain People* that Jews play a much smaller role in rock and roll than they have in other musical disciplines. Silberman paraphrases historian E. Anthony Rotundo's suggestion that "words are unimportant in rock, whereas in the popular music Jews write, words are crucial, for the songs tell a story—and Jews tend to be storytellers. Jews also tend to be uncomfortable with the kind of raw and uncontrolled emotions and sensuality that are central to rock." Neil Diamond and Carly Simon might disagree.

But all the speculation cannot disregard the fact that there have been some phenomenal contributions by American Jews to *all* kinds of American music. As a study it may be listless, but as a list it's priceless.

Music is resilience. It is love, hope, and happiness rolled into one. Words and music lift us when we're down and follow us like benevolent shadows through our entire lives, reminding us of the old days when the new ones get a little hard to bear. The Jewish contributions—like those of people from every conceivable heritage—have colored our world with every emotion, every shade, and every nuance. But it is a particular tribute to the Jew that, after so many centuries of living in societies that make no secrets of their disdain, we can still put a damn good spin on life through our music.

The Rockers and the Poppers

Herb Alpert   Grabbed the brass ring as one of the last pop-jazz band-leaders to make it in the Top 40. He arranged, played on, and produced many pop hits and cofounded A&M Records, one of the biggest labels in the 70s. Herb Alpert and his band, the Tijuana Brass, won a Grammy in 1965 for "A Taste of Honey."

Neil Diamond (1941–   )   Was subject to the blues now and then, but dealt with it musically as a composer and singer, digging for emotion and coming up with lots of gold. He wrote for The Monkees early in his career.

Bob Dylan   Blew in the wind and found a lot of people who wanted to hear what he had to say. This celebrated folk-rock poet, who became popular in the 1960s and won Grammys in 1979, 1995, and three of them in 1998, apparently never even needed a good voice.

"Mama" Cass Elliot   Stopped into a church and began to pray (at least in song), and was blessed with one of the most successful folk-rock careers of the 1960s. The Mamas and the Papas won a Grammy in 1966 for "Monday, Monday."

Billy Joel (1949–) Played us a melody as the last of the great ol' fashioned piano men. Joel, comfortable with a variety of styles, from blues to ballads, is the proud owner of four Grammys.

Carole King Felt the earth move in 1971 with four Grammys for writing and performing "It's Too Late," writing "You've Got a Friend," and for the phenomenally successful *Tapestry* album.

Barry Manilow Looked up, down, trying to get the feeling again after a hot career in the 1970s. He was Bette Midler's accompanist and arranger before "Mandy" gave him an audience of his own. He won a Grammy in 1978 for "Copacabana."

Bette Midler (1939–) Boogie woogied her way from Hawaii to cabarets to Top 40 and then rose to even greater heights on screen. She was one of Tevya's daughters on Broadway and the last Mama Rose on TV, and she also has two Grammys beneath her wings.

Neal Sedaka Made us hear laughter in the rain, even when breaking up was hard to do. With his nasal "comma comma down doobie do down down" he was an unlikely but enormously successful teen idol of the late 1950s and early 1960s who reemerged on the charts in the 1970s.

Gene Simmons (1950–) and **Paul Stanley** (1950–) Hated by critics, their phenomenally popular rock band Kiss thrilled kids and scared parents throughout the 1970s. The music was heavy metal and the shtick was Rocky Horror makeup, stage pyrotechnics, and simulated blood barfing and flame spitting. Simmons (born in Israel) and Stanley led the group to more than a dozen gold and platinum albums.

Carly Simon Anticipated a fantastic career as a sharp, clear-voiced, passionate pop songwriter and singer, and she was right. Her 1971 Grammy as Best New Artist was just the beginning—but that's the way she always thought it should be. She also writes children's books.

Paul Simon (1941–) and **Art Garfunkel** (1941–) Kept their customers satisfied—all but Mrs. Robinson, of course. One guitar, two voices, and a trunkful of great pop tunes that even became part of the SATs. Together they won four Grammy Awards, and Paul Simon won three more as a solo artist.

Barbra Streisand Became a person who loved people, especially when they just let her make her movies and stopped begging her to do concerts, even though that's what all her fans want. But she won an Academy Award in 1968 for *Funny Girl*, another one in 1976 for cowriting the song "Evergreen" (from *A Star Is Born*) and seven Grammys, so she has nothing to feel guilty about.

Peter Yarrow First sang at the Newport Jazz Festival in 1960, then hooked up with Paul Stookey and Mary Travers for a string of hits, including "If I

Had a Hammer;" "Where Have All the Flowers Gone," "Puff the Magic Dragon," "Blowing in the Wind," and "Leaving on a Jet Plane." A serious musician, Yarrow strives to use music to get people to improve humanity without violence.

Warren Zevon (1947–)   Uniquely distinctive singer/songwriter whose "Werewolves of London" doesn't even begin to tell the story. He studied classical piano, played at a piano bar in Spain, and toured with the Everly Brothers before hitting his stride. His sardonic story-songs, combined with skilled musicianship, made him a favorite of Linda Ronstadt and Jackson Browne. Albums include *Excitable Boy, Bad Luck Streak in Dancing School,* and *Sentimental Hygiene.*

Words and Music

Harold Arlen (1905–1986)   Lived, worked, and died in the most emerald of cities, New York, where he composed some of the most popular and timeless tunes ever, including "It's Only a Paper Moon," "Stormy Weather," and all the music for "The Wizard of Oz." After Arlen, original movie musicals were never the same because of the way the music began to carry the story and its characters.

Burt Bacharach   Put a hundred down and bought a car, which he drove to the Grammys in 1986 to pick up his award (with Carole Bayer Sager) for "That's What Friends Are For," one of his more conventional ballads. More typical Bacharach tunes have unusual tempo changes and stylized instrumentation, including "What the World Needs Now Is Love," "I'll Never Fall in Love Again," and "Raindrops Keep Falling On My Head." Long-time collaborators include Hal David and Dionne Warwick.

Jeff Barry   Like many Jewish songwriters who began in the late 1950s, he was a Brill Building regular who took us through the entire relationship process in song, from "Be My Baby" to "Then He Kissed Me" and finally "Going to the Chapel."

Irving Berlin   Blessed America with some of the most enduring popular songs of all time. His output was enormous and his talent was undeniable. His hit songs include "Alexander's Ragtime Band," "God Bless America," "Marie," and "When I Lost You." He wrote the Broadway musicals *Annie Get Your Gun* and *Call Me Madame,* and the scores for the films *Top Hat* (1935), *Easter Parade* (1948), *Holiday Inn* (1942), and *White Christmas* (1954). No style of music was foreign to him, and no one was more important to the development of popular American music.

Sammy Cahn   A musical institution you can't disparage. A lyricist who wrote for many of the great balladeers of the 1940s, 1950s and 1960s, his beautiful and popular songs include "Love and Marriage"; "I'll Walk Alone"; "Let It Snow, Let It Snow, Let It Snow"; "High Hopes"; "All the Way"; and "Call Me Irresponsible."

Lorenz Hart (1895–1943)   Never bewitched, bothered, or bewildered by his success, because he discovered his genius for lyrics early on. His songs, many written for Broadway and the movies, include "Blue Moon," "Isn't It Romantic," "The Lady Is a Tramp," and "The Most Beautiful Girl in the World."

Jerry Leiber (1933–   ) and **Mike Stoller** (1933–   )   They said the neon lights are bright on Broadway, and they were right, with the musical *Smokey Joe's Café* a recent success. Had they not paired up almost fifty years ago, the world wouldn't have "Charlie Brown," "Hound Dog," "Jailhouse Rock," "Kansas City," "Love Potion #9," "Spanish Harlem," "Stand By Me," "Yakety Yak," and countless other hits.

Frank Loesser (1910–1969)   Succeeded in show business not just by trying hard but by using his prodigious gifts well. A lyricist and composer, his classic Broadway triumphs include *Guys and Dolls, The Most Happy Fella,* and *How to Succeed in Business Without Really Trying.* He also wrote patriotic songs during World War II, such as "What Do You Do in the Infantry?"

Barry Mann and **Cynthia Weil**   Doo wop pop duo, from "Uptown" to "Walking in the Rain" and "You've Lost That Loving Feeling." They also wrote the score for Stephen Spielberg's animated feature *An American Tail.*

Albert (1878–1956) and **Harry Von Tilzer** (1872–1946)   Root toot tooted for each other as songwriting brothers—though they were not part-ners—and came up with such classics as Albert's "Take Me Out to the Ball Game" and "I'll Be With You in Apple Blossom Time," and Harry's "I Want a Girl Just Like the Girl That Married Dear Old Dad" and "Wait 'til the Sun Shines, Nellie." Together they were among the busiest residents of New York's Tin Pan Alley.

Swinging Stars

Bud Freeman (1906–   )   Blew his own horn throughout his career—in his case, the tenor saxophone—by doing what he wanted, when he wanted, and where he wanted. His playing, always bouncy and joyful, was used by Tommy Dorsey, Benny Goodman, and other bands, as well as with the famous Austin High Gang, creators of the Chicago sound.

Stan Getz   Played cool jazz even before it was cool. Though his hot saxophone was a fixture on the jazz scene by the early 1940s, he topped the 1960s charts as a prince of modern jazz—and bossa nova. His "Girl From Ipanema," which just about everyone recognizes, won a Record of the Year Grammy in 1964 (and he won two other Grammys that year, as well).

Benny Goodman His red-hot clarinet playing made blue skies bluer because of his skill, professionalism, perfectionism, and innovation. The King of Swing started performing at age twelve (with a professional union card), formed a swing band when he was twenty-five, and toured until his death in 1986. "Blue Skies," "Stardust," and "Avalon" were among his biggest numbers. His Carnegie Hall concert in 1938 ushered in the big-band jazz era.

Artie Shaw (1910–) Scaled the heights of popular swing music with a clarinet and a couple of high-caliber groups. He made sure to share his woodwind work's spotlight with the guys in his bands, and the bands became famous partially because they were the first with full string sections, ushering in a new and exciting sound. His was also the first white band to feature a black singer—the great Billie Holliday.

Paul Whiteman (1891–1967) Many other musical greats such as the Dorsey brothers, Bing Crosby, and Mildred Bailey got their start with his symphonic jazz, swing, and dance band arrangements. Primarily a conductor and arranger, he was the one who commissioned George Gershwin's "Rhapsody in Blue."

Style and Substance

Sammy Davis Jr. (1923–1987) Stopped the world with his tap dancing, singing, clowning, and acting. The only black Jewish rat packer in the history of the world, he had quite a varied and impressive career from Broadway to films to TV. "Candy Man" may have been fluff, but "Mr. Bojangles" was heartfelt and "I've Got To Be Me" was real.

Michael Feinstein A modern cabaret artist who sticks to the classics by Cole Porter, Irving Berlin, and George and Ira Gershwin. A singer and pianist, he brings his "purist" interpretations to the recording studio, exclusive hotels, TV talk shows, and one-man Broadway engagements. His 1985 album. *Pure Gershwin,* sold 40,000 copies.

Eddie Fisher (1928–) Lived a life far more dramatic (Debbie Reynolds, Elizabeth Taylor, etc. etc.) than any of his won songs, but nevertheless used a great voice to put much emotion behind "Oh! My Pa Pa"; "I'm Walking Behind You"; "Cindy, Oh Cindy"; and many other standards.

Al Jolson (1886–1950) The original jazz singer, in more ways than one. He did it on Broadway, in the movies—and lived it in real life. Much imitated but never duplicated, his passionate and sincere musical orations include "Swanee River," "Climb Upon My Knee, Sonny Boy," "Dear Old Mammy," and "Toot Toot Tootsie."

Steve Lawrence and **Eydie Gorme** Crooned and swooned together, thanks in part to Steve Allen, on whose TV shows in the 1950s they met. (Steve Lawrence began singing on a local Steve Allen show when he was seventeen years old.) Together, they have produced a long list of romantic pop albums and played thousands of gigs as a romantic duo, but separately they also made many TV appearances and recordings. In 1960, they won a Grammy for "We Got Us," and continue to perform together.

Tony Martin Had an operatic voice but romantic pop looks, and he skillfully combined the two for a career that included many fine albums, a stint with Glenn Miller's Air Force band, a couple of movies (including *The Big Store* [1941] with Groucho, Chico, and Harpo), and a marriage to Cyd Charisse.

Dinah Shore (1917–1994) Sang blues in the night, and during the day, on radio stations and jukeboxes all through 1940s and 1950s. Almost gospel in nature, her singing style was the perfect match between spirituality and romance, and between blues and pop. She also spent about twenty years hosting various variety and talk shows on TV.

Mel Tormé Singer, songwriter, composer, arranger, piano player, drummer known as "The Velvet Fog." At age fifteen he auditioned for Harry James's band singing a song he wrote, "Lament For Love." He didn't get the job, but James recorded the song and it became a hit. Soon after, Woody Herman and Les Brown persuaded a top manager to take him on, and he's been "on" ever since. His smooth, elegant tones and cool, breezy technique put him in a class of his own. He won a Grammy in 1983 for "Top Drawer."

Virtual Classics

Samuel Adler Put music to the word *prolific*. A composer with over two hundred published symphonic compositions; five stage works; seven string quartets; concerti for violin, flute, organ and piano, choral and chamber music; and liturgical works. He received the Army Medal of Honor, the Dallas Symphony Prize, a Guggenheim Fellowship, and he founded the Seventh Army Symphony Orchestra in Germany in 1952.

Leonard Bernstein Led the best of all popular lives for a classical musician, for he was able to conduct, compose, teach, lecture, entertain, and inspire, all with equal aplomb and success. He conducted the New

York City Symphony Orchestra and the New York Philharmonic for several years, composed the music for *West Side Story* and *Candide,* wrote symphonies and jazz, and organized and led the New York Philharmonic's Young People's Concerts on TV between 1958 and 1972. He won a half dozen Grammys between 1964 and 1992.

Aaron Copeland (1900–1990)   Wrote purely original and therefore purely American orchestral compositions, including the ballets *Billy the Kid* and *Rodeo,* and the orchestral pieces *El Salon Mexico, A Lincoln Portrait,* and *Appalachian Spring.*

Arthur Fiedler (1894–1979)   Helped make the modern orchestra popular during his forty-nine years as conductor of the world famous Boston Pops. Through his untiring devotion to the Pops, he taught several generations to appreciate popular band music.

Morton Gould (1913–1996)   Struck gold as a composer, conductor, and pianist in several musical styles. He wrote and played with the Radio City Music Hall orchestra, adapted jazz for classical styles, and used elements of folk and popular music in his compositions, which included *Lincoln Legend* for orchestra and *Fall River Legend* for ballet. He also wrote the score for the musical comedy *Billion Dollar Baby.*

Gary Graffman   Outstanding pianist who won his first major scholarship when he was eight years old and played New York when he was ten. In 1979, he began to lose the use of his right hand. He wrote about his life and the apparent loss of his career in a wonderful, funny, and insightful book, *I Really Ought to Be Practicing.*

Jascha Heifetz   Soloed, more or less, for eighty-two years, beginning when he was four years old. It didn't take long for his violin teachers to realize he had a keen sense of musicality, intense powers of concentration, and a singular technical proficiency that would make him a violin virtuoso of worldwide acclaim. And that's what he was for his entire life. He won several Grammys in the 1960s for chamber music recordings.

Vladimir Horowitz   Virtually owned the concept of piano playing. With speed and interpretive mechanics that can only be described as unique, he was a keyboard virtuoso of unparelleled accomplishment. He gave a famous televised concert in 1986 from Russia, to which he had returned for a visit after immigrating to the United States sixty-one years before. He won three classical-album Grammys.

Igor Kipnis   With forty solo albums to his name, performances around the globe, and numerous Grammy nominations, he is the best-known harpsichordist in the world. *Contemporary Keyboard* magazine named him the Best Harpsichordist of the Year in 1974, 1978, and 1980. He also revived the fortepiano, taught at the famous Tanglewood music festival school in Massachusetts, and had several compositions written for him by contemporary composers.

Ellis Kohs (1916–   )   Variations, asymmetry, and dissonance are three words often attributed to his compostions, which ranged from operas and orchestral pieces to chamber works and sonatas. Titles include *Night Watch for Flute, Horn, and Trumpet; Fatal Interview; Lord of the Ascendant; Etude in Memory of Bartok;* and *Fantasy on La, Sol, Fa, Re, Mi.*

James Levine (1943–   )   Conducted himself like a true artistic business professional on both sides of the podium. For nearly thirty years he conducted both the orchestra and the business affairs of the famed New York Metropolitan Opera before moving to the Chicago Symphony. He has won a half dozen Grammys for his efforts.

Yehudi Menuhin (1916–   )   Played for peace more than anyone. A wonderful violinist, he spent much of his career entertaining troops and playing for war refugees, including concentration camp survivors and citizens in postwar Japan. As a chamber music performer and a classical orchestra leader, he made sure music was used to promote humanitarian causes around the globe.

Robert Merrill (1919–   )   Won the Metropolitan Opera Auditions on the Air when he was very young, then made his debut with the company in 1945 in *La Traviata.* Long the Met's reigning baritone, he also sang with major American orchestras, performed on stage in *Fiddler on the Roof* and other musicals, and dabbled in artwork. He was briefly married to Roberta Peters.

Mitch Miller (1911–   )   Followed the bouncing ball from studio bands to record companies as both an expert oboist and a talented music executive. His stint at Columbia Records forged an association with talents like Tony Bennett, whose career took off with Miller's help. Miller's sing-along records introduced a unique and successful new concept to American popular music.

Eugene Ormandy (1899–1985)   Orchestrated a new respect for symphonic entertainment as the longtime conductor of the preeminent Philadelphia Orchestra. He also had a Ph.D. in music and had been a violin virtuoso.

Roberta Peters (1930–   )   Never really met her match as one of the best-loved sopranos of all time singing with New York's Metropolitan Opera for more than thirty-five years.

Artur Rubinstein (1887–1982)   Piano wizard—a child prodigy—who became the world's foremost interpreter of the music of Chopin. Both his

Roberta Peters. Courtesy The National Foundation for Jewish Culture; photo by Newey

worldwide tours and his popular recordings have covered the complete works of Chopin. His autobiographies were called *My Young Years* and *My Many Years.*

Beverly Sills   Bubbled everywhere she sang, beginning as a child radio star before becoming an opera star. She made her coloratura soprano debut in Philadelphia at age seventeen, joined the New York City Opera at age twenty-six, and appeared all over Europe in the 1960s and 1970s. She was the director of the New York City Opera for nine years.

Issac Stern   Fiddled his way to fame by playing the classics with virtuosity. His violin performances in New York, Japan, South America, the Soviet Union, and Israel are legendary. Active in cultural affairs in the United States and Israel, Stern has recorded or performed nearly every major violin piece by every major classical composer. He received the first Albert Schweitzer Music Award in 1975. In the early 1960s, he helped found the National Council on the Arts (which later became the National Endowment for the Arts). He provided the violin music for the film version of *Fiddler on the Roof* in 1971, and won a Grammy in 1991.

The Big Score

Elmer Bernstein   His first commandment of movie composing was to make the audience feel they were witnessing something real and very serious. *To Kill a Mockingbird, The Great Escape,* and the 1956 version of *The Ten Commandments* were among his classic film scores.

George (1898–1937) and **Ira Gershwin** (1896–1983) They rhapsodized about popularizing every style of music they knew. George's *Porgy and Bess* was a successful innovative opera, and "Rhapsody in Blue" is among the most popular pieces in American musical history because it successfully bridged jazz, classical, and American folk music. It has been instantly recognizable as an American classic for over seventy years. With Ira's lyrics, the Gershwins created other instant classics such as "I Got Rhythm," "'S Wonderful," and "Embraceable You."

Ernest Gold (1921–   )   Won an Oscar for the score to *Exodus.* He studied at the Vienna Academy of Music, directed the Santa Barbara Symphony Orchestra, and wrote the scores for *Inherit the Wind, Judgment at Nuremberg,* and *The Defiant Ones* in addition to writing some chamber music and piano pieces.

Morton Gould (1913–1996)   A composer and conductor who once hosted a TV show called *The World of Music With Morton Gould.* He scored for the movies, TV, and ballet, including *Billion Dollar Baby,* the *Holocaust* miniseries, *Fall River Legend* (choreographed by Agnes DeMille), and even the 1984 Olympics, for which he wrote "American Sing." He also won a Grammy for his work with the Chicago Symphony.

Marvin Hamlisch   A singular sensation with Oscars, Grammys, and Tonys for (respectively) *The Way We Were* (best score, 1973), Best New Artist of 1974, and *A Chorus Line* (best score, 1976). He also scored *The Sting* and wrote the music for *They're Playing Our Song* on Broadway.

Bernard Herrmann   First he worked for CBS Radio, then hooked up with Orson Welles and the Mercury Theatre. He followed Welles to Hollywood to score *Citizen Kane* (1941) and ended up doing more than sixty films there, including *Psycho* (1960), *The Man Who Knew Too Much* (1956), *North by Northwest* (1959), and *The Day the Earth Stood Still* (1951). He was an early user of electronic music in the movies to create new effects.

Jerome Kern (1885–1945)   Told great stories—through music. His compositions took American musical theatre to new heights of sophistication in the first decades of the century with such works as *Show Boat* and *Swingtime.* Among his tunes are "Ol' Man River" and "Smoke Gets in Your Eyes."

Irwin Kostal (1915–1994)   Won Oscars for the scores of *West Side Story* and *The Sound of Music.*

Randy Newman (1943–   )   First gained popularity, or notoriety, with song

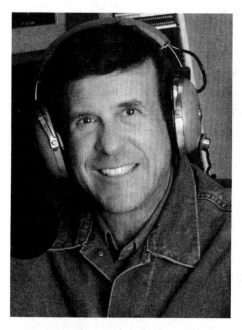

Another Brooklyn boy who made good music—without ever singing a note. "Cousin Brucie" Morrow, one of the pioneers of Top 40 radio in New York, began broadcasting in the late 1950s and is still going strong today. Courtesy WCBS FM, New York

parodies like "Short People," but he scored even bigger on screen by creating lush, evocative music for *The Natural, Avalon, Toy Story,* and other films.

Andre Previn (1929–   )   Scored big in several musical disciplines, including movies, chamber groups, and jazz. He won four Academy Awards (including one for orchestrating *My Fair Lady,* 1964), two Grammys (one for his jazz group recording of *West Side Story*), and was married to Mia Farrow.

Franz Waxman   Composed scores for some of the biggest movies of his day, from *Sunset Boulevard* (1950), *Stalag 17* (1953), and *Magnificent Obsession* (1954), *Captains Courageous* (1937), *Sayonara* (1957), and *The Philadelphia Story* (1940). He won an Oscar for *Sunset Boulevard.* Waxman also composed orchestral works and founded the Los Angeles Music Fesitval.

And then there are the novelty songs, where Jewish musical tummlers mix melodies with mirth, both for the fun and satire of it all. From Adam Sandler's "Chanukkah Song" to Kinky Friedman's "Ride 'em, Jewboy," novelty songs with Jewish genes are rare—but impactful because of their rarity and occasional irreverence. Mickey Katz had a string of them earlier in the century, such as "How Much Is That Pickle in the Window" and "Shleppin' My Baby Back Home." Benny Bell's "Pincus the Peddler," a rare serious-comedic song, was a New York–area hit in 1946. It told the tale of a poor Jewish peddler who hits hard times in Brooklyn and goes back to Russia, and Bell did it with a brilliant blend of pathos and sardonic humor. Forty years later, the mock rap group 2 Live Jews revisited the mini-genre of Jewish novelty songs with such ditties as "J.A.P. Rap," "As Kosher as They Wanna Be," and "Shake Your Tuchas."

Two of the biggest Top 40 radio deejays of all time are Jews—Cousin Brucie (Bruce Morrow) and Murray the K (Murray Kaufman), both of whom helped define Top 40 rock and roll on New York radio. The most popular Jews working in radio today are no longer involved in music (except for Cousin Brucie, who still has a show on WCBS-FM in New York), but instead provide radio talk, self-help, and whatever else it is that Howard Stern provides. Those who are offended by Stern need only remember that he is only "half Jewish," as he has been known to point out every once in a while.

The debate over whether Jewish musicians have an inherent Jewish style may have been rendered a non-debate, but we still have "White Christmas," "The Christmas Song" ("Chestnuts roasting on an open fire...."), and Elvis Presley's "Santa Claus Is Back in Town" to deal with. "White Christmas" was written by Irving Berlin, "The Christmas Song" was composed by Mel Torme, and the Presley number was penned by Leiber and Stoller. Are they Christian songs written by Jews or just great songs written by great songwriters?

Musicians must remain free to follow their inspirations, whatever they are, for if they don't, we may be left with nothing but the sound of silence.

18

Where the Wild Things Are Imagined

These Portraits of 37 Jewish-American Artists Only Begin to Paint the Picture

Paint the anguish of all the world. Let people see the pain. But create your own molds and your own play of forms for the pain. We must give a balance to the universe.

—from *My Name Is Asher Lev*, by Chaim Potok

As with all creative endeavors, one can say that artists are a dime a dozen. Anyone who has ever painted a landscape with a roller, sketched a pencil Elvis, slapped primary colors on secondary walls, shot a picture of a bald spot, or built a bison out of beer cans can call himself an artist.

That's true to some extent, but *true* artists are those who have the foresight to recognize their own talent, the courage to devote their lives to it, and the convictions to use it to do some good for the world. Or at least to entertain or make people think.

For a century, we have been entertained and challenged by Jewish-American artists whose works bravely reflect the internal or environmental forces that shaped their lives. Actually, it's been happening for *more* than a century. It has been suggested that silversmith Myer Myers, born in 1723 in New York, was America's first native-born artist. Myers reguarly made Jewish ritual objects and domestic wares. And Jewish photographer Solomon Nunes Carvalho accompanied John Charles Fremont on his expeditions of the American West in the 1840s and 1850s, where he painted portraits of Indians and pioneer rabbis.

In the early nineteenth century, Jews in Western Europe were liberated from the restrictions of joining guilds, and a vibrant Jewish artistic community grew there. A much smaller community of Jewish painters and sculptors in America seemed to pick up some of those vibrations. The wave of immigration to America between 1880 and 1920 brought with it a great number of European artists to join those already here. Together they contributed to the growth of a new kind of American art, characterized by a general disappearance of religion and mythology and a new appearance of secularism and abstract expressionism.

The internal and environmental forces that shaped Jewish-American artists were many and varied. Louise Nevelson's father was a junkman, and her own inclination to collect junk turned her into one the country's leading environmental sculptors. Maurice Sendak had an experience when he was a child that may have carved *his* path, as well. His maternal grandfather had been a rabbi who died young, and Maurice loved him very much. One night, Maurice had a high fever, and in his delerium, he walked over to a painting on the wall of his grandfather and reached out to it. His frightened mother was convinced her father was calling out to Maurice from the other side. Maurice Sendak has been drawing the products of childish imaginations ever since.

In short, Jewish-American painters, sculptors, photographers, cartoonists, and illustrators prove that true artists are not a dime a dozen, but one in a million.

Diane Arbus Avant-garde and documentary photographer who, throughout the 1950s and 1960s, redefined what constituted photographic art. Freaks, transvestites, the mentally retarded, nudists, and midgets became viable subjects in front of her lens because of the respect she seemed to give to every subject.

Lila Oliver Asher (1921–   ) Artist who produced 3,600 portrait sketches of U.S. servicemen in World War II, work that was included in a special Smithsonian traveling exhibition. She has also had over fifty one-person shows of her portraiture in the United States and abroad.

Richard Avedon (1923–   ) Once deemed one of the ten greatest photographers in the world by Popular Photography, Avedon was also at one time one of the highest-paid photographers in the world. He turned fashion photography into an art with a strict, studied approach to the visual presentation of any advertising or promotional idea communicated by photography.

Leonard Baskin (1922–   ) Humanist sculptor and printmaker. He said he tried to present ideas about morality and mortality in his works, which included sculptures in wood, bronze, and limestone. Termed by critics as "mystical" or "compassionate," the works had names like "Man With a Dead Bird" and "Man of Peace." His father was an Orthodox rabbi.

Saul Bass (1920–1996)   Artist and designer who moved from motion pictures to stamps to consumer products with ease and endless creativity. He designed the graphics, credits, or titles for more than sixty movies, including *The Shining* and *Anatomy of a Murder,* designed many postage stamps, trademarks, and logos, and had his work shown at the Museum of Modern Art in New York, the Library of Congress, and the Smithsonian.

Robert Blum (1899–   )   One of the most important figures in late nineteenth century American art, known for his distinct and personal style, which was based on English classicism.

Aaron Bohrod (1907–1992)   One of the best realists on the art scene. His still lifes were so realistic it was often reported that many gallery viewers tried to touch the canvases to see exactly what they were dealing with. Bohrod, who received many commissions (including one from *Life* magazine to document World War II) insisted realism was just the vision of the artist and not necessarily a realistic portrait of real life.

Mortimer Borne   Artist who invented color drypoint, originated a new method for woodcuts and drawings, and worked tirelessly until his death in 1987. His religious-inspired drawings have been shown in Washington, Jerusalem, and Tel Aviv and have been included in the books *The Visual Bible* and *Meet Moses.*

Jim Dine (1935–   )   Took abstract expressionism and let it develop into something new by using environmental and social influences in his creations. He combined everyday objects and conventional painting methods into a single entity. He painted subjects like screwdrivers, wrenches, and bathrobes. He also created artistic "happenings," such as one called Car Crash. He called his work "entertainment psychology."

Alfred Eisenstaedt (1898–1995)   First of the modern photojournalists. Finding the right moment to tell a news story was his specialty. He single-handedly let us forever remember the end of a terrible war with a wonderful image of a sailor kissing a nurse in New York City's Times Square.

Leonard Everett Fisher   Prolific painter and illustrator who was awarded the Pulitzer Prize for painting in 1950. He illustrated about two hundred books and designed ten U.S. postage stamps. His other awards include the National Jewish Book Award in 1981 and the Christopher Medal in 1980.

Adolf Gottlieb (1903–1974)   Abstract expressionist who at one time was considered one of the most traveled artists in the world, having studied and worked in Paris, Berlin, Munich, and other cities. He was known for his pictographs, which were compartmentalized pictures into which abstract concepts were drawn.

Al Hirschfeld (1903–)   Most famous theatrical caricaturist in history, a line king of the first order. His brilliant and respectful works, with their hidden Ninas (he frequently puts the name of his daughter within his drawings), have been part of the New York Times Arts & Leisure section for years. A gold medal recipient of the National Society of Arts and Letters, his work is also represented at the Metropolitan Museum of Art in New York, the Whitney Museum of Modern Art, the Brooklyn Museum, and other top artistic venues.

Lee Krasner (1908–1984)   Worked as a hat decorator, waitress, and factory worker before breaking out as an expressionist artist of note during and after her life with Jackson Pollock. (She was married to him and acted as his business manager.) She studied at Cooper Union, the National Academy of Design, and with German expressionist Hans Hoffman, and she was known for what has been termed "turbulent expressions of rage."

Annie Leibovitz   Photographer who has taken us into the hearts, minds, shadows, creases, and crevices of some of the biggest cultural superstars of the last three decades. Ignoring standard public conceptions of her subjects, she has shot intriguing portraits of John Lennon, Bruce Springsteen, Bob Dylan, Stevie Wonder, and others (including politicians and writers). Leibovitz lived on an Israeli kibbutz in 1969, and her Israel pictures and photos of a San Francisco peace march landed her a job with *Rolling Stone*, where she became chief photographer in 1973. She has had an exhibit in the National Portrait Gallery in Washington, D.C., and her books include *Annie Leibovitz: Photographs 1970–1990*, and *Olympic Portraits*.

Jack Levine (1915–)   Painter who stood out from the crowd because of his favorite subject matter: social protest and political manifestations. He won many prizes for his work and had many exhibitions, including major ones at the Museum of Modern Art and the Whitney Museum of American Art. He had also been a soldier artist in the U.S. Army.

Louise Nevelson   Her junk art, environmental sculptures, sculptured walls, and other creations made her an American original from the 1930s to the 1980s. Wood, aluminum, Plexiglas, steel—much of it scavanged—were her tools. Along with some paint and sometimes other objects to place in or around it all, her inspirations became artistic expressions and vice versa.

Barnett Newman (1905–1970) Painter and sculptor who pioneered color-field painting. Called an "action painter" by some, his somewhat controversial abstract expressionism nevertheless paved the way for the shaped canvas and minimal art scene of the 1960s.

Irving Penn (1917–) One of the first superstars of magazine fashion photography, he used sharp, deliberate compositions illuminated by stark, natural light, and he tried a variety of methods to achieve a certain look, style, and feel. His first book, *Moments Preserved,* featured three hundred travel, fashion, and portrait photos taken for *Vogue* magazine, and was well received by the critics. His work has appeared in the Smithsonian, the Metropolitan Museum of Art in New York, and the Art Institute of Chicago. He is the brother of film director Arthur Penn.

Robert Rauschenberg (1925–) Pop artist more than anything. His works included avant-garde multimedia productions, art as live performance, and bizarre combinations of objects. He also did silk screens and collages.

Man Ray (1890–1976) Some of his multimedia concoctions were called "inventions," even when they made fun of established artistic methods. One such invention, Rayographs, signalled the beginning of abstract photography. Man Ray, whose work was often met with controversy, combined real-life objects with paintings, produced avant-garde films, and generally went his own way through the entire mid-twentieth century.

Larry Rivers (1923–) His ideas and humor paved the way for Pop Art, but his own art was more varied because he imbued it with strong expressionistic views. Among his subjects were cigarette packs and print advertisements. He also painted nudes with body parts labeled in other languages. In addition to art, Rivers was a jazz saxophonist, poet, and stage designer.

Joe Rosenthal (1911–1974) Associated Press photographer whose news photos were often as much art as they were news. His most famous picture is of American troops raising the flag at Iwo Jima on February 23, 1945.

Mark Rothko (1903–1970) Abstract expressionist who, through large areas of solid colors and shifting colors, tried to create "simple expressions of the complex thought." Others said he destroyed illusion and revealed truth. His paintings in the 1950s and 1960s were shown in universities and galleries in the Uniteed States and England. Earlier on, he painted for the Federal Arts Project and cofounded an expressionist group called The Ten.

Maurice Sendak. Courtesy The National Foundation for Jewish Culture; photo by Chris Callis

Maurice Sendak (1928–   )   Children's book illustrator and author. His genius is in drawing and writing the ways in which children can truly identify. His goal is to "create the special world of the story," and that's just what he did in works such as *Higglety Pigglety Pop!; What Do You Say, Dear; A Very Special House; Very Far Away,* and the classic *Where the Wild Things Are.*

Ben Shahn (1898–1969)   Painter, designer, and photographer. Called a "social realist" painter, he created scenes of such real-life events as the Dreyfus case, street scenes, and other subjects with which he could make social commentary through his art. He also painted murals for Rockefeller Center and many buildings in Washington, D.C.

Art Spiegelman (1948–   )   Pulitzer Prize–winning comic book artist. His *Maus* series generated quite a bit of publicity, with Jews as mice, Germans as cats, Poles as pigs. More recently he published *Open Me— I'm a Dog!*

Alfred Stieglitz (1864–1946)   One of the earliest and strongest champions of photography-as-art. In addition to his own photo art, he formed a multimedia work group called PhotoSuccession Group, founded the magazine *Camera Work,* and ran several galleries where he had many exhibitions and competitions. His wife was the artist Georgia O'Keeffe, who became one of his favorite, frequent, and famous subjects—along with clouds and all of New York City.

"Sound in the Mulberry Tree" by Ben Shahn. Oil painting expressiveness without the oil: Shahn used a non-oil process known as tempera for this beautiful creation. Courtesy Smith College Museum of Art, Northampton, Massachusetts

There have been several Jewish artists who have made quite a colorful and comic sensation in the competitive world of popular cartooning. Among them are:

Al Capp   *Li'l Abner.*
Max Fleisher   *Popeye, Ko-Ko the Clown, Betty Boop.*
Rube Goldberg   Pulitzer Prize winner in 1947 for political cartoons; also created *Ike & Mike* and the cartoon columns *Foolish Questions* and *Inventions.*
Irwin Hasen   *Dondi*
Bob Kane   *Batman & Robin*
Stan Lee   *Spiderman*
Joe Shuster (with writer **Jerry Siegel**)   *Superman*

19

Golden Girls, Sunshine Boys

56 Cheers to These Oscar-
and Emmy-Winning Jews

*My mother said to me one day, "I really want people to see a
movie that you make someday that's about us and about who we
are, not as a people but as people." So this it it. This is for her.*
—Steven Spielberg, talking about *Schindler's List*

Wang Lung was patriarch of the Chinese family that is at the center of
Pearl Buck's memorable epic *The Good Earth*, and O-lan was his
long-suffering wife. In 1937, the story was brought to the screen with Wang
Lung and O-lan played by Paul Muni and Luise Rainer, both of whom were
Academy Award-winning film stars of the day, and both of whom were white
American Jews. No one raised an eyebrow.

Just a few seasons ago, by contrast, there was an uproar in New York's
theatrical community when the producers of the Broadway show *Miss Saigon*
cast non-Asians in Asian roles. For a few tense days, it seemed as if political
correctness, equal opportunity, artistic sensibilities, cultural pride, and other
initiatives were about to collide, twist, implode, and generally bury the
entertainment world under a cloud of anxiety.

Fortunately, that didn't happen. Everyone managed to get their heads
out of the clouds and put their feet back onto the good earth, and the show
went on. Without minimizing the need to adopt the best and most sensible
elements of each of those initiatives, isn't it the acting that really counts?

Jewish actors have been giving great performances on American screens,
large and small, since movies and television began. Theda Bara was a Jewish
silent screen star whose credits include *Carmen* (1915), *What Men Desire*

(1919), and *Madame Mystery* (1926) (with thirty-nine other films in between). And Jewish directors have been molding and developing those performances on cinematic canvases ever since. Can it be that Jews have a storytelling passion that is a reflection of their cultural heritage? Or that as a nation known for wandering around for centuries before jumping into the crowded American melting pot we have developed a special gift for observing, adapting, and mimicking the characteristics of so many others?

Maybe it is both reasons, maybe neither. As this list of Jewish Oscar and Emmy winners attests, it is the enjoyment *we* get out of it all that is of ultimate concern. It matters little that two members of the Corleone family (*The Godfather*) are Jewish in real life (James Caan and Abe Vigoda), or even that *Fiddler on the Roof* was *not* directed by a Jew (even though director Norman Jewison sounds like he should be). What is far more important is that *Fiddler on the Roof* is a warm, funny, joyful, evocative movie and that the hot-headed Sonny and quiet capo Tessio are as real as the people sitting next to us in the movie theater. It's storytelling at its best. And that's an offer no one should refuse.

Jack Albertson　Best Supporting Actor, *The Subject Was Roses*, 1968; Best Actor–Comedy Series, *Chico and the Man*, 1975–1976.
Woody Allen　Best Director, *Annie Hall*, 1977.
Roseanne Arnold　Best Actress–Comedy Series, *Roseanne*, 1992–1993.
Beatrice Arthur　Best Actress–Comedy Series, *Maude*, 1976–1977; Best Actress–Comedy Series, *Golden Girls*, 1987–1988.
Martin Balsam　Best Supporting Actor, *A Thousand Clowns*, 1965.

The number of roles some of these actors and actresses have played is nothing short of staggering, a testament as much to their likeability, energy, and agents as it is to their skill. Martin Balsam appeared in at least eighty films, including *Twelve Angry Men* (1957), *Psycho* (1960), and *Catch-22* (1970) and TV shows such as *Archie Bunker's Place* and *The Philco Television Playhouse*. Shelley Winters made over a hundred films, such as *A Place in the Sun* (1951), *The Greatest Story Ever Told* (1965), *Blume in Love* (1973), and *S.O.B.* (1981). Kirk Douglas topped eighty-five with such classics as *The Glass Menagerie* (1950), *Spartacus* (1960), *Seven Days in May* (1964), and *There Was a Crooked Man* (1970).

Jack Benny　Best Actor–Comedy, *The Jack Benny Show*, 1958–1959.
Gertrude Berg　Best Actress (TV), 1950.

George Burns Best Supporting Actor, *The Sunshine Boys*, 1975.

Red Buttons Best Supporting Actor, *Sayonara*, 1957.

Sid Caesar Best Actor (TV), 1951; Best Comedian, *Caesar's Hour*, 1956.

George Cukor Best Director, *My Fair Lady*, 1964.

Melvin Douglas Best Supporting Actor, *Hud*, 1963; Best Supporting Actor, *Being There*, 1979.

Richard Dreyfuss Best Actor, *The Goodbye Girl*, 1977.

Peter Falk Best Actor–Drama Series, *Columbo*, 1971–1972, 1975–1976, 1989–1990.

Not all of them started out as actors (and no doubt many of their mothers tried to talk them out of it). Peter Falk applied for a job with the CIA before becoming an actor and then worked as an efficiency expert. Bea Arthur is trained as a medical lab technician and actually worked in a Maryland hospital for a while.

Fyvush Finkel Best Supporting Actor–Drama Series, *Picket Fences*, 1993–1994.

William Friedkin Best Director, *The French Connection*, 1971.

Estelle Getty Best Supporting Actress–Comedy Series, *Golden Girls*, 1987–1988.

Lee Grant Best Supporting Actress–Drama Series, *Peyton Place*, 1965–1966; Best Supporting Actress, *Shampoo*, 1975.

Prior to her award-winning performances, the very talented Lee Grant suffered the fate of many Jewish entertainment personalities in the late 1940s and 1950s as members of the infamous Hollywood blacklist. She was on it only because her husband, playwright Arnold Manoff, was suspected of having communist ties. Other blacklisted Hollywood veterans, most of whom were denied jobs in the industry for several years, included actor Herschel Bernardi, who was in *Fiddler on the Roof* on stage, *Irma La Douce* on screen, and *Arnie* on TV; actor Howard da Silva, who starred in *They Live By Night* and *1776* on stage and screen; actor John Garfield, famous for *The Postman Always Rings Twice* and *Destination Tokyo*; actor Zero Mostel, known for his stage work with *Fiddler on the Roof* and *A Funny Thing Happened on the Way to the Forum*; actor Larry Parks, known for *The Jolson Story* and *Love Is Better Than Ever*; director Martin Ritt, who made *Hombre*, *Norma Rae*, and *Sounder*; director Robert Rosen, who helmed *Body and Soul* and *The*

Two-time Oscar and one-time Emmy winner Dustin Hoffman. Courtesy *The Jewish Week*, New York

Hustler; director Lewis Milestone, responsible for *All Quiet on the Western Front* and *A Walk in the Sun;* screenwriter Walter Bernstein, who wrote *The Front* (which was about the blacklist), and others.

Joel Grey   Best Supporting Actor, *Cabaret*, 1972.

Goldie Hawn   Best Supporting Actress, *Cactus Flower*, 1969.

Judd Hirsch   Best Actor–Comedy Series, *Taxi*, 1980–1981, 1982–1983.

Dustin Hoffman   Best Actor, *Kramer vs. Kramer*, 1979; Best Actor–Miniseries, *Death of a Salesman*, 1985–1986; Best Actor, *Rain Man*, 1988.

Judy Holliday   Best Actress, *Born Yesterday*, 1950.

Scott Jacoby   Best Supporting Actor–Drama or Drama Series, *That Certain Summer*, 1972–1973.

Carol Kane   Best Actress–Comedy Series, *Taxi*, 1981–1982; Best Supporting Actress–Comedy Series, *Taxi*, 1982–1983.

Julie Kavner   Best Supporting Actress–Comedy Series, *Rhoda*, 1977–1978.

Jack Klugman   Best Actor–Drama Series, *The Defenders*, 1963–1964; Best Actor–Comedy Series, *The Odd Couple*, 1970–1971, 1972–1973.

Martin Landau   Best Supporting Actor, *Ed Wood*, 1994.

Landau is a member of a very exclusive club: Jews in space. Between 1975 and 1979, he and Barbara Bain starred in *Space: 1999*, about an errant moon base. A decade earlier, two other Jewish actors spent a few years aboard the starship *Enterprise*. From 1966 to 1969, William Shatner, as Captain James T. Kirk, and Leonard Nimoy, as Science Officer Spock, took *Star Trek* where no man had gone before. It was about the same time, in 1968, that James Caan played an astronaut on his way to the moon in Robert Altman's critically acclaimed but little seen *Countdown*. In 1977, just when you thought it was safe to go out at night, Richard Dreyfuss entered a spaceship at the end of *Close Encounters of the Third Kind* for the flight of a lifetime. And in 1987, Mel Brooks played the president of a planet in *Spaceballs,* as well as a little guru named not the great, not the wise, but just the plain, Yogurt.

Ron Leibman   Best Actor–Drama Series, *Kaz,* 1978–1979.
Barry Levinson   Best Director, *Rain Man,* 1988.
Delbert Mann   Best Director, *Marty,* 1955.
Walter Matthau   Best Supporting Actor, *The Fortune Cookie,* 1966.
Lewis Mileston   Best Director, *All Quiet on the Western Front,* 1930.
Paul Muni   Best Actor, *The Story of Louis Pasteur,* 1936.

A Chinese farmer wasn't the only stretch for the talented Muni. Among his other roles were mobster Tony Camonte in *Scarface* (1932), Hispanic lawyer Johnny Ramirez in *Bordertown* (1935), French writer Emile Zola in *The Life of Emile Zola* (1937), and Mexican leader Benito Pablo Juarez in *Juarez* (1939). He also played Dr. Sam Abelman in *The Last Angry Man* (1959), his last picture. Lee J. Cobb made similar courageous choices, including a Siamese prime minister in *Anna and the King of Siam* (1946), a Spanish buccaneer in *Captain From Castile* (1947), and a Chinese warlord in *The Left Hand of God* (1955).

Mike Nichols   Best Director, *The Graduate,* 1967.
Mandy Patinkin   Best Actor–Drama Series, *Chicago Hope,* 1994–1995.
Rhea Perlman   Best Supporting Actress–Comedy Series, *Cheers,* 1983–1984, 1984–1985, 1985–1986, 1988–1989.
Sydney Pollack   Best Director, *Out of Africa,* 1985.
Luise Rainer   Best Actress, *The Great Ziegfeld,* 1936; Best Actress, *The Good Earth,* 1937.
Tony Randall   Best Actor–Comedy Series, *The Odd Couple,* 1974–1975.
Carl Reiner   Best Supporting Actor–Comedy Series, *Caesar's Hour,* 1957.

Reiner appeared on Sid Caesar's *Your Show of Shows* from 1950 to 1954 and worked with some of the funniest Jewish comedy writers in TV history, among them Mel Brooks, Larry Gelbart, Woody Allen, and Neil Simon. What was it like to be part of a team like that? A *Show of Shows*–type show was spoofed in the movie *My Favorite Year*, and Neil Simon himself wrote a play based on his experiences called *Laughter on the 27th Floor*. Perhaps a quick review of the post-*Your Show of Shows* comic output of that team tells a better story: *The Dick Van Dyke Show, The Thrill of It All, Dead Men Don't Wear Plaid* (Reiner); *The Producers, Blazing Saddles, Young Frankenstein, High Anxiety* (Brooks); *A Funny Thing Happened on the Way to the Forum, M°A°S°H, Tootsie, Oh, God!* (Gelbart); *Sleeper, Love and Death, Annie Hall, Broadway Danny Rose* (Allen); *Barefoot in the Park, The Odd Couple, The Goodbye Girl, The Sunshine Boys* (Simon). And that's a highly abridged list. In his book *Laughing Matters*, Gelbart recalls how he once was asked why all of Sid Caesar's writers were young and Jewish. Gelbart replied it was probably because all their parents were old and Jewish.

Rob Reiner   Best Supporting Actor–Comedy Series, *All in the Family,* 1973–1974, 1977–1978.

Jerome Robbins   Best Director, *West Side Story*, 1961.

Franklin Schaffner   Best Director, *Patton,* 1970.

Joseph Schildkraut   Best Supporting Actor, *The Life of Emile Zola,* 1937.

Norma Shearer   Best Actress, *The Divorcee*, 1930.

Phil Silvers   Best Actor (TV), *The Phil Silvers Show*, 1955; Best Comedian (TV), 1955.

Steven Spielberg   Best Director, *Schindler's List*, 1993.

Spielberg's *An American Tale* presented one of the few Jewish cartoon characters to play a significant role in a successful American film. Fievel is a young Russian immigrant mouse who is separated from his family in turn-of-the-century New York. Fievel has more kin on TV than he does in the movies. Jewish cartoon characters on the small screen include Krusty the Clown from *The Simpsons* (real name Hershel Krustofsky), Krusty's father, Rabbi Krustofsky (whose voice is supplied by Jackie Mason), and Grandma Minka and Grandpa Boris, who are Tommy

Pickles's grandparents in *Rugrats*. In the late 1960s and early 1970s there was a cartoon called *The Ant and the Aardvark* as part of *The Pink Panther Show* in which the Aardvark's voice, provided by John Byner, was distinctly Jackie Mason–like, which is to say that the aardvark itself was distinctively Jewish.

Barbra Streisand   Best Actress, *Funny Girl*, 1968 (tied with Katharine Hepburn, who starred in *The Lion in Winter*).

Elizabeth Taylor   Best Actress, *Butterfield 8*, 1960; Best Actress, *Who's Afraid of Virginia Woolf?*, 1966.

Eli Wallach   Best Supporting Actor–Drama, *The Poppy Is Also a Flower*, 1966–1967.

Billy Wilder   Best Director, *The Lost Weekend*, 1945; Best Director, *The Apartment*, 1960.

Shelley Winters   Best Supporting Actress, *The Diary of Anne Frank*, 1959; Best Actress–Drama Series, *Two Is the Number*, 1963–64; Best Supporting Actress, *A Patch of Blue*, 1965.

Robert Wise   Best Director, *West Side Story*, 1961; Best Director, *The Sound of Music*, 1965.

William Wyler   Best Director, *Mrs. Miniver*, 1942; Best Director, *The Best Years of Our Lives*, 1946; Best Director, *Ben-Hur*, 1959.

Fred Zinnemann   Best Director, *From Here to Eternity*, 1953; Best Director, *A Man for All Seasons*, 1966.

Without all the Jewish writers, producers, cinematographers, editors, orchestrators, production designers, costumers, lighting and sound technicians, camera operators, company assistants, and supporting cast members that are not mentioned here, there would not be a movie and television industry. It takes dozens and sometimes hundreds of people behind the lens to turn a Henry Winkler into an Arthur Fonzarelli .

Among the most innovative television producers of all time is Norman Lear, who brought *All in the Family, Sanford and Son, The Jeffersons, Good Times, Maude, One Day at a Time, Diff'rent Strokes, Mary Hartman, Mary Hartman,* and *Soap* to American TV, as well as the motion pictures *Divorce American Style* (1967), *The Night They Raided Minsky's* (1968), and *Cold Turkey* (1971). Leonard Goldberg and Aaron Spelling also stand out. Goldberg produced two of the most successful TV movies in history, *Something About Amelia* and *Brian's Song*, both of which won several Emmys and other awards. The Spelling/Goldberg team produced *Charlie's*

Angels, Starsky and Hutch, Fantasy Island, The Rookies, Hart to Hart, and *Family*, and Spelling gave life to *Vegas, The Mod Squad, The Love Boat, Hotel*, and *Beverly Hills 90210.*

When Hollywood makes its decisions on what movies to be greenlighted, usually one of two parameters has to be met: current trends, or the greatest common denominator in audience drawing power.

Movies primarily about Jews, Judaism, the Jewish-American experience, or even Jewish world history (including the Holocaust) have never been trendy subjects for mainstream Hollywood, nor do most studios and producers believe average American audiences coast to coast will flock to see such entertainments when other options are readily available.

Nevertheless, "Jewish" movies do come around every once in a while, and a majority of them are not only well received, but highly regarded as well. Hundreds of movies are released each year; only a few dozen over the least several decades have been intrinsically about the Jewish experience, American or otherwise. But what a few dozen they are! Based on critical reviews, popular reception, and professional response, the following is a Top 20 list of the best Jewish movies Hollywood has produced, offering Jews and non-Jews alike the Jewish experience as sheer entertainment or a palette onto which the way things really were are permanently etched. Most are available on videocassette.

Top 20 Jewish Movies

Annie Hall (1977)   Woody Allen, Diane Keaton, Tony Roberts, Paul Simon, Colleen Dewhurst, Christopher Walken. Directed by Woody Allen. Sophisticated, poignant, and very funny look at two neurotics—one Jewish, one not—who meet, live, love, leave, laugh, and long for other things throughout New York. Oscars for Best Picture, Best Director, Best Actress (Keaton), and Best Screenplay (Allen and Marshall Brickman).

The Apprenticeship of Duddy Kravitz (1974)   Richard Dreyfuss, Jack Warden, Randy Quaid, Micheline Lanctot, Joseph Wiseman, Denholm Elliott, Joe Silver. Directed by Ted Kotcheff. Canadian film about a very ambious young Jewish man from Montreal's Jewish ghetto in the 1940s who tries one scheme after another to get ahead.

Avalon (1990)   Aidan Quinn, Elizabeth Perkins, Armin Mueller-Stahl, Joan Plowright, Lou Jacobi, Kevin Pollack. Directed by Barry Levinson. Levinson's loving visual poem to the lives of Jewish immigrants and their children in Baltimore several decades ago.

The Chosen (1981)   Robby Benson, Barry Miller, Maximillian Schell, Rod

Steiger. Directed by Jeremy Paul Kagan. The special friendship between two Jews in 1940s Brooklyn, one hasidic and the other more secular. Based on Chaim Potok's excellent novel.

Crossing Delancey (1988)   Amy Irving, Peter Riegert, Reizl Bozyk, Jeroen Krabbe, Sylvia Miles. Directed by Joan Micklin Silver. A modern Jewish New York woman must deal with her grandmother's old-fashioned ways when the grandmother becomes determined to hire a matchmaker for her.

The Diary of Anne Frank (1959)   Millie Perkins, Joseph Schildkraut, Shelley Winters, Richard Beymer, Lou Jacobi, Dinae Baker, Ed Wynn. Directed by George Stevens. Adaptation of the play, which was an adaptation of the famous diary written by a girl whose family hid from the Nazis in an attic. Oscars for Best Supporting Actress (Winters) and Best Cinematography.

Enemies, a Love Story (1989)   Anjelica Huston, Ron Silver, Lena Olin, Margaret Sophie Stein, Alan King. Directed by Paul Mazursky. Isaac Bashevis Singer's quirky, funny, and intriguing tale of a Jewish survivor who comes to New York only to have to survive a triangle of women in his life.

Europa, Europa (1991)   Marco Hofschneider, Rene Hofschneider, Julie Delpy, Ashley Wanninger. Directed by Agnieszka Holland. French–German film about a Jewish teenager who escapes from the Nazis, changes his identity for survival, and is then drafted into Hitler's army.

Fiddler on the Roof (1971)   Topol, Norma Crane, Leonard Frey, Molly Picon, Paul Mann. Directed by Norman Jewison. Hearty, evocative adapation of the long-running Broadway musical about Tevya the milkman and his struggles to hold onto a few traditions in a changing and sometimes crazy world. Oscars for Best Cinematography and Best Scoring.

Gentleman's Agreement (1947)   Gregory Peck, Dorothy McGuire, John Garfield, Celeste Holm, Jane Wyatt, Dean Stockwell, Sam Jaffe. Directed by Elia Kazan. A writer poses as a Jew to investigate anti-Semitism. Oscars for Best Picture, Best Director, Best Supporting Actress (Holm).

Goodbye, Columbus (1969)   Richard Benjamin, Ali MacGraw, Jack Klugman, Nan Martin. Directed by Larry Peerce. Based on Philip Roth's novella of a young man who falls in love with the independent daughter of a socially affluent Jewish family.

Hester Street (1975)   Carol Kane, Steven Keats, Mel Howard, Doris Roberts. Directed by Joan Micklin Silver. A Jewish immigrant joins her husband in turn-of-the-century New York only to find him changed by the ways of the new world.

Joshua Then and Now (1985)   James Woods, Alan Arkin, Gabrielle Lazure, Michael Sarrazin. Directed by Ted Kotcheff. Canadian film about a Jewish writer and his experiences with his small-time gangster father, the upper-crust Gentile family he marries into, and other serio-comic episodes.

Lies My Father Told Me (1975)   Yossi Yadin, Len Birman, Marilyn Lightstone, Jeffrey Lynas. Directed by Jan Kadar. Canadian film, seen through the eyes of a young boy from the Jewish ghetto in the 1920s, who discovers many truths about life, family, and things in between.

The Pawnbroker (1965)   Rod Steiger, Geraldine Fitzgerald, Brock Peters. Directed by Sidney Lumet. Steiger's Sol Nazerman lives in New York—but his tortured memories never left the Nazi death camps.

Private Benjamin (1980)   Goldie Hawn, Armand Assante, Eileen Brennan, Sam Wanamaker, Albert Brooks. Directed by Howard Zieff. A Jewish-American Princess enlists in the army under false pretenses and unwittingly learns a thing or two about self-esteem and dignity.

Schindler's List (1993)   Liam Neeson, Ben Kingsley, Ralph Fiennes. Directed by Steven Spielberg. Highly acclaimed and much honored drama of Oskar Schindler, an ambitious and, at first, ambivalent businessman who saves the lives of hundreds of Jews marked for death by the Nazis by employing them in his factory. Oscars for Best Picture, Director, Adapted Screenplay, Original Score, and Cinematography.

The Shop on Main Street (1965)   Elmar Klos, Josef Kroner, Ida Kaminsky. Directed by Jan Kadar. A Czechoslovakian film about a woman in World War II who, to avoid persecution, must agree to have her button shop run by a man. Oscar for Best Foreign Film.

The Ten Commandments (1956)   Charlton Heston, Yul Brynner, Anne Baxter, Edward G. Robinson, Yvonne De Carlo, Debra Paget, John Derek. Directed by Cecil B. DeMille. Moses, slavery, the basket, the Pharoah's daughter, the secret, the leader, the plagues, the parting of the Red Sea, the Ten Commandments: An epic of biblical proportions.

Yentl (1983)   Barbra Streisand, Mandy Patinkin, Amy Irving, Nehemiah Persoff, Steven Hill. Directed by Barbra Streisand. Streisand produced, directed, cowrote (based on Isaac Bashevis Singer's short story) and sang the songs in this tale of a turn-of-the-century girl in Eastern Europe who poses as a boy in order to fullfill her Yeshiva dreams. Oscar for Best Original Score (Alan & Marilyn Bergman and Michel Legrand).

With three Academy Awards for Best Picture, three for Best Director, and many more in categories from acting to art and writing to music, these twenty films truly stand up as motion pictures that are as much about good moviemaking as they are about Jews.

In reviewing some of those responsible for these films, some interesting facts appear: two of the top twenty were directed by one woman, Joan Micklin Silver (*Hester Street, Crossing Delancey*); two were directed by Ted Kotcheff based on Mordecai Richter stories (*The Apprenticeship of Duddy Kravitz, Joshua Then and Now*); two were based on Isaac Bashevis Singer stories (*Enemies, a Love Story; Yentl*); and two starred Rod Steiger, who is not Jewish, as a Nazi concentration camp survivor (*The Pawnbroker*) and a hasidic rabbi (*The Chosen*).

5 Jewish Women Directors and Producers

Joan Micklin Silver is in good company where Jewish women directors and producers are concerned. There are not that many women in those areas of the motion picture industry in the first place; several of those who have made their mark have been Jewish. They include:

Sherry Lansing who as a top studio executive and independent producer has been responsible for several hits, including *Fatal Attraction* and *Indecent Proposal*.

Susan Seidelman a director whose *Desperately Seeking Susan* began the film careers of several actors, including Madonna, and whose other credits include *Making Mr. Right* and *Smithereens*.

Dawn Steel was both a studio executive and an independent producer whose credits include *Cool Runnings, Sister Act 2*, and *Honey, I Blew Up the Kid*.

Barbara Streisand who produced many of her own films and also directed and starred in *Yentl* and *The Prince of Tides*.

Claudia Weill lensed films on both sides of the budget spectrum, from *Girlfriends* to *It's My Turn*.

In addition to *Hester Street* and *Crossing Delancey*, Joan Micklin Silver's directorial efforts include *Between the Lines* and *Chilly Scenes of Winter*.

Rod Steiger tells a story about an incident in Israel when he was there to promote the opening of *The Pawnbroker*. An Orthodox Jew at a publicity event noticed the actor's obvious reticence at being there. When the man inquired, Steiger admitted that he didn't want to desecrate the memory of the Holocaust victims by participating so visibly in the event, since he wasn't Jewish. The Orthodox man asked if he was the actor who played Sol Nazerman in the picture. Steiger replied that he was. The Orthodox man said to him, "Don't worry. You're Jewish."

TV's Top Ten Best-Loved Openly Jewish Characters

Molly Goldberg from *The Goldbergs* was played by Gertrude Berg from 1949 to 1955. Created by Berg on radio in 1929, Molly, residing at 1038 West Tremont Avenue in the Bronx, was America's first coast-to-coast Jewish mother. The show was produced and written by Berg.

Buddy Sorrell from *The Dick Van Dyke Show* was played by Morey Amsterdam from 1961 to 1966. Buddy, one of the writers of The Alan Brady Show, was an entire act by himself, even without the comic support of Rob, Sally, and Mel. He even joked at his own bar mitzvah, which he celebrated on the series as a grown man as a present to his mother.

Bernie Steinberg from *Bridget Loves Bernie,* was played by David Birney (who is not Jewish) from 1972 to 1973. For a series with an extremely short life, this show seems to have kvetched its way into our memories. Perhaps that's because in real life Bernie married Bridget (Meredith Baxter, although they are now divorced). In the show, aspiring writer Bernie falls in love with teacher Bridget Theresa Mary Coleen Fitzgerald.

Dr. Sidney Freedman from *M**A*S*H was played by Alan Arbus from 1972 to 1983. The gentle Jewish psychiatrist for the 4077th stepped in and out sporadically to help keep the madcap surgeons from going insane. If he hadn't *M**A*S*H might have turned into a tragedy.

Rhoda Morgenstern from *Rhoda* was played by Valerie Harper (who is not Jewish) from 1974 to 1978. Mary Richards's neighbor moved back to New York from Minneapolis to find a job and a husband. She got both—in addition to some of the most neurotic and enigmatic acquaintances in TV land (including Carlton the doorman), not to mention a meddling mom. Rhoda and her husband, Joe, were divorced in the fourth year of the series.

Brenda Morgenstern from *Rhoda* was played by Julie Kavner. Rhoda's sister was unabashedly neurotic herself, and just as funny. Her trials and tribulations—including boyfriends like Benny Goodwin—provided her with enough comic baggage to make it seem as if it were her show as much as her sister's.

Paul Pfeiffer from *The Wonder Years* was played by Josh Saviano from 1988 to 1993. There was a geeky Paul in every junior and senior high school in America throughout the 1970s, when this series took place. The lead character's awkward best friend through thick and thin, Paul somehow seemed destined to turn out okay, and he did.

Jerry Seinfeld from *Seinfeld* was played by Jerry Seinfeld, one of the most popular and innovative comedies of all time, from 1989 to 1998. He was the calm in the middle of a storm called living and loving in Manhattan. Jerry's TV parents, played by Elizabeth Sheridan and Barney Martin, also get adoring nods.

Paul Buckman   from *Mad About You* is played by Paul Reiser. The show first aired in 1992. Paul, a documentary filmmaker, is mad about Jamie (Helen Hunt), and their own living and loving in Manhattan scenario is more realistic than Seinfeld's, and often just as funny. Paul's cousin Ira, played by John Pankow, is another favorite.

Fran Fine   from *The Nanny* is played by Fran Drescher. The show first aired in 1993. That voice from Flushing should be enough to turn anyone away from stereotypical Jewish characters, but apparently Fran's got something extra. The popularity of her series proves it. Fran's mother, Sylvia, played by Elaine May, is another classic Jewish mother—in the extreme.

And As Moses...

- Mel Brooks, in *History of the World, Part I* (1984)

- Charleton Heston, in *The Ten Commandments* (1956)

- Ben Kingsley, in *Moses* (1996 TV Miniseries)

- Burt Lancaster, in *Moses, the Lawgiver* (1975 TV miniseries, then theatrical release)

- Dudley Moore, in *Wholly Moses* (1980)

- Theodore Roberts, in *The Ten Commandments* (1923)

- Soupy Sales, in *...And God Spoke* (1993)

20

A Funny Thing Happened on the Way to the Theater

63 Jews on Broadway

You don't have to be Jewish to love Tevye.
—Norman Nadel, *World–Telegram & Sun*

Although American Jews got their collective theatrical feet wet in Yiddish theatre, there is nothing particularly religious or ethnic about their later contributions to the development of the American stage and particularly the Broadway musical. Other than a few shows with a decidedly Jewish bearing (*The Tenth Man, Fiddler on the Roof, Funny Girl*), the musical stage entertainment written, composed, adapted, designed, directed, choreographed, and acted by Jews has been for everyone, regardless of race, creed, or color, as their popularity confirms.

But it was not *just* the sound of their music that gave Jews a front row center seat in Broadway history. Several of the most important impressarios on the Great White Way were Jewish, as well:

David Belasco (1853–1931) Around the early part of the twentieth century, took the theatre to its outer limits of staging and technical innovations with new kinds of lighting and special effects. Just having him as the producer of a show was a big box-office draw.

Alexander H. Cohen (1920–) Has produced one hundred shows in his career so far, more than sixty of them on Broadway, including *Angel Street, The Homecoming,* and *The Herbal Bed*. He also directed his energies toward the Actor's Fund, for which he raised a lot of money to support, among other things, the Actor's Home extended care facility in

Englewood, New Jersey, and he produced twenty Tony Awards telecasts and other TV specials.

Sol Hurok (1890–1974)   Several years after Belasco, skillfully and methodically turned American stages into palaces of both enchantment and fortune.

Marcus Loew and **Adolph Zukor**   Two Jewish furriers who built a successful vaudeville circuit, beginning in 1909, throughout Brooklyn and New Jersey. (Zukor subsequently founded Paramount Pictures in 1917.)

Billy Rose   Who started out as a speedy shorthand writer for financier Bernard Baruch, eventually began to write songs, then branched into nightclubs, and finally produced many Broadway spectacles, such as *Carman Jones* (1943) and *The Seven Lively Arts* (1944). He also owned the Ziegfeld and Billy Rose theatres.

Sam (1875–1905), **Lee** (1876–1953), and **Jacob Shubert,** (1887–1962)   Sons of a peddler in upstate New York, they built their own theater row from one end of Broadway to the other. They filled their stages with over five hundred plays and helped advance the careers of Al Jolson, Eddie Cantor, and Fanny Brice.

Florenz Ziegfeld   Was the ultimate showman who celebrated American female beauty and grace in his Ziegfeld Follies, popular Broadway reviews that ran from 1906 to 1931. Spectacular sets and costumes were the icing on the cake.

Two of the greatest and most influential dramatic acting teachers of all time were Jewish, Lee Strasberg and Stella Adler. Among their students were Marlon Brando, Robert DeNiro, Kim Hunter, Paul Newman, Al Pacino, Geraldine Page, and Warren Beatty. Strasberg was a founder of the famed Group Theatre in 1931 with another Jew, the critic Harold Clurman, and among the Jewish actors who were in the company at the beginning were Adler and the famous Shakespearean Morris Carnovsky.

Dozens of famous, groundbreaking, and award-winning plays have been written by Jews, many of them based on memory or experience, others simply on the natural ability of each playwright to see life on some of its most poignant, pitiful, or hilarious levels. Some of the theater's most intriguing Jewish playwrights include:

Paddy Chayefsky (1923–1981)   *The Tenth Man, Gideon, The Latent Heterosexual.*

Bruce Jay Friedman (1930–)   *Steambath, Scuba Duba, Have You Spoken to Any Jews Lately?*

Herb Gardner (1934–)   *Conversations With My Father, I'm Not Rappaport, A Thousand Clowns.*

Broadway Bound

There are dozens of plays that explore the Jewish-American experience. Here are ten of the most intriguing, haunting, and consistently enjoyable.

• *Awake and Sing,* by Clifford Odets (1935). A multigenerational family saga set in the Bronx.

• *Brighton Beach Memoirs,* by Neil Simon (1982). The first of the three Simon semiautobiographical serious-comedies about life, love, and the pursuit of dreams.

• *Broken Glass,* by Arthur Miller (1994). A portrait of a Jewish marriage that is shattering, like the windows during Kristalnacht which echo in the wife's memory.

• *Counsellor-at-Law,* by Elmer Rice (1931). A gifted Jewish lawyer deals with a somewhat alien environment.

• *Crossing Delancey,* by Susan Sandler (1986). A modern young Jewish woman looks for love with an old-fashioned *bubbe* looking out for her.

• *Home of the Brave,* by Arthur Laurents (1945). A Jewish soldier deals with personal battles, from friendships to religion.

• *The Old Neighborhood,* by David Mamet (1997). Three short plays that touch on some long divisions: *The Disappearances of the Jews, Jolly,* and *Deeny.*

• *A Shayna Maidel,* by Barbara Lebow (1985). Two sisters of the Holocaust, separated in childhood, are reunited in New York.

• *The Sisters Rosensweig,* by Wendy Wasserstein (1991). Three Jewish-American women in London look for love, identity, and fulfillment.

• *The Tenth Man,* by Paddy Chayefsky (1959). The "exorcism" of a troubled Jewish man on Long Island.

Moss Hart (1904–1961) and **George S. Kaufman** (1889–1961) *The Man Who Came to Dinner, You Can't Take It With You.*

Ben Hecht (1894–1961) *The Front Page* (with Charles MacArthur), *A Flag Is Born.*

Lillian Hellman (1905–1984) *The Children's Hour, The Little Foxes, Toys in the Attic.*

Israel Horovitz (1939–) *The Indian Wants the Bronx, The Primary English Class, It's Called the Sugar Plum, The Honest-to-God Schnozzola.*

Playwright Arthur Miller was married from 1956 to 1961 to actress Marilyn Monroe, who had converted to Judaism. Miller created many tragic characters, but none as tragic as Monroe. Courtesy Archive Photos

Tony Kushner (1957–   ) *Angels in America: Millennium Approaches* (Pulitzer Prize for drama), *Angels in America: Perestroika.*

Arthur Laurents (1918–   )   *Home of the Brave, The Bird Cage.*

David Mamet (1947–   )   *American Buffalo, Glengarry Glen Ross, Sexual Perversity in Chicago, The Old Neighborhood.*

Sidney Michaels (1927–   )   *Ben Franklin in Paris, Dylan.*

Arthur Miller (1915–   )   *After the Fall, All My Sons, The Crucible, Death of a Salesman, A View from the Bridge.*

Clifford Odets (1906–1963)   *Awake and Sing, Golden Boy, Waiting for Lefty.*

Elmer Rice (1892–1966)   *The Adding Machine, American Landscape, Street Scene, On Trial.*

Murray Schisgal (1926–   )   *Luv, The Typists, The Tiger, Jimmy Shine.*

Neil Simon (1927–   )   *Barefoot in the Park, Broadway Bound, The Odd Couple, The Sunshine Boys, Lost in Yonkers, Laughter on the 23rd Floor.*

Wendy Wasserstein (1959–   )   *An American Daughter, The Heidi Chronicles.*

Herman Wouk (1915–   )   *The Caine Mutiny Court-Martial, The Traitor, Nature's Way.*

There have been hundreds of Broadway musicals. Every once in a while a show comes along that alters the course of American musical theater, usually in very exciting ways, and usually forever. *Show Boat* did it in 1927, setting new standards for combining theatrical spectacle with a serious plot. *Oklahoma!* did it again in 1943 as the first musical to successfully combine literary drama and theatrical ballet without giving up any of its comedy or show-stopping numbers. The music for *Show Boat* and *Oklahoma!* were written by Jews—**Jerome Kern** and **Richard Rodgers**, respectively. *Show Boat* was based on a book by Jewish author **Edna Ferber**.

There would still be Broadway musicals if it weren't for Jewish talent. It just wouldn't be one of our favorite things.

Here are just some of theater's greatest Jewish composers and lyricists and a few of the most popular shows they brought to Broadway:

Leonard Bernstein (1918–1990) (music):   *On the Town, Candide, West Side Story* (lyrics by Stephen Sondheim).

Jerry Bock (1928–   ) (music) and **Sheldon Harnick** (lyrics):   *The Body Beautiful, Fiddler on the Roof, Fiorello, Mr. Wonderful, She Loves Me, Tenderloin.*

Cy Coleman (1929–   ) (music):   *Little Me, Sweet Charity, Seesaw, I Love My Wife, On the 20th Century, Barnum, City of Angels.*

Betty Comden (1916–   ) and **Adolph Green** (1915–   ) (book and lyrics):   *Bells Are Ringing, On the Town, Two on the Aisle.*

Marvin Hamlisch (1944–   ) (music):   *A Chorus Line, They're Playing Our Song.*

John Kander (1927–   ) (music):   *The Act, Cabaret, Chicago, Zorba.*

Alan J. Lerner (1918–1986) (lyrics) and **Frederick Loewe** (1904–1988) (music):   *Brigadoon, Camelot, My Fair Lady, Paint Your Wagon.*

Frank Loesser (1910–1969) (music and lyrics):   *Guys & Dolls, How to Succeed in Business Without Really Trying, The Most Happy Fella, Where's Charlie?*

Richard Rodgers (1902–1979) (music, with lyrics by Oscar Hammerstein II):   *Carousel, Flower Drum Song, The King and I, Oklahoma!, The Sound of Music, South Pacific.*

Stephen Sondheim (1930–   ) (music and lyrics):   *Follies, A Funny Thing Happened on the Way to the Forum, Into the Woods, A Little Night Music, Pacific Overtures, Sunday in the Park With George, Sweeney Todd.*

Jule Styne (1905–1994)(music):   *Bells Are Ringing, Funny Girl, Gentlemen Prefer Blondes, Gypsy.*

Almost all of them have won the prestigious Tony award at least once; Stephen Sondheim has won it for his scores to *Company, A Little Night Music, Sweeney Todd,* and *Into the Woods.* Two Jewish-American Broadway heroes who have won Tonys several times for categories other than music are **Hal Prince** and **Jerome Robbins.** Prince, one of the most successful pros in Broadway history, won it for producing *Fiddler on the Roof,* and directing *Sweeney Todd, Evita, Phantom of the Opera,* and the revivals of *Candide* (1974) and *Show Boat* (1995). Jerome Robbins picked up the statuette for choreographing *High Button Shoes, West Side Story,* directing and choreographing *Fiddler on the Roof,* and directing *Jerome Robbins' Broadway.* Robbins had been associate artistic director of the New York City Ballet in the late 1940s and early 1950s, but has also been involved in about two dozen Broadway shows, including the choreography for *The King and I,* directing and co-choreographing *The Pajama Game,* and directing and choreographing *Gypsy.* He died in 1998.

Our Broadway memories are usually wonderful even when the reviews are not. What do you say about a show that's been less-than-embraced by some critics yet goes on to win the hearts of audiences as well as many awards and to build some careers to stratospheric heights? Is there a Jewish resilience gene? Or is it that you just can't argue with enjoyment? (Notice how one list absent from this book is a list of critics.)

Fiddler on the Roof

I think it might be an altogether charming musical if only the people of Anatevka did not pause every now and then to give their regard to Broadway, with remembrances to Herald Square. [The show] is a very-near-miss, and I very much miss what it might have been.

—Walter Kerr, *Herald Tribune*

Funny Girl

Hail to thee, Barbra Streisand; Fanny Brice thou never wert! But there you have the whole paradox of this show—one spectacular talent in the role of another spectacular talent, but never becoming, or perhaps even trying to become, the woman this play is about.

—Norman Nadel, *World–Telegram & Sun*

The star's passion has many colors, her phrasing has many colors, but her voice does not have *that* many. One feels that the management is trying to cram an entire evening into one show.

—Walter Kerr, *Herald Tribune*

While the dedicated work of all concerned with it has had some pleasant results, I can't help feeling that it remains a disappointing entertainment.

—Richard Watts Jr., *New York Post*

A *Funny Thing Happened on the Way to the Forum*

A boy entering the Alvin Theatre last night called loudly to his companion (three feet away): "If this isn't a hit, I'm going to lynch your brother." I just hope the lad had some second thoughts about his attitude today, while lynching his friend's brother. Maybe he will learn in time to be grateful for small favors. Small indeed are the favors afforded this new musical....

—Norman Nadel, *World–Telegram & Sun*

The Sound of Music

I can only wish that someone had not been moved to abandon the snowflakes and substitute cornflakes. Before *The Sound of Music* is halfway through its promising chores it becomes not only too sweet for words but almost too sweet for music.... There are seven tots necessary to the narrative, and I am not against tots. But must they bounce into bed in their nightgowns so often, and so armingly?

—Walter Kerr, *Herald Tribune*

West Side Story

The show is, in general, not well sung. It is grudgingly acted. And it is, apart from the spine tingling velocity of the dances, almost never emotionally affecting.... This is the show that could have danced all night, and nearly did. But the dancing is it. Don't look for laughter or—for that matter—tears.

—Walter Kerr, *Herald Tribune*

It is a marvel peculiar to this country. Here we breed evil in our cities, but here we also parade a Bernstein and a Robbins so that a big part of this tortured world may say, "America must be proud of boys like these." And theatre-going Americans may reply, "You're darn tootin' we are."

—Frank Ashton, *World–Telegram and Star*

Among the Jewish actors who picked up Tony nods for nonmusical roles on Broadway were:

Martin Balsam *You Know I Can't Hear You When the Water's Running* (1968).
Gertrude Berg *A Majority of One* (1959).
Harvey Fierstein *Torch Song Trilogy* (1983).
Cliff Gorman *Lenny* (1972).
Judd Hirsch *I'm Not Rappaport* (1986) and *Conversations With My Father* (1992).

Madeline Kahn   *The Sisters Rosensweig* (1993).
Linda Lavin   *Broadway Bound* (1987).
Ron Leibman   *Angels in America: Millenium Approaches* (1993).
Walter Matthau   *A Shot in the Dark* (1962) and *The Odd Couple* (1965).
Barry Miller   *Biloxi Blues* (1985).
Zero Mostel   *Rhinoceros* (1961).
Paul Muni   *Inherit the Wind* (1956).
John Rubinstein   *Children of a Lesser God* (1980).
Ron Silver   *Speed the Plow (1988).*

21

The Names They
Are A-Changing

112 Real Names of Famous People

Mr. O'Brien, your mother Mrs. Horowitz is here to see you.
—from the comedy album *You Don't Have to Be Jewish*

The suave, handsome, and talented young man looked to the heavens on the day he decided to become an actor and said, "God, if you're there, can you answer me one question? Did you *have* to name me Ira Grossel?"

Whether Ira received an answer is unknown, but somewhere along the line Ira Grossel became Jeffrey Chandler and went on to make over forty motion pictures between 1947 and 1962.

He had a lot of company—from William Rosenberg, who became Billy Rose, to Pauline Esther Friedman, who became Ann Landers, to Jacob Cohen, who became Rodney Dangerfield.

Early in his career, comedian Leonard Hacker's agent changed Leonard's name to Buddy Hackett, without so much as an explanation, or even Leonard's permission. But that was not uncommon. Many entertainers, Jewish or otherwise, had their given names changed on the order or advice of all-knowing agents and producers. Sometimes, however, the names were changed for them by harried and careless immigration officials, like Melvin Torma's father, whose name was erroneously transcribed as Torme. (Mel added the accent, Tormé, years later when he was beginning to establish himself as a musician.) Still others changed their names based on idols or influences, as in the case of young Robert Zimmerman, who, because he emulated poet Dylan Thomas, changed his name to Bob Dylan..

Of course, there were also cases in which performers felt their given names were simply *too Jewish* for their intended audiences. Anglicizing names wasn't exclusively a Jewish province, but Jews were certainly in the majority. One statistic states that of the fifty thousand Americans who legally changed their names in the late 1940s and early 1950s, 80 percent were Jewish.

Fortunately Jewish entertainers have gotten a lot braver, or simply prouder, in the past few decades. Jonathan Silverman, Jerry Seinfeld, Tovah Feldshuh, and hundreds of others whose names once may have been too Jewish use their real names today without giving it a second thought. As far as the old days are concerned, the jury is still out on whether or not sheer talent could have overridden the quirkinesss of an original name even if the original name was Harold Lipshitz. While we may never know if a Benjamin Kubelsky routine would have been as good as one by Jack Benny, we do know that "Walter Matuschanskayasky" would never have fit on the billboard for *The Odd Couple*.

ORIGINAL NAMES AND PROFESSIONAL NAMES OF JEWISH-AMERICAN MEDIA PERSONALITIES

Original names	Stage names
Maximilian Adelbert	Max Baer
Hyman Arluck	Harold Arlen
Arthur Arshawsky	Artie Shaw
Israel Baline	Irving Berlin
Rosine Bernard	Sarah Bernhardt
Alfred Caplin	Al Capp
Jack Chakrin	Jack Carter
Ellen Cohen	Mama "Cass" Elliott
Howard Cohen	Howard Cosell
Jacob Cohen	Rodney Dangerfield
Sam Cohen	Sammy Cahn
Issur Danielovich	Kirk Douglas
Albert Einstein	Albert Brooks
Fivel Feldman	Phil Foster
Sophie Feldman	Totie Fields
Bernice Frankel	Bea Arthur
Esther Friedman	Ann Landers
Pauline Friedman	Abigail Van Buren
Samille Diane Friesan	Dyan Cannon
Julius Garfinkle	John Garfield

Schmuel Gelbfisz	Sam Goldwyn
Jacob Gellman	Jack Gilford
Israel Gershvin	Ira Gershwin
Avron Goldbogen	Mike Todd
Emanuel Goldenberg	Edward G. Robinson
Elliot Goldstein	Elliot Gould
Theodosia Goodman	Theda Bara
Sheldon Greenfield	Shecky Greene
Jay Scott Greenspan	Jason Alexander
Ira Grossel	Jeff Chandler
Leonard Hacker	Buddy Hackett
Melvyn Hesselberg	Melvyn Douglas
Catherine Holzman	Kitty Carlisle
Winona Horowitz	Winona Ryder
Barbara Huffman	Barbara Eden
Martin Ingerman	Marty Ingels
Isidor Iskowitch	Eddie Cantor
Melvin Israel	Mel Allen
Lee Jacob	Lee J. Cobb
Murray Janofsky	Jan Murray
Melvyn Kaminsky	Mel Brooks
Joel Katz	Joel Grey
Seymour Kaufman	Cy Coleman
Eugene Klass	Gene Barry
Samuel Klausman	Larry Parks
Carole Klein	Carole King
Richard Klein	Calvin Klein
Irwin Knilberg	Alan King
David Kominsky	Danny Kaye
Allan Konigsberg	Woody Allen
David Kotkin	David Copperfield
Benjamin Kubelsky	Jack Benny
Irving Lahrheim	Bert Lahr
Pincus Leff	Pinky Lee
Benjamin Leiner	Benny Leonard
Isaiah Leopold	Ed Wynn
Pauline Levee	Paulette Goddard
Joseph Levitch	Jerry Lewis
Sidney Liebowitz	Steve Lawrence
Ralph Lifshitz	Ralph Laren
Lorne Lipowitz	Lorne Michaels

Harold Lipshitz	Hal Linden
Laszlo Lowenstein	Peter Lorre
Walter Matuschanskayasky	Walter Matthau
Yacov Maza	Jackie Mason
Bruce Meyerowitz	"Cousin Brucie" Morrow
Moishe Miller	Robert Merrill
Joan Molinsky	Joan Rivers
Alvin Morris	Tony Martin
Jill Oppenheimer	Jill St. John
Michael Orowitz	Michael Landon
Betty Joan Perske	Lauren Bacall
Michael Peschkowsky	Mike Nichols
Barry Alan Pincus	Barry Manilow
Andreas Priwin	Andre Previn
Emanuel Radnitsky	Man Ray
William Rosenberg	Billy Rose
Martin Rosenblatt	Ross Martin
Leonard Rosenthal	Tony Randall
Lyova Rosenthal	Lee Grant
Barnet Rosofsky	Barney Ross
Harold Rubin	Harold Robbins
Leonard Scheider	Lenny Bruce
Shirley Schrift	Shelly Winters
Richard Schulefand	Dick Shawn
Bernard Schwartz	Tony Curtis
David Shapiro	David Frye
Francis Rose Shore	Dinah Shore
Jerome Silberman	Gene Wilder
Harold Silverblatt	Howard de Silva
Belle Silverman	Beverly Sills
Philip Silversmith	Phil Silvers
Andrew Silverstein	Andrew "Dice" Clay
Julius Stein	Jule Styne
Herbert Streicher	Harry Reems
Milton Supman	Soupy Sales
William Szathmary	Bill Dana
Irving Tennebaum	Irving Stone
Arthur Teichman	Arthur Murray
Michael Thomashevsky	Michael Tilson Thomas
Melvin Torma	Mel Tormé
Sonia Kalish	Sophie Tucker

Judith Tuvim	Judy Holliday
Myron Wallace	Mike Wallace
Nathan Weinstein	Nathaniel West
Muni Weisenfreund	Paul Muni
Erich Weiss	Harry Houdini
Chaim Wietz	Gene Simmons
Robert Widerman	Robert Clary
Asa Yoelson	Al Jolson
Lawrence Zeiger	Larry King
Robert Zimmerman	Bob Dylan

In The Name of God

There are many ways Jews refer to God in prayer, worship, and written documents, from both the Bible and in post-biblical usage, and both in Hebrew and English. Twelve of the most common are:

- Lord

- Adonai (Lord)

- Elohim (God)

- YHWH (Hebrew consonants from the phrase Ineffible Name of God)

- King of Kings

- Hashem (meaning "the name")

- Master of the Universe

- El Elyon (meaning Most High God)

- Almighty

- Shaddai (Almighty)

- Ha-Kadosh Baruch Hu (Holy One Blessed Be He)

- G–D

and of course God.

22

Some Like It Jewish

The World of Converts

*Who would have imagined that my witnessing of the lighting of
Shabbos candles would open my mind and heart to a religion I
had once believed to be false?*

—John David Scalamonti, former Roman Catholic priest,
now an Orthodox Jew

Not all famous Jewish personalities started out famous—or even Jewish,
for that matter. Sometimes love's got a lot to do with it.

Actress **Norma Shearer,** who starred in *The Women* (1939), *Idiot's
Delight* (1939), and many other motion pictures, converted to Judaism after
marrying producer Irving Thalberg and became enormously devoted to the
faith during the course of their marriage. When **Elizabeth Taylor** was
married to Jewish producer Mike Todd she told him she wanted to convert,
but Todd urged her not to take the decision lightly and to think about it for a
while. Todd died suddenly in an airplane crash, and then Taylor fell in love
with Eddie Fisher, who also was Jewish. That's when she made the final
decision to convert. **Marilyn Monroe** converted after marrying Jewish
playwright Arthur Miller.

In November 1954, **Sammy Davis Jr.** was in a serious automobile
accident. Eddie Cantor, who previously had presented Sammy with a
mezuzah, visited the entertainer in the hospital. It was at about that time
when Sammy started pondering the affinity between Jews and blacks as
historically oppressed people. He asked a Hollywood rabbi, Nussbaum, to
help him convert and Nussbaum readily agreed, feeling that Davis's desire
was genuine. Sammy's wanting to convert, the rabbi said, did not come from
marital or childrearing issues or conflicts but from his heart.

Other famous converts include singer **Helen Reddy** and actress **Kate Capshaw**, Steven Spielberg's wife.

A 1990 survey by the Council of Jewish Federations estimated there are 185,000 Jews-by-choice in the United States (meaning both those who formally converted and those who did not officially convert but follow Jewish practice and consider themselves Jewish). About 135,000 are formal converts.

Typically, a person who wants to convert is discouraged three times, giving them ample opportunity to prove their seriousness and commitment. There seems to be a biblical precedent to this. Ruth, a Moabite, became a widow and was told three times by her mother-in-law, Naomi, to return to her own people. But Ruth felt the need to stay, and stay she did, joining the people of Israel and starting the lineage that led to King David. According to the Talmud the Messiah will be a direct descendent of Ruth.

It is said that when one converts to Judaism, one remains a Jew forever. It is further said that because such a person chooses a path that requires the courage to leave a part of themselves behind, God offers extra-special protection to that person throughout his or her life.

One of the earliest recorded converts in the United States was **Warder Cresson**, a public servant whose Quaker family lived in Philadelphia. Cresson was the first U.S. consul in Jerusalem between 1944 and 1948, and when his term was over he fell in love with Judaism. His family tried to have him committed for reasons of insanity, but Cresson returned to Palestine and lived there for the rest of his life as an Orthodox Jew.

Rachel Cowan had an Old Testament name but a New Testament background. Her husband, writer Paul Cowan, born a Jew but raised without religion, rediscovered his connection to the faith when he was in his thirties. Rachel, who stood by him through each phase of his return, discovered something on her own: she, too, wanted to be Jewish. "I used to think that conversion meant that you stopped being one thing in order to become another, and therefore I resisted it," she says in her husband's book, *An Orphan in History.* "But the Israeli Rabbi Adin Steinsaltz gave me a more organic metaphor. Conversion, he said, is like marriage. You are joined to a new community, but you bring to the union the strengths and the values that have been your foundation all your life."

John David Scalamonti, born and raised a Roman Catholic in Jessup, Pennsylvania, was a priest for sixteen years. Having grown disenchanted with many aspects of the priesthood and Catholic doctrine, he left the church, explored Judaism, and in 1972 converted. In his 1992 book, *Ordained to Be a Jew,* he says he liked Judaism's uncomplicated theology, compassionate understanding of the human condition, colorful rituals, and warm home life.

"Judaism views the world as good, unlike Christianity, which sees it as a threat to achieving eternal salvation," he wrote. "For the Jew the world is a beautiful place, no doubt far from perfect, but designed by the hand of God, and offering many opportunities for love, family and friendship."

Lawrence J. Epstein wrote a book about conversion called *Conversion to Judaism: A Guidebook* and had been helping people interested in conversion by connecting them to helpful rabbis in various parts of the world via the Internet. Before long he saw the need to set up an actual site of his own, which he calls "The Conversion to Judaism Home Page" (*http:www.convert.org*). It gets about 2,000 visits a month.

Epstein doesn't have a clear-cut reason for his interest in helping people convert. Neither he nor his wife are converts, nor is anyone in his immediate family. "I thought converts would reduce the intermarriage rate and increase the Jewish population," he states. "After an examination of Judaism's most fundamental beliefs, I have concluded that it is a religious obligation for Jews to welcome converts." Raised in a secular home, Epstein reconnected with his Jewishness in his twenties, and when he did so it was almost like a conversion in itself. That, he says, is why he is so sympathetic to those who wish to *really* convert. Proselytizing, he emphasizes, is not a Jewish tradition and through his book and his Internet site he insists he is simply "stating the availability of conversion for those who are interested—and who must take the first step themselves."

23

U.S. Steal

30 Jewish Criminals From a Different Golden Age

I'm reviewing the situation...
—Fagin, in the musical *Oliver!*

Not every Jewish mother wants her son's name to appear on a list. Especially this list.

There have been naughty Jews ever since there have been Jews. Some people like to propose economic reasons for their naughtiness while others just like to make movies about them. Of the former, author Stephen Birmingham suggests that prohibition provided the impetus for several poor Jewish immigrants in tenement flats to become dapper dons of high society through nefarious means. Of the latter, director Barry Levenson, for one, in 1991's *Bugsy*, shows how Benjamin Siegel's monumental lusts and visions could not coexist.

There is a little truth to it all. The Jewish gangsters of the 1920s, 1930s, and 1940s have the tenor of their times and the glossy filter of Hollywood to cast an innocuous shadow on their lives. But they did exist, and they were once "nice Jewish boys" who, even throughout their lives of crime, stayed attached to their families.

In Jewish crime's golden age it was not incomprehensible even for boys from nice Jewish families to turn to crime in the densely populated ghettos. It was a way out. It was a chance to get ahead, make a mark, get things done. Bootlegging, perhaps the greatest inspiration for the early ones, was exciting, lucrative, and challenging. Some even justified it by saying they were only giving people what they really wanted. During and after prohibition, many of these boys inherited the oft-mentioned Jewish "gift" for business planning and finance, skills that aided them on their way up. Others were just mean, *very* mean. It has often been said that Jewish influence in organized crime in the 1920s and 1930s matched that of Italian influence. It is a very dubious honor roll indeed:

Isadore "Kid Cann" Blumenthal
Louis "Lepke" Buchalter
Gangy Cohen
"Little Farvel" Cohen
"Dopey" Benny Fein
Arthur "Dutch Schultz" Flegenheimer
"Bugsy" Goldstein
Harry "Big Greenie" Greenberg
Jacob "Greedy Thumb" Guzik
Max "Boo Boo" Hoff
Samuel "The Greener" Jacobson
"Dandy Phil" Kastel
Phil "The Stick" Kovalick
Louis "Shadows" Kravitz
"Pretty" Levine
Samuel "Nails" Morton
Abe "Kid Twist" Reles
Frank "Lefty" Rosenthal
Arnold "The Brain" Rothstein
Benjamin "Bugsy" Siegel
Jake "Gurrah" Shapiro
Charles "King" Solomon
"Pep" Strauss
"Tick-Tock" Tannenbaum
Solomon "Cutcher-Head-Off" Weissman
Moey "Dimples " Wolensky
Charlie "The Bug" Workman
"Big" Jack Zelig
Abner "Longie" Zwillman

Every moniker has a story as good as anything Damon Runyon came up with. Jacob Guzik became "Greedy Thumb" because he was unrelenting when collecting bribes. Abner Zwillman became "Longie" because of the rumored length of one of his appendages.

Speaking of Damon Runyon, Arnold Rothstein, a gambler and

reportedly the guy who fixed the 1919 World Series, is said to have been the inspiration for Nathan Detroit in Runyon's *Guys and Dolls*. Allegedly Rothstein was asked by authorities in New York to help end the garment district strike of 1926. It wasn't the only time Jewish gangsters were asked to lend a hand. It has long been insinuated that they were asked to help secure arms during Israel's war for independence.

Meyer Lansky, bootlegger extraordinaire and a gambling czar in the United States, Cuba, and the Bahamas, was as erudite as he was ruthless. He also considered himself a pious Jew and always kept the Sabbath. An FBI agent once remarked about him, "He would have been the chairman of General Motors if he'd gone into legitimate business."

24

I Do, I Do, I Do

The Word on Polygamy

...Love and marriage go together like a horse and carriage.
—Songwriter Sammy Cahn

Many Jewish societies between the first and tenth centuries felt that any woman who did not have a husband was in danger of falling victim to social and economic ills. So, if a man who was already married wished to marry a woman who could not find a husband, the polygamous union was allowed, sometimes even encouraged.

A thousand or more years ago many Jews, particularly in Central Europe, traveled far and wide in pursuit of commercial interests, spending a lot of time in each city where business was done. Some of them found it quite useful to keep families in more than one place.

Polygamy is not expressly forbidden in the Bible or the Talmud. After all, King David had eight wives, Isaac's son Esau had three, and Jacob four. And who can forget King Solomon, who had seven hundred wives and an additional three hundred concubines?

Still, the Jewish conscience in general, and more specifically the countless decrees and proclamations by rabbis and sages throughout the ages, have always regarded monogamy as the only true course of marriage.

Ultimately those inclined toward polygamous unions must deal more with the laws of their own nations than the edicts of their religious forefathers. Polygamy is illegal in the United States and not permitted in Israel. Up until the mid-twentieth century, however, polygamy was widely practiced among the Jews of Yemen.

A little less than a thousand years ago several talmudic and rabbinic courts enacted reforms or issued rulings called *takkanahs* banning polygamy. In many instances such rulings expire after a thousand years—which brings us right to the start of the twenty-first century. For husbands whose idea of bliss is buying gifts for more than one wife, next Chanukah may bring their heavenly rewards.

25

Jewwww.weird.com

10 Unusual Jewish Web Sites to Kvetch About

Jews are a singular confusion—difficult to define, awkward to describe, impossible to understand. All the virtues, all the vices, every pleasure, every pain—nothing is spared them.
—Israel Shenker, *A Coat of Many Colors*

Now that the world is on the web, outsiders are in, oddballs are getting even, and anyone with an idea and a mouse can come out of the woodwork.

With literally thousands of Jewish-oriented web sites, there are the inevitable few our rabbis might not want us to know about and other religious leaders would feel are just a waste of our precious time. Nevertheless such sites do effectively show Judaism's emotional pull, for even the strangest of the bunch take efforts to discuss, describe, debate, but never deride their Jewishness. Judiasm doesn't attracts these types, they were there to begin with and simply found a way to make themselves available on-line.*

Jewish Dylan Anecdotes *http://www.well.com/user/yudel/Anecdote.html*
A couple of pages blowin' on the net all about Robert Zimmerman's (Bob Dylan) Jewishness, Jewish heritage, and Jewish-related events. Brief anecdotes are provided on his bar mitzvah, the time he was a guest at someone else's bar mitzvah, a Passover Seder he attended, and more.

---

*Web sites often move (change addresses), are revised, or become defunct in short periods of time. With some Web surfing, all of these sites (which were accurate at the time of publication), or at least new or altered versions of them, can probably be found.

The site was created by the publisher of RadioHazak: Israeli Music on the Internet.

Jewish Pickup Lines *http://www.wam.umd.edu/~baldrick/textiles/jewish Pickup.txt* "Your father must have been a rabbi. He stole the vowels from the Torah and put them in your eyes." Or, "Want to wander through my desert?" Or, "Can I put my Torah in your ark?" And more, if you need them. Actually, this is one of several related and linked sites, such as Jewish Mother Jokes, *http://www.lovelink.co.il/fun/Mother.htm* ("What's the difference between a Jewish mother and a Rottweiler? Eventually the Rottweiler lets go") and Jewish Men and Women Jokes, *http://www.lovelink.co.il/fun/men&woma.htm* ("What do you call a Jewish man who's lost 95 percent of his brains? A widower"). And so on.

Kvetch *www.kvetch.com* A website that allows anyone to, well, kvetch—to complain about anything to anyone who cares to listen. It also allows anyone who listens to respond with confirming or rebutting kvetches of their own. Kvetch, according to kvetch.com, "came from the twisted mind of Derek M. Powazek," who says the site is "an experiment in randomized, pseudo-interactive, confessional, oracle-ish bitching and moaning." Kvetch topics, which seem limitless, have so far included family matters, love, politics, work, driving, and lots more.

The Lilith Shrine *http://www.cjnetworks.com/lilitu/lilith/* An "online shrine to my role model as an uppity Jewish woman," says the site's mysterious and basically anonymous webmistress. Lilith, it is said, is the most well-known demoness or goddess created by God at the same time as Adam. Unlike Eve, who was created from Adam's rib, Lilith refused to submit to Adam's will. This site is all about Liliths past and present and has graphics and stories to match as well as a message board and links to other related sites.

NuYenta *http://www.nuyenta.com* A membership Internet service where Jewish gay, lesbian, bisexual, and transgender singles can meet in the pursuit of happiness, friendship, and love. It is kept strictly confidential. The site's tag line is, "Jewish matchmaking for the rest of us," and with anonymous Internet technology at its disposal, only you and your chosen paramours will know who "the rest of us" are.

The Official Jewish American Princess Home Page *www.comfo.ca/us/jap/* This page is strictly for laughs—apparently. With jokes, essays, and ruminations, it will either advance the cause of pride through levity, or set back stereotypes by thirty-five years. "You might be a Jewish American Princess," the site says, "if Neiman Marcus is #2 on your cellular's speed dial, if your favorite wine is *I wanna go to Miami…*" and so on. Among the topics you can click on are Oy Gevalt, Yenta Chat, Fehrklemp and Feh, Feh, Feh.

Porn Again Jews *www.lukeford.com/indexa57.html*   Luke Ford has many pages on the web devoted to Jews in the pornography industry. "Jews dominate the production and distribution of porn," he says. His site retells dozens of stories about Jewish porn performers—about their families, how they got into porn, their views on Jewish heritage, their views of Jews in porn, and more. A few of the performers, Ford says, have brothers or sisters who are Orthodox Jews, and one of the performers even wanted to be a rabbi. Richard Pacheco auditioned for a porn film and didn't get the job, but five years later he auditioned again. "That very day," Pacheco says in a story on the web site, "I also interviewed at Hebrew Union Seminary to do rabbinical study. I made the choice that the kind of rabbi I would be, if I became one, was one that could perform in sex films as part of his experience."

The Surfing Rabbi *www.surfsoul.virtual.co.il*   Rabbi Nachum Shifren, the Surfing Rabbi, publishes a Surf and Soul Internet newsletter in which he tells inspirational stories often with a surfing theme. Rabbi Shifren, a native of Southern California, currently lives in Israel with his wife and three children. A lifelong physical fitness fan, Rabbi Shifren lectures, gives surfing lessons, writes articles, performs outreach work for students, and continually stresses the benefits of physical fitness. He was also a competitive swimmer, runner, and triathlete and was a Los Angeles County lifeguard. He has taught language and speaks Spanish, German, Hebrew, and Yiddish. His studies in Israel included work at Toras Chayim Yeshiva in Jerusalem and Yeshiva Tomchei Tmomon in Kfar Chabad, where he received his Rabbinical ordination. On his Internet Surf and Soul newsletter, Rabbi Shifrin talks of searching for the perfect wave, which he calls soul surfing. Evocative and provocative, he brings existential class to Web surfing.

Twice Blessed *http://www.usc.edu/Library/oneigla/tb/Announce.html*   In short, everything gay, lesbian, bisexual, transgender, and Jewish. It is comprehensive, highly varied, and quite serious. Included in its many pages are e-mail discussions (under themes such as "Nice Jewish Girls: A Discussion for Jewish Lesbian and Bisexual Women"), cartoons like "Rabbi Tony's Guide to Sexuality," dozens of links to gay Jewish news on legal issues, politics, the arts, and Israel, and many other notes and postings for people wishing to get involved in gay Jewish activities.

The Uncircumcised Jews of America *www.cyberhighway.net/~glennw/ foreskin.htm*   The home page of Anton Yakovlevitch Borodovsky, a Ukranian Jew who now lives in the United States and formed what he calls "the most exclusive club in America." He says that when he came to America in the late 1970s, he became keenly aware of the difference between himself and his fellow Jews. "I realized that I, like my father before me, was one foreskin ahead of the pack. Even though I reveled in my unique nature, it began to feel lonely at the top." Borodovsky confesses that the current membership of his club "could fit in a Volkswagen" and, through the Web, is searching for new members. On his website he professes his Jewishness, offers a test for anyone to take online to see if they can join, and presents his official club motto. As weird sites go, this one makes the cut.

26

Weathering Many a Storm

76 Jewish Organizations for Every Need

Being a Jew is like walking in the wind or swimming: you are touched at all points and conscious everywhere.
—Lionel Trilling

It often it seems there are more Jewish organizations, federations, societies, and clubs than there are Jews. And yet sometimes it doesn't seem as if there are enough.

Judaism is a religion with thousands of years of history, and one that during those centuries has had a thousand reasons to pray for its survival. Doesn't a religion like that *need* a disproportionate number of alliances? And because Judaism accepts—albeit grudgingly at times and only in certain pockets—those with nonconformist views or unconventional lifestyles the list of organizations gets longer every year, joining dozens of groups that promote more conventional Jewish pursuits, in the arts, sciences, physical fitness, and other endeavors.

Moreover, Judaism has a long and profound tradition of charity and community responsibility. There are many national organizations that address that tradition and thousands that exist on the regional level as well. Many are nonprofit and volunteer-based, providing services such as outreach programs, religious education, endowments, juvenile and camp services, local political action, and more. (By and large, such local groups are not included simply because there are too many for one list. Many are local chapters of well-known national organizations like B'nai B'rith, United Jewish Appeal, and Jewish Community Centers, or JCC.)

Arts and Media

American Guild of Judaic Art
P.O. Box 1794
Murray Hill Station
New York, NY 10156-0609
212-889-7581
212-770-9015 (fax)

Membership organization for people interested in Judaic arts, and a resource center for contemporary Jewish artists and the general public.

American Society for Jewish Music
170 West 74th Street
New York, NY 10023
212-874-4456
212-874-8605 (fax)

Promotes the knowledge, appreciation, and development of Jewish music of the past and present for professional and lay audiences.

Association of Jewish Book Publishers
P.O. Box 237
Woodstock, VT 05091
802-457-4000
802-457-4004 (fax)

Non-profit group that provides a forum for the discussion of ideas, topics, and issues of mutual interest among Jewish publishers.

International Jewish Media Association
c/o St. Louis Jewish Light
12 Millstone Campus Drive
St. Louis, MO 63146
314-432-3353
314-432-0515 (fax)
stlouislgt@aol.com

Worldwide network of Jewish journalists, publishers, and others who seek to enhance the status of the Jewish media and Jewish journalists by exchanging materials and ideas.

Jewish Book Council
15 East 26th Street

New York, NY 10010
212-532-4949 ext. 297
carolynhessel@jewishbooks.org

Serves as the literary arm of the American Jewish community and as a clearing house for Jewish-context literature.

Jewish Heritage Project
150 Franklin Street, #1W
New York, NY 10013
212-925-9067

An effort to bring to the broadest possible audience authentic works of literary and historical value relating to Jewish history and culture.

National Center for Jewish Film
Brandeis University, Lown Building #102
Waltham, MA 02254-9110
617-899-7044
617-736-2070 (fax)
ncjf@logos.cc.brandeis.edu

An archive and library of films related to the Jewish experience.

Family and Family Issues

Association of Jewish Genealogical Societies
P.O. Box 50245
Palo Alto, CA 94303
415-424-1622
RWeissJGS@aol.com
www.jewishgen.org

Encourages Jews to research their family histories and promotes membership in various associated societies.

National Center for Jewish Healing
120 West 57th Street
New York, NY 10019
212-632-4705

Provides references on Healing Centers nationwide; publishes newletters with information for caregivers and those in need of care; and offers books, audiotapes, prayer cards, and other applicable items.

National Jewish Hospitality Committee
P.O. Box 53691
Philadelphia, PA 19105
800-745-0301

Group that assists people interested in Judaism for intermarriage, conversion, response to missionaries, or general information.

Outreach Judaism
710 Edison Court
Monsey, NY 10952
800-315-JEWS
tovia@j51.com

Formerly Jews for Judaism, this group responds to issues raised by missionaries and cults.

Stars of David International, Inc.
3175 Commercial Avenue
Suite 100
Northbrook, IL 60002
800-STAR-349

http://www.starsofdavid.org
starsdavid@aol.com

Nonprofit organization that provides information as well as a social and support network for Jewish and partly-Jewish adoptive families.

Holocaust

American Gathering of Jewish Holocaust Survivors
122 West 30th Street, #205
New York, NY 10001
212-239-4230
212-279-2926 (fax)

Dedicated to documenting the past and passing on a legacy of remembrance concerning the Holocaust. The group compiles the National Registry of Jewish Holocaust Survivors, visible at the U.S. Holocaust Memorial Museum in Washington D.C.

The Blue Card
2121 Broadway, Suite 402

New York, NY 10023
212-873-7400
212-496-5736 (fax)

Nationwide group founded in 1940 that supports Holocaust survivors in the United States, with grants to prevent institutionalization and poverty.

International Network of Children of Jewish Holocaust Survivors
3000 NW 145th Street
North Miami, FL 33181-3600
305-940-5690
305-940-5691 (fax)
xholocau@fiu.edu

Links second-generation groups and individuals throughout the world and represents their shared views and interests.

Simon Wiesenthal Center
9760 W. Pico Blvd.
Los Angeles, CA 90035-4701
310-553-9036
310-553-8007 (fax)

The largest institution of its kind in North America dedicated to the study of the Holocaust, its contemporary implications, and related issues.

Survivors of the Shoah Visual History Foundation
P.O. Box 3168
Los Angeles, CA 90078-3168

Founded by filmmaker Steven Spielberg to videotape and preserve interviews with Holocaust survivors throughout the world.

Jewish Culture, Ideals, and Ethics

American Academy for Jewish Research
3080 Broadway
New York, NY 10027
212-678-8864
212-678-8947 (fax)

Educational society that encourages Jewish learning and research through meetings, awards, and grants.

American Council for Judaism
P.O. Box 9009
Alexandria, VA 22304
703-836-2546

Seeks to advance the universal principles of Judaism and to promote the integration of American Jews into all manner of national, civic, cultural, and social institutions.

American Jewish Historical Society
2 Thornton Road
Waltham, MA 02154
617-891-8110
617-899-9208 (fax)
ajhs@jhs.org

Collects, catalogs, publishes, and displays material on the history of Jews in America.

American Sephardi Federation
305 Seventh Avenue
New York, NY 10001
212-366-7223
212-366-7263 (fax)

Umbrella organization for all Sephardic congregations, societies, and agencies.

Association of Jewish Family and Children's Agencies
3086 State Highway 27, Suite 11
P.O. Box 248
Kendall Park, NJ 08824
800-634-7346
732-821-0493 (fax)

Provides information, problem-solving, recruitment assistance, research, planning, and other support services to more than one hundred Jewish human service agencies in the United States and Canada in a continuing effort to enhance and sustain the quality of Jewish and communal life.

Congress for Jewish Culture
25 East 21ˢᵗ Street
New York, NY 10010
212-505-8040

Umbrella group of sixteen organizations working toward the enhancement of Jewish creative expression in the United States and abroad, including Yiddish cultural life.

Institute for Jewish Medical Ethics

645 14th Avenue
San Francisco, CA 94118
415-725-7333

Professionals who work to identify the underlying principles of Jewish law in biblical, talmudic, and other Jewish scholarship as they relate to the practice of medicine, and to review various modern policies accordingly.

Jewish Peace Fellowship

P.O. Box 271
Nyack, NY 10960
914-358-4601
914-358-4924 (fax)

Unites those who believe that Jewish ideals and experience provide inspiration for a nonviolent philosophy and way of life.

The Jewish Professionals Institute

40 Exchange Place, Suite 441
New York, NY 10005-2701
212-742-0092
212-382-0067 (fax)

Through education, lectures, classes, and events it provides mature, sophisticated Jewish adults in modern professions (medicine, accounting, academics, etc.) the opportunity to get acquainted with their heritage.

National American Conference of Ethiopian Jewry

16 East 56th Street
New York, NY 10022
212-752-6340

Provides financial support to Ethiopian Jews living in Israel to enable them to get good educations leading to college or technical schools.

National Council of Young Israel

3 West 16th Street
New York, NY 10011
212-929-1526

Promotes spiritual, cultural, social, and communal acitivity programs to advance traditional Judaism.

National Foundation for Jewish Culture
330 Seventh Avenue, 21st Floor
New York, NY 10001
212-629-0500
212-629-0508 (fax)
nfjc@jewisculture.org

Foundation developed to promote Jewish culture in the United States through endowments, fellowships, and conferences.

Sephardic House
2112 Broadway, Suite 200A
New York, NY 10023
212-496-2173
212-496-2264 (fax)

Organization dedicated to fostering Sephardic history and culture through classes, programs, films, festivals, and summer programs.

Yivo Institute for Jewish Renewal
555 West 57th Street, Suite 1100
New York, NY 10019
212-246-6080

Dedicated to the study and preservation of the Eastern European Jewish heritage. Founded in 1925, Yivo has become the world's preeminent research institute and academic center for Eastern European Jewish studies.

Lifestyles

Jewish Activist Gays and Lesbians
c/o Lesbian and Gay Community Services Center
208 West 13th Street
New York, NY
212-479-8501

Organization of young gay, lesbian, and bisexual Jews who struggle against homophobia in the Jewish community and anti-Semitism in the gay world.

Jewish Vegan Lifestyle
5501 North 7th Avenue, Suite 227
Phoenix, AZ 85013-1755
602-249-3351
jewish@vegetarians.com

Support and educational group of Jews who promote a vegetarian lifestyle.

World Congress of Gay and Lesbian Jewish Orgnaizations
P.O. Box 233379
Washington, DC 20026-3379
leewalzer@mindspring.com

Umbrella organization that supports and represents over sixty-five gay and lesbian Jewish groups around the world.

Rights and Freedoms

American Jewish Committee
165 East 56th Street
New York, NY 10022
212-751-4000
212-750-0326 (fax)
National committee designed to protect the rights and freedoms of Jews everywhere, to combat bigotry and anti-Semitism, and to promote human rights for all.

American Jewish Congress
15 East 84th Street
New York, NY 10028
212-879-4500
212-249-3672 (fax)

Large organization that works to foster the creative survival of Jews and to help Israel develop in peace, freedom, and security.

Anti-Defamation League of B'nai B'rith
823 United Nations Plaza
New York, NY 10017
212-490-2525
212-867-0779 (fax)
www.adl.org

Combats anti-Semitism and works to secure justice and fairness for all citizens through laws, education, and community relations.

Jews for Racial and Economic Justice
64 Fulton Street, #605
New York, NY 10038
212-964-9210

Group of active participants in the struggle for racial and economic justice, primarily in New York City.

World Jewish Congress
501 Madison Avenue, 17th Floor
New York, NY 10022
212-755-5883 (fax)

Major alliance that seeks to intensify bonds of world Jewry among Jews everywhere, with a special concentration on Israel as the central force in Jewish life.

Singles

Jewish Connections
1040 North Kings Highway, Suite 602
Cherry Hill, NJ 08034-1921
609-667-7047
215-922-7723
908-246-4646

Service that matches Jewish singles in New York, New Jersey, Pennsylvania, Delaware, Maryland, and Washington, D.C.

Jewish Outdoor Group of Singles
P.O. Box 390
Linden, NJ 07036
908-925-3836
hpkatseff@monmouth.com

Group that promotes outdoor activities among Jewish singles.

Special Groups

Council of Jewish Organizations in Civil Service
45 East 33rd Street

New York, NY 10016
212-689-2015

Encourages recruitment of Jewish youth to government service.

Jewish War Veterans of the United States of America
1811 R Street NW
Washington, DC 20009
202-265-6280
202-234-5662 (fax)

Seeks to foster allegiance to the United States, combat bigotry, prevent defamation of Jews, encourage universal liberty and equal rights, and foster education of ex-servicemen and women.

Jews for the Preservation of Firearms Ownership
2872 South Wentworth Avenue
Milwaukee, WI 53207
414-769-0760
414-483-8435
Non-profit membership organization that uses intellectual research to promote the belief that ownership of firearms is a civil right, not a privilege.

Sports and Recreation

Jewish Sports Congress
P.O. Box 4549
Old Village Station
Great Neck, NY 11023
516-482-5550

Promotes and supports athletics and physical fitness with the international Jewish community.

Mosaic Outdoor Clubs of America
262 S. Coconut Lane
Miami Beach, FL 33139
1-888-MOSAICS
www.mosaics.org

Organization designed to bring Jewish people together to enjoy the outdoors through many regional chapters.

National Jewish Committee on Scouting
1325 West Walnut Hill Lane
P.O. Box 152079
Irving, TX 75015-2079
972-580-2119
972-580-7870 (fax)

Assists Jewish institutions in meeting their needs and concerns through scouting.

National Jewish Girl Scout Committee
33 Central Drive
Bronxville, NY 10708
914-738-3986; 914-738-6752
914-252-6072 (fax)

Assists in organizing Girl Scout troops in Jewish communities and in forming local Jewish Girl Scout committees.

Shomrei Adamah/Keepers of the Earth
c/o Surprise Lake Camp
50 West 17th Street
New York, NY 10011
212-807-6376
212-924-5112

Through workshops and retreats, promotes understanding that love of nature and environmental protection are values deeply imbedded in Jewish tradition and texts.

Students

B'nai B'rith Youth Organization
1640 Rhode Island Avenue NW
Washington, DC 20036
202-857-7733
202-857-6568 (fax)

Helps Jewish teenagers achieve self-fulfillment and make worthwhile contributions to their communities and to their country.

Kadima
155 Fifth Avenue

New York, NY 10010-6802

212-533-7800

71263.400@compuserve.com

Involves Jewish preteens in a meaningful religious, educational, and fraternal environment through chapter programs and events.

National Jewish Law Students Association

233 Bay State Road

Boston, MA 02215

617-353-7210 ext. 31

617-353-7214 (fax)

njlsa@aol.com

Fosters Jewish identity in the legal profession and among law students and promotes their involvement in the Jewish community.

Support Groups

Association of Jewish Family and Children's Agencies

3086 State Highway 27, Suite 11

P.O. Box 248

Kendall Park, NJ 08824-0248

1-800-634-7346

Provides links to and supervision on any kind of medical care or support a family might need for elder care.

International Jewish AIDS Network

c/o Union of American Hebrew Congregations

555 Skokie Boulevard #225

Northbrook, IL 60062-2833

773-327-1733

773-327-1791 (fax)

Provides assistance for people with AIDS and acts as clearinghouse for information and other AIDS services.

JACS (Jewish Alcoholics, Chemically dependent persons, and Significant others)

426 West 58th Street

New York, NY 10019

212-397-4197

212-489-6229 (fax)
jacs@jacsweb.org

Provides education, outreach, and support to Jews and their families
whose lives have been affected by alcoholism and substance abuse.

Jewish Heritage for the Blind
1655 East 24th Street
Brooklyn, NY 11229
718-338-4999

Helps the blind and visually impaired participate fully in Jewish life by
providing Braille and large-type publications, audiotapes for children and
adults, health and medical information, and participation in synagogue and
community affairs.

Jewish Prisoner Services International
P.O. Box 85840
Seattle, WA 98145
206-528-03363
206-7113 (fax)
garyfriedman@msn.com

Dedicated to serving the needs of Jewish prisoners and their families.

Kaddish Foundation
3618 Shannon Road
Cleveland Heights, OH 44118
216-321-5557
www.mnemotrix.com/kaddish

Nonprofit organization dedicated to helping perpetuate the soul of the
departed and linking it to the living (through observation of Yahrzeits, for
example), and allocating funds to Jewish children with special educational
needs.

Tzvi Aryeh AIDS Foundation
P.O. Box 150
New York, NY 10023
212-866-6306

An AIDS information hotline with assistance in English, Yiddish, and
Hebrew. The group also provides the names and numbers of rabbis of every
denomination who can offer spiritual assistance, for those who request it.

United Jewish Appeal
99 Park Avenue, Suite 300
New York, NY 10016
212-818-9100
212-818-9509 (fax)

Works to help the imperiled, care for the vulnerable, and revitalize Jewish life by raising funds for humanitarian causes and social services here and abroad. Works with more than 150 local Jewish federations.

Wolk Center for the Jewish Deaf
Interfaith Center
1 Lomb Memorial Drive
Rochester, NY 14623
716-475-5171

Allows deaf Jewish students to become familiar with and express their identities as Jews.

Technology

Institute for Computers in Jewish Life
7074 N. Western Avenue
Chicago, IL 60645
312-262-9200
312-262-9298 (fax)
rosirv@aol.com

Explores applications of computer technology to parts of Jewish life, with an emphasis on education.

U.S.-Israel Biotech Council
1628 Martha Terrace
Rockville, MD 20852
410-468-2915

Nonprofit orgranization dedicated to promoting strategic alliances between growing North American and Israeli life-sciences industries through networking, information exchange, and public policy initiatives.

Women's Issues

Agunah, Inc.
P.O. Box 236

Midwood Station
Brooklyn, NY 11230
718-434-6246

Nonprofit organization dealing exclusively with helping women whose husbands are withholding a *get* (Jewish divorce).

Amit Women
817 Broadway, 4th Floor
New York, NY 10003
212-477-4720, ext. 119

Focuses on Zionism and traditional Judaism in America.

Hadassah, The Women's Zionist Organization of America
50 West 58th Street
New York, NY 10019
212-303-8222
212-303-8282 (fax)

Helps American Jews strengthen partnerships with Israel, ensure Jewish continuity, and realize their potential impact on American society. The organization recently founded the National Commission on American Jewish Women.

International Research Institute on Jewish Women
Brandeis University
P.O. Box 9110
Waltham, MA 02254-9110
617-736-4200

Conducts research programs on the history and role of Jewish women.

Jewish Orthodox Feminist Alliance
3333 Henry Hudson Parkway, #115
Riverdale, NY 10463
718-601-3769

Provides support for college students and networking for rabbis.

Jewish Women International
1828 L Street NW, Suite 250
Washington, DC 20036
202-857-1300

Supports Jewish women in their quest to strengthen their roles as they relate to family values, intermarriage, children, and other important life initiatives.

Jewish Women's Archive
68 Howard Street
Brookline, MA 02146
617-232-2258

New group created to document Jewish women's lives in twentieth century America

Jewish Women's Resource Center
9 East 69th Street
New York, NY 10021
212-575-5900
JWRCNCJW@aol.com

Volunteer organization that is a wing of the National Council for Jewish Women devoted to promoting Jewish values, social justice, and empowerment for women and children through community-based services, advocacy, education, and leadership development. The group has branches in New York and Los Angeles.

National Council for Jewish Women
53 West 23rd Street, 6th Floor
New York, NY 10010
212-645-4048

Provides community service, advocacy, and couseling for children, women, and the elderly.

Project Kesher
1134 Judson Avenue
Evanston, IL 60202
708-332-1994
708-332-2134
74771.142@compuserve.com

Nonprofit organization connecting Jewish women around the world in an effort to empower them to build and deepen their Jewish identities.

Women of Reform Judaism
838 Fifth Avenue
New York, NY 10028
212-650-4050

Serves the needs of sisterhood organizations at Reform synagogues.

Women's League for Conservative Judaism
48 East 74th Street
New York, NY 10021
212-0628-1600

Provides programs and resources in Conservative Jewish education, social action, and leadership training.

Women's Tefilla Network
811 Palisade Avenue
Teaneck, NJ 07666
201-801-0701

Umbrella organization for Orthodox women's prayer groups.

27

The Jewish Observers

31 Newspapers and Magazines for American Jews Nationwide

The foremost problem in the Jewish religion is how to get the Jews to take the Bible seriously without taking it literally.
—Rabbi Mordecai Kaplan

Believe it or not, the Jewish press has us covered. While just a tiny patch of blue and white within all that is published by the Fourth Estate, Jewish newspapers and magazines observe, debate, investigate, castigate, publicize, empathize, and emphasize virtually all aspects of Judaism in general, and American Judaism in particular. And they've been doing it since 1823 when Solomon Jackson founded the first Jewish newspaper in America, *The Jew.*

"Sometimes magazines like ours have the challenge of being taken seriously even within the Jewish world," comments *Lilith* editor Susan Weidman Schneider. "Not surprisingly, readers often put more weight on what periodicals like *Newsweek* and *Time* have to say than in what Jewish magazines have to say."

Challenged or not, many Jewish publications have gone to great lengths to bring the quality of their reporting, writing, and graphic presentation up to the level of more mainstream magazines. It has paid off. *Lilith* has been around since 1976, *Moment* since 1977, *Jewish Monthly* since way back in 1885. Local Jewish newspapers also have been carving out solid reputations with interesting feature stories, volatile issues, and lively layouts.

"We're independent and answer only to ourselves and our readers," states Suzanne Singer, managing editor of *Moment.* Some Jewish magazines have the additional challenge of answering to the organizations that own and support them, such as the governing bodies of Judaic movements and some other major federations. Still many cover topics such as assisted suicide and drug addiction, albeit from their unique perspectives.

There are also more than 150 local Jewish newspapers in the nation, most of which are owned and operated by local chapters of major Jewish federations. This list features publications basically national in nature or, if they are regional, that serve a readership much larger than most other regional publications.

Akivon
25 West 26th Street
New York, NY 10010
212-889-5260

Monthly that features articles, stories, and games on Judaism and Israel for elementary school students.

Apples & Honey
350 South Dahlia
Denver, CO 80226
303-399-2660

Newsletter for parents interested in creating a Jewish home for their young children.

Bible Review
4710 41st Street NW
Washington, DC 20016
202-264-3300

Bimonthly published by the Biblical Archeology Society

Commentary
155 East 56th Street
New York, NY 10022
212-751-4000

Prominent, long-standing monthly that covers Jewish society and political concerns; founded by the American Jewish Committee.

Common Quest
Box 781
Howard University
Washington, DC 20059

202-806-6705

Published three times a year by the American Jewish Committee and Howard University as a magazine of black–Jewish relations.

The Forward
45 East 33rd Street
New York, NY 10016
1-800-849-1825
www.forward.com

One of the most famous Jewish newspapers in the world, founded in 1897.

Good Fortune
1527 53rd Street
Brooklyn, NY 11219-3961
718-438-0939

Monthly about Jewish personalities.

Hadassah Magazine
50 West 58th Street
New York, NY 10019-2590
212-355-7900

84-year-old monthly on social, economic, educational, and cultural aspects of world Jewry.

Inside
226 S. 16th Street
Philadelphia, PA 19102
215-893-5700

Philadelphia-based quarterly of Jewish life and style.

Jewish Action
333 Seventh Avenue
New York, NY 10001
212-563-4000

Quarterly publication of the Union of Orthodox Jewish Congregations of America.

Jewish Braille Review
110 East 30th Street

New York, NY 10016-7375
212-889-2525

Monthly digest of Judaic articles and prose in braille.

Jewish Education
426 West 58ᵗʰ Street
New York, NY 10019-1190
212-713-0290

Quarterly devoted to exploring current thinking and practice in the field of Jewish education.

The Jewish Monthly
1640 Rhode Island Avenue NW
Washington, DC 20036
202-857-6560

B'nai B'rith publication devoted to politics, culture, and social issues.

The Jewish News
P.O. Box 269
Northampton, MA 01061
413-582-9847 (fax)
jwnews18@aol.com

New England–based newspaper that covers world Judaism and the arts.

The Jewish Press
338 Third Avenue
Brooklyn, NY 11215-1897
718-330-0900

Largest independent Anglo-Jewish weekly newspaper.

The Jewish Spectator
250 West 57ᵗʰ Street
New York, NY 10019

Seasoned, intellectual monthly noted for its many editorial columns about American–Jewish affairs.

The Jewish Standard
1086 Teaneck Road
Teaneck, NJ 07666
201-837-8818

New Jersey's oldest Jewish weekly newspaper.

Jewish Veteran
1811 R Street NW
Washington, DC 20009-1603
202-265-6280

Quarterly with features and news of interest to Jewish veterans.

Jewish Week
1501 Broadway
New York, NY 10036
212-921-7822

Largest circulation American Jewish weekly with emphasis on U.S. foreign policy in the mideast.

The Jewish World
1104 Central Avenue
Albany, NY 1205-3428
518-459-8455

Weekly for active Jewish civic, fraternal, and synagogue groups featuring national and international news.

Lilith
250 West 57th Street, Suite 2432
New York, NY 10107
212-757-0818
lilithmag@aol.com

Independent Jewish woman's magazine.

Moment
4710 41st Street NW
Washington, DC 20016
202-364-3300

Issues- and culture-oriented magazine for a wide-spectrum Jewish readership.

The New York Jewish Week
1501 Broadway
New York, NY 10036
212-921-7822
editor@jewishweek.org

Weekly newspaper serving the Jewish community of Greater New York.

Americana Judaica

In addition to such divine legacies as the Ten Commandments and such spirited gifts as the Sabbath, Judaism has given America (and the world) some additional rewards.

• Movies and plays like *Raiders of the Lost Ark,* Steven Spielberg's 1981 film starring Harrison Ford, which concerns a quest to retrieve the biblical treasure—the Ark of the Covenant—from Nazi thieves; and *Joseph and the Amazing Technicolor Dreamcoat,* an early Andrew Lloyd Weber–Tim Rice collaboration about the biblical Jacob's favorite son and the special ornamental robe he wore.

• Flowers and plants—like *Rose of Sharon* and *Jacob's Ladder*—that received their prominence (or at least their names) from Bible stories. Rose of Sharon is a beautiful bell-shaped hibiscus that flowers at the end of summer, named from the Song of Solomon, a psalm which compares a wonderful lover to Sharon, a particularly fertile area in what is now Israel. Jacob's Ladder is an herb with blue or white flowers and a stalk with leaves placed like the rungs of a ladder, reminiscent of the ladder Jacob dreamt about that stretched from the earth to heaven.

• *The Olive Branch,* an almost universally accepted symbol of peace, which comes from Genesis, the First Book of Moses, when Noah sends a dove out from the ark he had built to rescue the world from hate and violence after God flooded all the lands. "The dove came back to him toward evening, and there in its bill was a plucked-off olive leaf. Then Noah knew the waters had decreased on earth." Apparently God had made peace with man; hence the continued significance of the olive branch.

• *The Catskills.* Jewish boardinghouses started dotting the hills and valleys of Ellenville, Liberty, and other upstate New York villages in the Catskill Mountains as early as 1890, with kosher food and entertainment and, a few years later, children's playgrounds, pools, bowling, and billiards. Grossingers started as a seven-room farmhouse in 1914 and by the 1960s had grown into a mini-city of lodging, leisure, sports, and entertainment. It is now just a memory, having closed for good in 1996 (except for the golf course). Up until the 1970s, the Catskills was one of the most famous summer resort and entertainment areas for Jews from New York City, Long Island, and elsewhere, and the training ground for several generations of singers and comedians.

- *The Vulcan greeting.* Jewish actor Leonard Nimoy reportedly was the one who chose the sign of the Kohen, the Jewish High Priest, to use as a live-long-and-prosper greeting for his Vulcan character Spock on TV's *Star Trek*. The sign—five fingers held upright and split between the middle and ring fingers—is seen on many religious and temple ornaments.

- *The Lincoln Penny.* Ever since it was commissioned by the Treasury Department and assigned to Jewish artist Victor David Brenner to design in 1909, the Lincoln penny has been one of the most ubiquitous, indispensable, and often obtrusive American coins in our nation's history. The 1909 commission was also the first U.S. coin to honor an American President. Brenner based his design on a photographic portrait of Abraham Lincoln taken by famed Civil War photographer Mathew Brady.

Pakn-Treger
1021 West Street
Amherst, MA 01002-3375
800-535-3595

Published four times a year by the National Yiddish Book Center as a continuing discussion of Yiddish roots and modern Jewish culture.

Reconstructionism Today
30 Old Whitfield Road
Accord, NY 12403

Contemporary Judaica and Jewish culture from the Reconstructionist perspective.

Reform Judaism
838 Fifth Avenue
New York, NY 10021
212-650-4240
http://uahc.org/rjmag

Quarterly published by the Union of Hebrew Congregations.

The Reporter
315 Park Avenue South
New York, NY 10010
212-674-3057

Jewish topics of interest to women.

Synagogue/Kosher Life
47 Beekman Street

New York, NY 10038-1510
212-227-7543

Quarterly with profiles on personalities and articles on trends in American-Jewish life, including kosher food, products, and restaurant reviews.

Tikkun
120 West 44th Street
Suite 704
New York, NY 10036

Bimonthly Jewish critique of politics, culture, and society.

United Synagogue Review
Rapaport House
155 Fifth Avenue
New York, NY 10010
212-533-7800 ext. 2601
www.uscj.org

Quarterly published by the United Synagogue of Conservative Judaism.

Young Israel Viewpoint
3 West 16th Street
New York, NY 10011-6393
212-929-1525

Bimonthly Jewish community publication serving over three hundred Orthodox synagogues in the United States, Canada, and Israel.

28

Treasures From Home

A Travel, Vacation, and Study Guide to 40 Jewish Places of Interest in the United States

I marvel at the resilience of the Jewish people. Their best characteristic is their desire to remember. No other people has such an obsession with memory.

—Elie Wiesel

Home. It can mean a little village on the Russian–Polish border thousands of miles from here, or a town twenty minutes from Penn Station. To American Jews who take an interest in the history of the Jewish people, home can be a confusing, debatable, emotive term. But to the directors, supervisors, and curators of Jewish-American places of interest, it means anything and everything that bring us together as a people; the faith itself, in many respects, is our home, and those directors, supervisors, and curators are the people who keep it nice and tidy.

On one hand, there aren't that many places to begin with, at least in relation to the size of the country. But on the other hand, Jews comprise only 2 percent of the American population, so why should there be? On one hand, we've been here as long as America has been here, and even helped win our independence. But on the other hand, the vast majority of us got here by boat less than a century ago and had almost nothing to do with American independence.

With so many hands to consider, who has time to visit any places at all?

Still, many like to—or need to—make such an effort, for their children, for their ancestors, and for themselves.

Each synagogue has an interesting story to tell because of the people who built it and the people it served (and in most cases continues to serve). Each museum and library has some of the most memorable and consequential works by renowned artists, writers, and craftsmen of yesterday and today. And each monument brings us a little closer to the meaning of resilience, faith, hope, and pride.

And home.

Synagogues

Central Synagogue
652 Lexington Avenue
New York, NY 10022

A Moorish-style structure built in 1872, designed by the first Jewish architect in America, Henry Fernbach. It is the oldest synagogue in New York still in use, and is a National Historic Landmark.

Congregation B'nai Yosef
1616 Ocean Parkway
Brooklyn, NY 11223
718-627-9861

An eight thousand-square-foot temple with two levels, completely covered with murals by artist Archie Rand that depict thirty-seven different themes.

Congregation Mikveh Israel
44 North Fourth Street
Philadelphia, PA 19102
215-922-5446

Dating back to the 1740s, this is one of the first organized Jewish congregations in the nation. It is commonly known as the Synagogue of the American Revolution. Benjamin Franklin contributed to the building fund and congregants included Haym Salomon, Rebecca Gratz, and Isaac Leeser, the first American to translate the Bible into English.

Congregation Shearith Israel
2 West 70th Street
New York, NY 10023
212-873-0300

A Spanish and Portuguese synagogue that is one of the oldest in New York City and the nation, with an extensive archive of manuscripts in its possession.

Kahai Kadosh Beth Elohim
90 Hassell
Charleston, SC
304-346-2366

Built in 1840, this synagogue was designated a National Historic Landmark in 1980. It is the second oldest existing temple building in the United States, although it suffered major damage on three separate occasions—once during a fire, another time from Union shells during the Civil War, and a third time in an 1886 earthquake.

The Lloyd Street Synagogue
15 Lloyd Street
Baltimore, MD 21202
410-342-7561

Third oldest synagogue in America, and the first in Maryland, founded in 1845. Now an official National Historic Landmark, the Greek Revival–style synagogue still has many of its original features. Other architectural features have been faithfully reconstructed.

Touro Synagogue
72 Touro Street
Newport, RI 02840
401-847-4794

Organized by the Sephardic Jews who arrived in Newport as early as 1658. The oldest existing Jewish synagogue in the United States, the structure was built in 1759. Gloriously decorated, there are several unique features, including a trap door that was used as a means of escape, if one was necessary, during the Revolutionary War.

Union Temple
17 Eastern Parkway
Brooklyn, NY 11238
718-638-9861

At twelve stories high, this may be the world's tallest synagogue. It has a frescoed ceiling that depicts the temple's history.

Museums, Libraries, and Monuments

The Archives Museum
20 East Gordon Street

Savannah, GA 31401
912-233-1547

Located in the oldest synagogue in the South—and the third oldest in the nation (Temple Mikveh Israel)—the Archives has artifacts of Jewish life from the eighteenth through the twentieth centuries.

The Benjamin and Dr. Edgar R. Cofeld Judaic Museum of Temple Beth Zion
805 Delaware Avenue
Buffalo, NY 14209
716-886-7150

Features Judaic artifacts from the tenth century to the present, including coins, books, Holocaust remembrances, folk art, and textiles.

The Bloom Southwest Jewish Archive
1052 N. Highland Avenue
Tucson, AZ 85721
520-621-5774

At the University of Arizona, these archives comprise a distinguished research center dedicated to collecting and recording the dramatic history of pioneer Jews in the desert of the Southwest, particularly Arizona, New Mexico, and Western Texas.

B'nai B'rith Klutznick Museum
1640 Rhode Island Avenue NW
Washington, DC 20036
202-857-6583

Has a collection of hundreds of Jewish ceremonial and folk art objects, prints and drawings, paintings and sculpture, thousands of documents and coins, letters between George Washington and Moses Seixas, and more.

Congregation Emanu-El Museum
1 East 65th Street
New York, NY 10021
212-744-1400

Art and commemorative items commissioned by the synagogue itself are a major part of this museum's displays in addition to liturgical items used by synagogues and homes.

The Ellis Island Immigration Museum
New York Harbor
212-629-5755

Located a few hundred yards north of the Statue of Liberty, Ellis Island is where the largest human migration in modern history took place, between 1892 and 1954. The museum describes the experience of the twelve million immigrants who were processed there and uses interactive devices, computers, and taped reminiscences of the immigrants themselves.

Fenster Museum of Jewish Art
1223 East 17ᵗʰ Place
Tulsa, OK 74120
918-582-3732

Along with its one thousand-volume library, the Fenster has exhibits that emphasize Jewish history, culture, and art from biblical times to the present day.

The Jane L. and Robert H. Weiner Judaic Museum
6125 Montrose Road
Rockville, MD 20852
301-881-0100

Museum that features many various items of Judaica in the fields of ethnology and archaeology.

The Jewish Museum
1109 Fifth Avenue
New York, NY 10128
212-423-3200

Housed in the former Warburg Mansion, this museum contains one of the largest and most comprehensive collections of Jewish ceremonial objects from all parts of the world, including several Torah accessories such as arks and pointers.

Judaica Museum of Central Synagogue
123 East 55ᵗʰ Street
New York, NY 10022
212-838-5122

A mid-Manhattan treasure of Judiac coins, medals, textiles, paintings and sculpture.

The Judaica Museum of the Hebrew Home for the Aged at Riverdale
5961 Palisade Avenue
Bronx, NY 10471
718-548-1006

Features Jewish ceremonial objects, silver, gold, pewter, textiles, books, and more.

The Liberty Bell
Independence Hall
Philadelphia, PA

On July 8, 1776, the Liberty Bell rang for the first time from the tower at Independence Hall, summoning citizens to hear the first public reading of the Declaration of Independence. The Pennsylvania Assembly had ordered the bell in 1751 to commemorate the fiftieth anniversary of William Penn's 1701 Charter of Privileges. A passage from Leviticus is inscribed upon the Liberty Bell: "Proclaim liberty throughout all the land, unto all the inhabitants thereof."

The Library of Congress
101 Independence Avenue SE
Washington, DC 20540
202-707-8000

In addition to its research capabilities for any aspect of American life, religious and otherwise, the Library of Congress contains the largest collection of rare Hebrew and Yiddish texts in any government collection.

Lillian and Albert Small Jewish Museum
701 Third Street NW
Washington, DC 20001-2624
202-789-0900

The only archive and display center of Jewish historical objects related to the nation's capital, and a link to the early days of Washington's Jewish community. It also serves as the headquarters of the Jewish Historical Society of Greater Washington.

Lower East Side Tenement Museum
90 Orchard Street
New York, NY 10002
212-431-0233

Opened in 1988 in a former tenement building, this museum preserves and interprets the history of the immigrant experience on the Lower East Side. It is the first museum in the United States to take a preserved tenement and have it designated a National Historic Site.

Today it is the Lillian and Albert Small Jewish Museum of Washington. In 1876 it was the Adas Israel Synagogue. In between it was a church and a grocery store. In 1969, when its site was selected as the new home of the Washington Metro, the structure was moved three blocks, restored and rededicated. Courtesy Jewish Historical Society of Greater Washington

Martyrs Memorial and Museum of the Holocaust
6505 Wilshire Blvd.
Los Angeles, CA 90018
213-852-3242

Photo-narrative museum and resource center dedicated to Holocaust history, issues of genocide and prejudice, and curriculum development.

Martyrs Monument to Jewish Victims of the Holocaust
Benjamin Franklin Parkway and 16th at the Arch
Philadelphia, PA

An eighteen-foot bronze sculpture created by Nathan Rappaport.

The Morton B. Weiss Museum of Judaica
1100 Hyde Park Blvd.
Chicago, IL 60615
312-924-1234

Among the most valued objects in its possession are a three-hundred-year-old white-jade Chinese mezuzah and a tenth-century silver Purim megilah. Also included are artifacts of American-Jewish living and of European and Asian roots of many American Jews.

The Museum of Jewish Heritage, a Living Memorial to the Holocaust
18 First Place; Battery Park City
New York, NY 10004-1484
212-687-9141

A museum designed to educate people of all ages and backgrounds about twentieth-century Jewish history before, during, and after the Holocaust, from the perspective of those who lived it. Its several exhibitions are located inside a thirty-thousand-square-foot building with a symbolic six-sided shape.

Museum of the Jewish Family
P.O. Box 1526
Durham, NC 27702-1526
919-682-5095

Functions as a museum without walls, with exhibitions at locations such as Duke University, North Carolina Museum of History, Chapel Hill Town Hall, and others. One recent exhibit was "Images of Israel in Postage Stamp Art." There is also a permanent gallery, The Rosenzweig Gallery, in the Judea Reform Congregation, with exhibits and special shows.

Museum of the Southern Jewish Experience
4915 I-55 North, Suite 20413
Jackson, MS 39236
601-362-6357

From a purely Southern perspective, this museum features Jewish ritual and ceremonial items, as well as furniture, architectural pieces, historic photos, and other memorabilia.

Museum of Tolerance
9786 West Pico Blvd.
Los Angeles, CA 90035
310-553-8403

Affiliated with The Simon Wiesenthal Center, the Museum of Tolerance focuses on two themes in its interactive exhibits: the dynamics of racism and prejudice in America and the history of the Holocaust. One recent exhibit displayed fifty years of Israeli photography, and the museum's permanent collection includes letters, artwork, and artifacts from Holocaust survivors.

National Museum of American Jewish History
55 North 5ᵗʰ Street
Philadelphia, PA
215-923-3811

Opened on July 4, 1976, across from Independence Mall, this is the only museum in the nation dedicated exclusively to collecting, preserving, and interpreting artifacts pertaining to the American Jewish experience, with more than ten thousand items in its collections.

National Museum of American Jewish Military History
1811 R Street NW
Washington, DC 20009
202-265-6280

Under the auspices of the Jewish War Veterans of the United States, this museum documents and preserves the contributions of Jewish-Americans to the peace and freedom of the United States and educates the public on courage, heroism, and sacrifices made by Jewish-Americans in the armed forces.

Philadelphia Museum of Judaica
615 North Broad Street
Philadelphia, PA 19123
215-627-6747

Housed in the oldest German synagogue in the Western Hemisphere (Congregation Rodeph Shalom), this museum presents Jewish art and religious ceremonal items.

Skirball Cultural Center
2701 N. Sepulveda Boulevard
Los Angeles, CA 90049-6833
310-440-4500

Presents a full range of cultural programs, including temporary exhibitions, concerts, lectures, performances, readings, symposia, films, and video screenings, to share the American-Jewish experience for people of all ages and backgrounds. It has, among other things, a museum, a 350-seat auditorium, classroom facilities, and a Discovery Center where ancient chapters of Jewish history come alive for young people. Exhibits have included *Project Americana Study Gallery,* with over 1,300 items reflecting Jewish life in America, and *Archaeology of Ancient Lands,* in which new interpretations, excavations, and techniques in the Middle East were explored.

The Skirball Cultural Center in Los Angeles holding onto tradition...and passing it down. Courtesy The Skirball Center; photo by Timothy Hursley

Spertus Museum of Judaica
618 S. Michigan Avenue
Chicago, IL 60605
312-922-9012

Part of the Spertus College of Judaica and affiliated with its Asher Library, this is the first college-affiliated museum and the second museum of Judaica to be accredited by the American Association of Museums (in 1976). It has over three hundred items of ceremonial art, textiles, costumes, and Holocaust artifacts.

The Statue of Liberty
Liberty Island, NY (accessible by ferry from Battery Park in Manhattan or Liberty State Park in New Jersey).
212-363-3200

The Statue of Liberty, an American centennial gift from France, is one of the most famous symbols of freedom in the United States, and a monument to millions of immigrants who came here to be free. "The New Colossus," by Jewish-American poet Emma Lazarus, is inscribed on the statue ("Give me your tired, your poor, your huddled masses yearning to be free...").

Mixing Americana with Judaica, this menorah by artist Manfred Anson celebrates the Statue of Liberty, another symbol of freedom. Courtesy The Skirball Cultural Center; photo by Susan Einstein

Sylvia Plotkin Judaica Museum
3310 North 10ᵗʰ Avenue
Phoenix, AZ 85013
602-264-4428

Supported by a twelve-thousand-volume library with books on Judaic studies, art, and history, the Sylvia Plotkin features Jewish art and ceremonials from 1600 C.E. to the present, including Israeli archeology items.

The Temple Museum of Religious Art
26000 Shaker Boulevard
Beachwood, OH 44122

The oldest remaining Jewish presence in the Cleveland area, this museum has antiques from Israel and ritual objects from Jewish communities around the world.

The United States Holocaust Memorial Museum
100 Raoul Wallenburg Place SW
Washington, DC 20024-2150
202-488-0400

Chartered by a unanimous Act of Congress in 1980, this is America's national institution for the documentation, study, and interpretation of Holocaust history, and it serves as the country's official memorial to broaden public understanding of the history of the Holocaust through exhibitions, public understanding of the history of the Holocaust through exhibitions, collections, research, publications, and a variety of programs.

The William Breman Jewish Heritage Museum
1440 Spring Street NW
Atlanta, GA 3039-1661
404-873-1661

Dedicated to collecting, preserving, studying, and interpreting the history and culture of Atlanta's Jewish community.

Yeshiva University Museum
2520 Amsterdam Avenue
New York, NY 10033
212-960-5390

Noted for its fine collections of Jewish ceremonial objects, rare scrolls and books, photographs and fine arts, and even scale models of historic synagogues.

29

The Jewish Tree of Life

11 Branches of Judaism

God knows that the best synagogue is the human heart.
—Hasidic saying

The Queens-Midtown Tunnel was like a *Star Trek* transporter that beamed you instantaneously into a different world. With it, the suburban plain magically turned into a metropolis that was anything but plain: skyscrapers, marquees, people of every shape and color coming from or going to what I imagined to be an endless parade of activities, some good, some bad, all real.

My fifth-grade class hopped onto a bus early one morning in front of our school in Westbury, Long Island. About forty minutes later we were in Manhattan, heading toward the American Museum of Natural History. Two dozen fifth-grade faces pressed against the windows as if seeing this exotic island for the very first time and some of what we saw did indeed look foreign: from aproned hotdog vendors and mini-skirted secretaries, to sari-wrapped Hindus and dark-coated Hasids.

A boy named Wayne turned to me and asked, "Is that a Jewish rabbi over there?"

"Well," I joked, "it ain't a Christian rabbi!"

Wayne ignored my lame attempt at humor.

"Could be a rabbi," I said. "But actually they're just called Hasidim."

"How come you don't dress like that?" Wayne asked.

I looked back out at the man, with the dark trousers, long black coat, big black hat under which the long sidecurls hung out. "Because I'm normal," I wanted to say—but thought better of it. As the only Jew in class, I didn't want to make it any harder on myself than it already was. While there was no

American branches: Conformist and conventional to some, extreme and extraneous to others, but real and relevant to those who are true to their beliefs. Here, Jews in Manhattan take time off from work to pray in a local synagogue. Courtesy *The Jewish Week*, New York

outward prejudice in my school, and while I suffered no defeats or discriminations because of my religion, it was still tough at times because there were always so many explanations to make. The problem was that I never felt qualified to make them. My Conservative Jewish education and home life did not prepare me to discuss the Jewish holidays or Jewish history—let alone what the hasidic people were all about.

Before this I hadn't had a single question about the so-called branches of Judaism. It didn't affect me. Besides, I thought there were only three. After Wayne, I became a little more curious—and alot more confused. While I knew the Hasidim were not my cup of tea, when I visited a Reform synagogue and saw how *they* did things, that didn't seem entirely right to me either.

So thank you Wayne, wherever you are. You began my never-ending quest for "branch knowledge," one which I have pursued to the point where I discovered more than I intended, perhaps too much for comfort. But then again, one thing I learned is that we're *all* Jews if indeed we want to believe we are.

"The present day in Judaism means 1800 onward," says Herman Wouk in *This Is My God.* "That was when the enlightenment struck the ghetto; the enlightenment, that bolt which shattered old Jewry into the boil of parties it is today. Writing the tale of Judaism after 1800, one must write *The Iliad,* or one must be brief as a telegram."

Here, then, for Jewish and non-Jewish Waynes across the land, is my telegram.

Conservative   Conservative Judaism strives to embrace Jewish observance, bringing open-mindedness to a serious, critical evaluation of sacred texts, and a positive outlook on modern culture. While Conservative Judaism holds forth that the laws of the Torah and Talmud are of divine origin, there is a human element that requires modern scholarship—even if that means considering the influence of other ideas and cultures. Conservatives also believe that God's will is made known to humanity through revelation in many ways and that it can happen even today. Among Conservative innovations over the years are family seating in the synagogue, the freedom to drive to synagogue on the Sabbath, and major prayerbook reforms.

Humanistic Judaism   A nontheistic alternative to more traditional Judaism that affirms a "human centered philosophy combining rational thinking with a celebration of Jewish culture and identity." Established in 1963, Humanistic Judaism embraces Jewish history and culture while acknowledging the power and responsibility all humans have in shaping their own lives, independent of supernatural authority.

Jewish Renewal   A movement that fosters a renewed encounter with God and an understanding of Jewish history as a series of such renewed encounters, particularly at times following crises during which God or belief in God has been seriously obscured. Jewish Renewal seeks to rekindle a Judaic spark, to nurture communities that "dance and wrestle with God," and to assist in the spiritual growth and healing of people and societies. In Jewish Renewal, men and women are equal partners in shaping the future of Judaism, those who are sometimes dispossessed (such as gays and converts) are welcomed, and other spiritual paths, such as Buddhism and Sufism, are respected.

Jews for Jesus   Apparently, it began as a slogan, became a movement, and is now an international organization whose purpose is to "proclaim the message that Jesus is the Messiah of Israel and the Savior of the world." By their own estimates, there are between 25,000 and 60,000 Jews for Jesus in the United States. When asked about the contradictions of being Jews who believe in the deity of Jesus, they typically say that Christianity is a Jewish religion, that the entire messianic concept is rooted in Judaism, and that all the first Christians were Jews who never renounced their Jewishness. (Mainstream Judaism does not recognize Jews for Jesus as being Judaism in any way. Mainstream Judaism maintains that those who believe that redemption from sin can come only through a commitment to Jesus as the son of God are not Jews but Christians.)

Messianic Judaism   To a great degree indistinguishable from Jews for Jesus, Messianic Jews believe that God chose the Jewish people to bring His knowledge, standards, grace, and power of forgiveness and redemption to the world through the Messiah. A Messianic Jew is one who is Jewish by birth and accepts that Yeshua of Nazareth (Jesus) is the long-awaited Messiah. Messianic Jews believe that the Bible and the New Testament comprise the complete, infallible, and literal word of God, and they base their faith and practice on the life of Yeshua and his disciples.

Orthodox   The unifying feature among all Orthodox Jews is an unfailing belief in the written and oral laws and practices of the Torah. Like the terms Conservative and Reform, Orthodox is a rather new invention; in the past, you either were religious or you weren't, differing from your religious neighbors only in terms of how observant you were. Today, even within Orthodoxy there are several movements, including the Hasidic and Yeshiva movements. The two most important features of Orthodox Judaism are that the Torah is the precise word of God that does not represent any human influence, and that it is appropriate to ask what God requires of us only if we are willing to look for the answer among the laws, values, and narratives He gave us.

Reconstructionism   Puts forth the idea that Jewish tradition must be reconstructed by each generation to reflect new understandings about our world and the world of our ancestors. Founded in 1968, Reconstructionism strives to find ways to enable American Jews to live fully in two cultures—American and Jewish—by adapting and embracing rational thought and believing in the power of nature and the universe over more traditional concepts of God. Reconstructionist synagogues are known for their creativity, experimentation, and egalitarian approach to religious life and learning.

Reform   Reform Jews believe that, as heirs to the vast body of beliefs and practices embodied in the Torah, Jews are in fact created in God's image and dedicated to the improvement of the world. But Reform Jews also recognize that it is a heritage that has evolved over the centuries, capable of evolution and reform. It does not demand uniformity of belief or practice among all Jews for them to be good Jews. It is important to study the traditions but not necessarily to follow those that have little or no meaning for us today. Among the reformed traditions are the option of not wearing yarmulkes in temple and broader rules of who may be considered a Jew.

Of the Other 603 Commandments

In addition to the ten commandments which Moses brought down from Mt. Sinai, Jews throughout the ages have been required to follow more than six hundred others mentioned in the Torah and the Talmud. Of these 613 commandments quite a few are specific to the needs, understandings, beliefs, and sensibilities of the times in which they were written and seem rather archaic or unnecessary today. On the other hand, it is not unusual to find quite a few of enormous understanding and sensibility even for today, which is a reflection of Judaism's universal devotion to charity, benevolence, the sanctity of life, justice, and other positive attributes. So, of the other 603, here are ten we all need to remember, and ten most of us might just as soon forget.

Ten to Remember

1. Honor the old and the wise.
2. Do not break your word, even without an oath.
3. Do not deny charity to the poor.
4. Do not plant an entire field without leaving corners for the poor.
5. Do not hesitate to save the life of a person in danger.
6. Do not destroy houses of worship or holy books.
7. Do not destroy fruit trees, even in time of war.
8. Do not refuse to help a man or an animal collapsing with burden.
9. A judge is never to commit unrighteousness.
10. A judge is not to favor or be partial to a litigant.

Ten to Forget

1. Do not lend to another Jew with interest.
2. Do not curse a ruler.
3. Do not make figures of human beings.
4. Women should not wear men's clothing.
5. A violator must marry the virgin or maiden he has violated.
6. Do not wear a mixture of wool and linen.
7. Do not shave your head.
8. Do not eat bread baked by non-Jews.
9. Kings must write a copy of the Torah for themselves.
10. Do not tell tales.

Synagogue 2000   More of a think tank than an actual branch at the moment, Synagogue 2000 is a transdenominational organization dedicated to helping synagogues plan for the future in order to meet the changing needs of Jews in America. Funded by grants, the group currently is in partnership with sixteen synagogues across the country, which are working with materials prepared by Synagogue 2000 to determine how the visions will be reached. The synagogues convene once a year "to dream together about how to get where we all want to go."

Traditional Judaism   Not really a separate branch as much as an attempt to bring as many Jews as possible closer to an open-minded, observant Jewish lifestyle. Traditional Judaism used to be called Conservadox because it is somewhat a branch of Conservatism with a strong philosophical bent toward Orthodoxy. Those who adhere to Traditional Judaism try to be Orthodox but with a leniency the truly Orthodox would not accept, embracing as they do some minor compromises in customs and lifestyle.

Universal Judaism   An embryonic theologic movement that is closer to modern Humanism than it is to the other traditional branches. Its focus and goal is globalism; Universal Judaism strives to recognize, adopt, and share the insights that people throughout the entire global village can effectively use to celebrate life. The movement has a framework for experiencing a Jewishness that is at once original and inclusive of other ideals.

30

Miracle Days

A Refresher Course in 6 Major
Jewish Holidays and Festivals

I have forty-two thousand children. And not one comes to visit.
—Mel Brooks as the Two Thousand-Year-Old Man

Holidays and festivals do a lot more than remind us of the miracles and misfortunes of Jewish history. They also give us a good excuse for battling the Long Island Expressway.

These days, with families spread so wide and responsibilities taking up so much time, many look forward to the Jewish holidays simply as ways to plan our far-too-infrequent family reunions (not to mention the licensed overindulgence on good food). Sometimes, too, holidays enable us to return to at least a few of the traditions and customs we may have lost along the way. Not every Jewish family in America keeps a kosher home or has a mezuzah on every doorpost. Not every Jewish family goes to temple more than twice a year. Many of us still do get married under a chupah and have a bris and then a bar mitzvah for our sons (and a bat mitzvah for our daughters), but often that's about it. Ignoring customs and traditions does not make us less Jewish, but stealing a moment or two of that old time religion can make us feel good—and feeling good is as much a Jewish tradition as thanking God.

Holidays are easy to steal, particularly since they were ours to begin with.

"It has been said that if all Jewish houses of worship were to close, Jewish religious life would continue intact, because the religious life would be sustained in our homes," wrote Rabbi Morris N. Kertzer in *What Is a Jew?*, "but if Jews stop practicing Judaism in their homes, the synagogues by themselves would not be able to sustain Jewish commitment for more than a generation." Just what constitutes practicing is ripe for a little debate: the way we live our lives or how many sets of dishes we own?

This is not to say that a family that previously kept its Jewishness in its heart instead of its kitchen would not enjoy and appreciate relearning the customs and traditions their great- and great-great-grandparents subscribed to without even thinking about it. So much of it is fascinating stuff. For instance, what is the purpose of *kashrut* (keeping kosher)? There seem to be many reasons, much of it having to do with compassion, such as to limit the number of animals a Jew is permitted to eat, to eat animals that were slaughtered in as painless a way as possible, to avoid celebrating the shedding of blood, to instill self-discipline. Why are Jewish males circumcised? It is a pact between the son and God that he will never be anything but Jewish. Some Jewish philosophers have suggested that God gave us the useless foreskin to teach us that we have to work to try to make an imperfect world a little more perfect.

What about the *chupah*? Originally it was an enclosed chamber for the consummation of marriage, or to symbolize that what once was two lives apart becomes one life together. The stomping on the wine glass? There have been several explanations. One is that the noise of the shattering glass scares away evil. Another is that it represents the desire for the marriage to last until all the pieces come back together. A third is that it is the only destructive act in a constructive celebration, to remind everyone that life, like the glass itself, is a fragile thing.

The mezuzah? Inside each one is a piece of handwritten parchment with Hebrew text from the Bible. In Deuteronomy, we are commanded to "write the words of God upon our doorposts" as a constant reminder of our commitment. Any reason for a bar mitzvah, beyond a glorified thirteenth birthday party? It actually goes back only about five hundred years and is said to derive from the story of Abraham, who became a man at age thirteen when he realized the idols his father built and worshiped were worthless stone carvings and he found the courage and the words of wisdom to tell him so.

Like the faith itself, Jewish holidays and festivals are celebrations of life. Often, they give a more immediate sense of belonging, a fuller sense of pride, than certain other customs and traditions. Judaism also is an embracing faith, a forgiving faith, and those who have stayed away, or who have forgotten, or merely wander in and out of their own religious convictions, can easily take part in and appreciate any or all of the holidays and festivals. All it takes is a good ear for some great stories, and a hearty appetite. For them, here's a miracle days summary.

Rosh Hashanah   The Jewish New Year. The birth of the world. Judgment day. Our acknowledgment of God as King and Redeemer. For non-religious Jews, a day to leave work early without guilt. On this day, Jews commemorate God's greatest gift to the world—its very creation—and we pray that we should all be inscribed in the Book of Life for the coming year. The shofar, a ram's horn, is blown by the rabbi to acknowledge the Creator, to remind us that we are his to be judged, and to signify the beginning of a ten-day period of spiritual self-evaluation. The ram's horn is used because it reminds us of the story of Abraham and Isaac. God commanded Abraham to sacrifice his son Isaac as a sign of his devotion, but as Abraham was about to do so, God stopped him and told him to sacrifice a ram instead. Many American Jews celebrate Rosh Hashanah. Typically, it is one of two days (the other being Yom Kippur) on which many temples see more of their congregants than any other day. After services, we go home to have festive meals. One fine and lasting tradition is to begin the meal by dipping an apple in honey in hopes of a sweet year for all.

Yom Kippur   The Day of Atonement. The holiest day of the year. A shot at redemption. A day when we fill ourselves with the knowledge of the goodness of life while virtually starving to death at the same time. It is said that we fast on Yom Kippur to emulate the angels who do not eat, drink, wash, or do anything to reduce their humility for being in heaven. Of course, humans have to do a lot more than angels, such as open the front door when the cat wants to go out, or use toilet paper—yet these are some of the things that are not allowed on Yom Kippur (at least in Orthodox homes). For the ten days before this most holiest of holidays, we have been repenting and we have been judged. On this day, we receive our judgment. The evening before is always met with a huge feast. This is meant to give us the strength to make it through the following day without food. After the meal there is a temple service. Jews make peace with their neighbors, with God, and with themselves. The cantor sings the Kol Nidre, which absolves us of unkept vows in the previous year while asserting our desire to keep all our vows for the new one. The shofar is blown once more and we are free to begin the new year with open hearts and minds.

Sukkot   The harvest festival. The Feast of the Tabernacles. A time of joy. A homecoming. Thanksgiving. A truly festive holiday, Sukkot commemorates the joy the people of Israel felt in being protected by God while wandering in the desert after escaping Egypt. The nine-day festival is renowned for its use of the sukkah, which means covering, symbolizing the thatched huts the Israelites used throughout the desert. Many Jews who celebrate Sukkot begin building sukkahs the day after Yom Kippur. Meals are eaten in the sukkah, and thanks is given for the fruits of the harvest. Typically, the sukkah is decorated with apples, pears, grapes, pumpkins, corn, leaves, and branches. The last day, Simchat Torah, marks the completion of the reading of the Torah for the new year. Sukkot brings us closer to God and reminds us how dependent we are to Him, to nature, and to each other.

Chanukah   The Festival of Lights. The day of a thousand miracles. The holiday of a million spellings. Unfortunately Chanukah has reached mall-class status in less than half a century, at least in America, because of its proximity to Christmas. At its best, Chanukah (or Hanuka, Hanukah, or Hanukkah) gives Jewish children something to look forward to in the cold, dark days surrounding the winter solstice when all their gentile friends are enjoying celebrations with gaily decorated trees, blinking lights, and big fat men in red suits. At its worst, Chanukah becomes an annual rite of keeping up with the Joneses. Still, it does have meaning and, despite its minor standing in the Jewish calendar, the story of Chanukah is among the best known by young Jews, no matter how religious they are. It concerns the tale of Judah the Maccabee, whose small army of freedom fighters defeated the Greeks, who were set on destroying them and their holy temple. Judah's victory was nothing short of a miracle. His first task was to fix, clean, and rededicate the temple (Chanukah means dedication). They had only one jar of oil, which should have lasted for one day, to light the candles. It lasted for eight. This was a miracle indeed, and every year since then Jews around the world have been celebrating these miracles and the resilience that went along with them, as well as the spirit, the faith, and the dogged determination to avoid outside influences (which is why putting up Christmas trees and stockings in Jewish homes "for the sake of the kids" is a particularly foolish thing to do). The dreidels we spin on Chanukah have Hebrew letters on them standing for the words *Nes Gadol Haya Sham,* meaning, "A great miracle happened there." Little known is Chanukah's celebration of women. The women with Judah's freedom fighters were equally resilient. According to one legend, the maiden Judith, a beautiful widow, slipped into the tent of the Greek army's top general, seduced him, beseeched him to sleep, and then cut off his head, forcing the army to retreat.

Purim   The festive festival. The story of Esther. The Jewish Halloween. Typically festive as Chanukah can be, traditionally Purim is an even bigger deal, celebrating Esther's rescue of the Jews of Persia from the wicked Haman's diabolical plans to annihilate them. Therefore, like

Chanukah, it is also very much a celebration of women. Haman was the evil advisor to the King of Persia, who was angered at the entire Jewish people because a man named Mordechai refused to bow to him. During Purim, we retell the story of Esther from a scroll called the Megillah. In temple and home celebrations, when the name Haman is uttered, children are allowed, indeed encouraged, to make as much noise as they can, often with little noisemaking toys. In some religious homes, schools, and communities, children dress up as characters from the Purim story. There is much merrymaking, eating, and drinking. Tradition commands Jews to give gifts to the poor and food to a friend. *Hamantashen* is the food of record—a three-cornered pastry filled with fruit or poppy seeds representing Haman's hat. The word Purim is derived from the word *pur*, meaning lot; Haman chose lots to decide on which day he would destroy the Jews.

Passover   The holiday of redemption. The celebration of freedom. The birthday of the Jewish people. At the Passover Seder, Jews retell the story of the Hebrew slaves in Egypt and of Moses, who demanded that Pharaoh let his people go. Pharaoh refused, and God unleashed a series of plagues on Egypt. Still, Pharaoh refused to set them free. So, as a final plague, God sent his Angel of Death to slay the firstborn male of each Egyptian household. The Hebrews put lamb's blood on their doorposts as a signal to the Angel of Death to *pass over* their houses. Pharaoh suffered the death of his own son, and finally freed the slaves. But once they were free, he changed his mind and sent his army after them. God, working through Moses, parted the Red Sea, allowing the Hebrews to cross, but not Pharoah's soldiers. The first commandment ("I am the Lord thy God, who brought you out of the land of Egypt...") is the story in a nutshell, and also the story of Passover. Exodus, the First Book of Moses, is the unabridged version, and *The Ten Commandments* with Charlton Heston and Yul Brynner is the Hollywood version. At the traditional Passover Seder, food and wine are used in many creative ways to commemorate hardships or evoke emotions associated with the story. Bitter herbs remind us of the bitterness of slavery; eating matzoh signifies the haste with which the Hebrews left Egypt; *charoses* (a mixture of chopped apples and nuts) are meant to resemble the mortar used by the Hebrews to build Pharoah's Egyptian cities. Nutshelled, unabridged, or glitterized, it is one of the greatest stories ever told, and one of the best holidays around.

There are many additional holidays and celebrations, most of which are minor, but no listing of Jewish customs would be complete without special

In Other Words

Most of us know what these twenty-five words refer to—but not what they actually mean!

• *Aliya*   Hebrew for calling up. Refers both to the reading of blessings over the Torah in synagogue, and to Jewish immigration to Israel.

• *Anti-Semitism*   Though Semites were descendants of Shem, one of Noah's three sons, the term has been used since the tenth century to denote a hatred of all Jews. In modern linguistics, Semite refers to people who have phonetic and grammatical similarities, which means that both Jews and Arabs are Semites.

• *Bar Mitzvah*   Hebrew for son of the commandment, the designation given to Jewish boys when they become adult members of the Jewish community at age thirteen.

• *B'nai B'rith*   Hebrew for sons of the covenant. The organization that took this as its name was founded in New York City in 1843 and now has more than 350,000 members in the United States alone.

• *Bris*   Hebrew for covenant. A Jewish baby boy's circumcision, whereby both father and son make a covenant with God to follow His laws and commandments.

• *Cantor*   In Hebrew the word is *hazan,* which is a servant of the synagogue, but since the nineteenth century, the word cantor, meaning singer and borrowed from several languages, has been used to describe the synagogue's song and hymn leader and interpreter.

• *Haftarah*   Hebrew for conclusion. Refers to one of several sections from one of the biblical books of prophets, which are read after the Torah portions on the Sabbath and during festivals, including bar mitzvahs.

• *Haggadah*   From Hebrew for to tell. Refers to the book used on Passover to recount the story of the exodus from Egypt of the freed Hebrew slaves.

• *Hasid*   Hebrew for pious man. Hasidism originated in Poland in the eighteenth century.

• *Hillel*   The organization designed for Jewish college students was named after a first century B.C. Jewish scholar and rabbi who founded a school known as the House of Hillel.

• *Jew*   From the Hebrew for Yehudi, meaning Judean, which was a member of the tribe of Judah shortly after the death of King Solomon.

• *Kabbalah* Hebrew for tradition. Refers to all Jewish mystical beliefs, traditions, practices, and stories.

• *Klezmer* Yiddish for musical instrument. Refers to Eastern European Jewish folk music and the musicians who play it.

• *Kosher* Hebrew for fit. Refers to food that is ritually pure.

• *Menorah* Hebrew for candelabra. Primarily known today as a lantern used on Hanukah with nine candles, but in ancient times it was the name of the golden seven-branched lantern used in every temple all year long.

• *Messiah* Hebrew for anointed one. It originally referred to high priests, kings, and other special individuals, but later came to mean the divinely chosen Redeemer.

• *Mezuzah* Hebrew for doorpost. A tiny container in which is kept a scroll of parchment, onto which is written a portion from Deuteronomy.

• *Rabbi* Hebrew for my master. Reserved for men—and now women—who are competent to decide questions of Jewish law and lead the Jewish community, and ordained to do so.

• *Shiva* Hebrew for seven, referring to the seven days of mourning for the deceased by close relatives.

• *Tallis* Hebrew for prayer shawl. Long, rectangular shawl made of silk or wool, with a blue or black stripe and fringes on both ends, which are to remind Jews of all the commandments of the Lord.

• *Talmud* Hebrew for teaching or instruction. The most authoritative source of Judaism, comprised of the Mishnah (code of laws) and the Gemara (an elaboration on the Mishnah).

• *Torah* Hebrew for law. The Five Books of Moses.

• *Tzedakah* Many think it means charity, but it is really a Hebrew word meaning righteousness or justice. Helping others is a Jewish tradition born of a sense of duty, not pity.

• *Yarmulke* The specific origin of this word is unknown, although it likely derives from words in several Eastern European languages meaning small hat, raincoat, or rain. The skullcap worn by men in synagogue and by very religious Jewish men at all times.

• *Zionism* Coined in the 1890s, it means the desire to return to Zion, the poetic name for Palestine.

Sabbath ritual: A Jewish-American family holding onto tradition, and passing it down. Courtesy The Museum of the Jewish Family

and hallowed mention of the Sabbath. God rested on the seventh day, and so then must we. The fourth commandment decrees it. Time is precious, time is sanctified, time must be treated with respect, and the Sabbath gives us the means to honor, sanctify, and respect time, which after all is also among God's greatest gifts to mankind. Sabbath begins at sunset each Friday and lasts until sunset on Saturday. The Sabbath meal is a special meal. The day is one on which all Jews are urged to commune with God. And while it may not say it in the ten commandments, it is also the perfect day to spend with your family. God likes that, too.

31

Ferklemp, Bothered, and Bewildered

The 33 Most Popular Yiddish Words

I really do not speak Yiddish. Ah—maybe a bisl.
—Colin Powell

Several years ago Mary Tyler Moore was a presenter at a televised awards ceremony and, after being introduced, she strode to the podium, took a breath, looked at the audience, and said to the world, "I'm so *ferklemp!*"

That was Mary. MTM. Mary Richards. Laura Petrie. One of the loveliest *shikses* of prime time, and she spoke like a true *yenta*. Part of the reason, one can reasonably assume, was that she was happily married to a Jewish man (a Jewish doctor, no less), and may have come to love, through her husband's family, many of the marvelous, imminently expressive words of the Yiddish language. But even without marriage as a catalyst, it is the very expressiveness of these words that makes the language the frequent choice of Jews and non-Jews alike in many a private and public situation.

Yiddish is a mixture of Hebrew, German, and Slavic, and its origins can more or less be traced to central Europe over a thousand years ago. A few hundred years later, gaining more expressiveness with each generation of *kvetchers* and *tummlers,* it spread to other Eastern European communities and eventually became a Jewish language of its own. It is not Hebrew, which was and is the established language of Jewish prayer and all manner of religious ceremony. It is a separate language, although some of it has proven to adapt easily into American English because of how much fun we get out of using it. But in its entirety, it also has the capacity to die from disuse. In fact, its "death" has been reported time and time again.

Leo Rosten, author of *The Joys of Yiddish* and *Hooray for Yiddish,* called Yiddish the Robin Hood of languages. "It developed a phenomenal variety of comic uses, an extraordinary range of observational nuances, a striking skill in delineating psychological insight, and remarkable modalities of sarcasm, irony, paradox, and mockery."

It is a language Jews, even American Jews, used to be able to call their own, which was important in a new world where so many traditions and customs were beginning to disappear with each year of assimilation. But with tenements crowded with people of diverse ethnic backgrounds hearing those words daily, and with so many Jewish novelists, comedians, and TV writers coming out of those tenements to share them with everyone else, the joys of Yiddish were bound to spread well beyond familial borders. Now we have to share it with everyone. How many times have you heard Howard Stern call someone a *schmuck* on the air? How many times have you seen the word *schlemiel* in a review of a Woody Allen movie? If it is dying, it is the slowest death on record, thank God.

But sharing it is not a bad thing. First, it's something to be proud of, and second, everybody knows it's ours. We get a vicarious pleasure from hearing other people use it. A survey taken for this book reveals that there is a significant number of Yiddish words with which non-Jews are quite familiar. They are words Rosten termed Yinglish. But he last wrote about it in 1989 (he died in 1997), while Yinglish continues to be *shmeered* into the national tongue.

That is not to say that there aren't some significant misconceptions. Generally speaking, the most popular and well-understood Yiddish word among non-Jews, according to the survey, is *schmuck,* followed by *shmooze* and then *kvetch.* Most people seem to know that *schmuck* is commonly used derogatorily to refer to someone of a less than princely nature. Many people also know it is commonly regarded to mean penis—although it actually stems from a German word meaning ornament. (Incidentally, many are also aware of the penis connection to the words *schlong* and *putz* as well.)

Shmooze, meaning to talk or gossip, has become so common that many regard it as purely English. It has been described by non-Jews as meaning, among other things, the ultimate sales job or kissing *tuchis.*

Conversely, the most *mis*understood Yiddish words among non-Jews are *shlep* and *shnook. Shlep* is a verb, meaning to drag or pull, but many people think it means a jerk, a slob, or a klutz. One survey respondent thought it meant "to do menial work," while another was pretty sure *shlep* was one of the Three Stooges. A *shnook,* which is a meek, unassertive person, was variously described as "a little weasel," "the act of being cuddly," and "an eskimo" (probably by the same person who thought *shlep* was one of the Three Stooges).

So as long as we have to share the language, we might as well get to know which words (based on the survey) we can easily share with our non-Jewish brethren, and which words just make us all sound like *putzes*.

Bisl   A little bit. Not widely used anymore, especially in bagel stores, because no matter what language you use to ask for a *bisl* of butter, people who work there invariably *shmeer* on gobs of it (see separate entry for *shmeer*).

Boychik   Little boy. From the English word "boy" and the common Yiddish-German diminutive *chik*. Jack Gilford used to call Billy Crystal *boychik* on *Soap*. Declining in use. Our grandparents and great-grandparents used it much more frequently, although some non-Jews seem to like using it today to sound irreverent.

Bubee   A term of endearment. A Hebrew word meaning little doll or little grandmother but used to show affection for male friends, business associates, and clients (as in "Don't worry, *bubee,* I'll get you a guest shot on Letterman by next month"). Comic Jewish characters in many TV shows—Jack Carter types—were known to use it with more frequency than necessary. (*Bubele* is a variation used quite often.)

Bupkes   Almost nothing, or absolutely nothing. From the Russian word for beans. Usually meant to convey disgust, as in "You know what kind of bonus I got? *Bupkes* is what I got." It's just so much more expressive than "nothing," but can't really get you into trouble like some other expletives. There was an episode of *The Dick Van Dyke Show* where Rob had written a song called "Bupkes," which is exactly what the song was about. (On the show, it became a hit on the radio.) In *Rocky*, Sylvester Stallone's dog was named Bupkes.

Chutzpah   Gall, presumptiousness, brashness—although it is sometimes used as a compliment. It comes from a Hebrew word meaning audacity. Used with equal aplomb and effectiveness by Jews and non-Jews alike. Rosie O'Donnell uses it. Alan Dershowitz, who used it as a title of his book, calls it "boldness, assertiveness, a willingness to demand what is due, to defy tradition, to challenge authority, to raise eyebrows."

Dreck   Worthless junk. From the German word for excrement. Sounds like what it is. "That exhibit was *dreck.*" Someone in the survey thought it meant coffee grounds, presumably after the coffee is made, in which case it isn't entirely incorrect. Someone else thought it meant taking a long trip, which, depending on whom you are with, could also be accurate.

Farmisht   Mixed up and confused (at least temporarily). From the German to mix or blend. When your grandmother calls you Jack even though your name is Joel and she calls your sister Renée even though her name is Irene, it's because she's a little *farmisht*.

Ferklemp   Bewildered. Nearly interchangeable with *farmisht* (as well as with certain other words like *farblunjet* and *farshteist*). Many people seem to think *ferklempt* is a more serious bewilderment, as opposed to a mild bewilderment.

Gelt   Money. From the German for money. Money is money. The first time I bought a car, in 1980, the salesman, who was from an Italian background, finished his pitch by saying, "Just give me the *gelt* and we're all done."

Gevalt   A frustrated, annoyed exclamation meaning, "Oh God, oy vey, oh no, darnit!" It's from the German word meaning a force or a power. Several writers have put it into the mouths of non-Jewish characters to make them sound like non-Jewish characters trying desperately to say something Jewish.

Goy   Anyone who isn't Jewish. Interestingly, it's from a Hebrew word meaning nation. It's not really derogatory, but sometimes it comes out that way, especially when said with little interest in or patience for the person or persons about which it was being said (not uncommon among close-knit, unassimilated immigrants). Most non-Jews know what it means and take no offense, particularly today where it is used mostly in jest—frequently by the goys themselves. A male goy is a *shaygets*, which is not well known among non-Jews, and a female goy is a *shiksa*, which *is* well known.

Kibitz   To joke around or tease. From the German, closely related to busybody. Has become quite English. "What a *kibitzer*." "Will you quit *kibitzing* around and put your hands back on the steering wheel?" Has also been thought of as sticking your nose in other people's business, which might be the case if the kibitzer is a real *nudnick*.

Kvetch   To complain. From the German word for squeezing, because it originally was used to describe, for instance, how you would want to *kvetch* out a few dollars for a vacation. Now it means to complain incessantly about not being able to do that. A person who *kvetches* is a *kvetcher*. A *kvetcher* who is in the process of complaining is *kvetching*.

Maven   An expert or connoisseur. From the Hebrew word for understanding. No one thinks twice when they see it in a newspaper or magazine describing someone with a particular expertise. "Advice *maven* Ann Landers got divorced yesterday...."

Mensch   An admirable, honorable, and very worthy person. A real man.

From the German word meaning person. One of those juicy words that allow you to say it the way you mean it. "He's a real *mensch.*" Technically there's nothing that forbids it from being used to describe a female, although *menschela* has become an acceptable alternative for female *mensches.*

Meshuggener   Crazy person, someone who acts in a bizarre or obsessive manner. Slight differentiation between male and female: *meshuggener* with an *r* means crazy man, and *meshuggeneh* with an *eh* means a crazy woman...although the more you try to explain it, the more *meshugge* you get.

Mishegaas   Craziness, madness, insanity. From the Hebrew word for insane. Not really too well known, but a great word nonetheless and can very well catch on, particularly since it describes most of what goes on in the world.

Nebbish   An unfortunate, inept loser. Someone who gets walked on by a wife, a boss, a neighbor, and even his own children is a *nebbish.* It used to also be an interjection meaning unforunately (with a *ch* at the end instead of an *sh*), as in "My car needs $2,000 worth of work, *nebbich.*" Many respondents know what it means, basically, using such terms as milquetoast or annoying little man to describe it. One thought it was a good deed and another thought it was an hors d'oeuvre.

Plotz   To faint with exhaustion, die from laughing, burst with frustration. Pretty well known, although some think of it in other closely related terms, such as to expel gases from the body or just sit down with a heavy thump. (Of course, there's always one in the crowd who thinks it's a Jewish burial place.)

Shlemiel   A fool, a clumsy, gullible victim. Said to come from the name Shlumiel, a character in the Book of Numbers, a general who was always losing his battles. A *shlemiel* trips, spills, falls, misplaces, mixes up, screws up, misspeaks. A lot of comics have made money doing it, a lot of politicans have inadvertently become comics doing it. Laverne and Shirley used it in the opening chant of their show, along with *shlimazel.*

Shlimazel   A loser, a luckless misfit. Often confused with *shlemiel, nebbish, shlump, shnook, shmendrick,* and *shmegegge,* although there are slight differences among them. *Shlimazel* is a combination of the German *shlimm,* meaning bad, and the Hebrew *mazel,* meaning luck.

Shlock   Cheap merchandise. From the German *schlag,* meaning a blow. Used quite freely to describe all manner of certain catalog items, TV shows, and gifts given to trade magazine editors at the end of press conferences.

Shmaltz   Corny. Overly sentimental mush. From the German word for melted fat. Lawrence Welk was the king of *shmaltz,* music division, while the Waltons held the distinction on TV.

Shmatte A cheap, rag-like piece of clothing. From the Polish word for rag. A growing favorite among many, including some talk-show hosts.

Shmeer To smear or spread. From the German meaning to grease or bribe. Used to have a much different meaning directly related to its bribe origins. People spoke of *shmeering* officials, for instance, which meant greasing their palms. Today it is just a Yiddishization of smear, as in putting cream cheese on a bagel.

Shmoe A nicer version of *schmuck.*

Shnoz Slang for nose. From the German for snout. Jimmy Durante was known as The Shnoz. It's been used to describe other celebrities as well, only not as affectionately.

Shtup Vulgar reference to the act of fornication. It's from a German word meaning to push.

Tchotchke Inexpensive trinket. Its Slavic origin means to play pranks. *Tchotchkes* can be good or bad, depending on where you buy them, who gives them to you, or what purpose they serve. It's rather an enigma, for it is both well understood and misunderstood. As many respondents as there were who knew what it meant, there were just as many who assigned such meanings as ballsy, grandpa, and Jewish maracas.

Tuchis Buttocks. From the Hebrew word meaning under or beneath. Radio talk-show hosts used to use it a lot to sound daring and vulgar without being either. Has a very specific pronunciation, which most non-Jews (and even many Jews) find difficult to master.

Tumel Multiple derivations generally meaning disorder, commotion, or craziness that can drive someone nuts. A *tummler,* which is a jokester, prankster, or clown, creates *tumel.*

Yenta A gossip or blabbermouth. Its origins are unknown, although it is generally believed to be a distortion of a French or Spanish name. Nobody wants to be called a *yenta.* The word got a reprieve in *Fiddler on the Roof* with the character Yenta the Matchmaker, who was much funnier and endearing than she was coarse. Still, enough people recognize its original intent to know they are being insulted when they're called a *yenta.*

Zaftig Plump, buxom, full-figured. From the German word for juicy. Relatively well known, although most non-Jews put the emphasis on the bosom, and not always with bad intentions.

Jewish Dozen

The twelve most popular "Jewish foods" in America:

1. *Bagels*   Most of the arguments about whether or not these flour and water wonders are a Jewish delicacy are quite genially conducted over coffee and bagels, and, after a while, it just doesn't matter anymore.

2. *Blintzes*   A fried, folded pancake usually filled with cheese, and if it isn't, it should be.

3. *Challah*   Large loaf of holiday or Sabbath bread that can be carved, ripped, or excavated.

4. *Chicken soup*   Chicken, water, veggies, seasonings as desired. Also known as Jewish penicillin.

5. *Gefilte fish*   A couple of different fish in one. Other than that, there isn't much to say about gefilte fish.

6. *Kasha varnishkes*   Buckweat and bow-tie noodles. Hard to keep on a fork, but good nonetheless. Colloquially, it is slowly taking the place of chopped liver, as in, "What am I, kasha varnishkes?"

7. *Kreplach*   Fried dumpling with meat that no one makes as well as Jewish grandmothers born between 1900 and 1915.

8. *Kugel*   Casserole of egg noodles, nutmeg, raisins. Popular chip-in item for holiday family get-togethers, as in "I'll bring the kugel." Also known as noodle pudding.

9. *Latkes*   Potatoes, onions, eggs, matzo meal. A Chanukah treat. Usually people make enough to feed an army—but it's always all gone by the end of the night.

10. *Lox*   Smoked salmon. Unimaginable without bagels to give it some sense of purpose.

11. *Matzo balls*   Eggs, chicken fat, matzo meal, salt and made almost exclusively for chicken soup. Arguments abound over whether or not they should be hard or soft.

12. *Stuffed cabbage*   Cabbage that's stuffed. Onions, celery, pepper, bread crumbs, and lots of other stuff that by rights should not equal such a messy and ordinary dish.

32

On Being Divinely Aware

What 20 People Say About
the Joys of Judaism

The Jews had light, and gladness, and joy, and honor.
—The Book of Esther

You don't have to be Jewish to love life, but it doesn't hurt, especially if you want loving life to be the focus of your existence. And not just loving life: loving love, too. And sex. And while we're at it, loving food, celebrations, animals, forgiveness.

Jewish author Henry Miller once wrote, "The aim of life is to live, and to live means to be aware, joyously, drunkenly, serenely, divinely aware." Judaism gives us the tools to tap into that awareness by showing us how sharing the planet with all living things and acting wisely on our natural urges makes living even more worthwhile.

There are many laws, beliefs, and customs that can make anyone proud to be a Jew—too many for any one discussion. But just scratching the surface is enough to get the ball rolling. For example, Jews are taught that making love to one's spouse is both a blessing and a requirement. Judaism also teaches us to avoid the cruel treatment of animals at all costs. Hunting for sport is forbidden. Are laws and commandments bendable? No question. When a life is threatened, Jews are directed to break any laws or commandments to save it, for saving a life is to save the world.

Furthermore, we are allowed to be imperfect. As humans, we are capable of losing sight of our righteousness from time to time, capable of sin. But as long as we recognize and acknowledge our sins and resolve not to lose sight again, we are forgiven and can go on. God knows our limitations, frailties, and weaknesses. We may have been created in His image, but we picked up a few weird instincts along the way. Writer and lecturer Dennis Prager explains, "Instead of denying or denigrating our animal-like activities, Judaism attempts to sanctify them through its laws of holiness....We can eat or engage in sexual relations just as animals do, or we can elevate the way we engage in these activities."

Speaking of food, we celebrate our heroes and victories, and remember our villains and defeats, in many joyful, family oriented rituals and feasts—which means that, while we may not harm animals needlessly we can murder our own digestive systems dozens of times each year. Nevertheless, the memories that are part of these celebrations provide at least a portion of the glue that has held us together for thousands of years.

Millions of words have been written on Judaism's love of love, life, latkes, and laughter. But the words that really count are the ones spoken by Jews in America today—rabbis, students, professionals, writers—who will bring American Jewry into the twenty-first century. Here, mixed in with some special guests and thoughts from beyond, are some of those words.

> The Hebrew word for life is *hayyim,* a plural form that tells us life is intrinsically diverse and dialectical, filled with ups and downs, twists and turns. Our lives consist of many lives. Because *hayyim* contains the two letters for God in its center bracketed by two letters that make the word for meaning, we further understand that a Jew lives both with inner spirit and outer passion.
>
> —Rabbi James S. Diamond,
> Center for Jewish Life, Princeton University

> Judaism and food: to me, the two are nearly synonymous. I was just talking with a Jewish colleague about the meals his grandmother used to prepare and both our mouths started to water.
>
> —Randy Danto, attorney and Internet correspondent

> In Judaism there is a blessing for everything life has to offer. We eat—we bless. We marry—we bless. We see a rainbow—we bless. One saying goes, It is a great mitzvah to be happy all the time.
>
> —Dr. Tzvie Zahavy,
> The Jewish Communications Network (www.jcn.com)

> Hate stirs up strife, but love covers all transgressions.
>
> —Proverbs 10:2

Judaism is very much a family oriented religion of the home, and so many holidays have specific and traditional foods, therefore the body and the spirit are nourished together.

—Ellen S. Goodrich, registered nurse,
Milledgeville, Georgia

And if our good fortune never comes, here's to whatever comes...

—From "To Life," in *Fiddler on the Roof*

Judaism regards sex as the cord that secures the union of two lovers for life: for shared strength, pleasure, and ease, and for the rearing of children.

—Herman Wouk, in *This Is My God*

When a man is in union with his wife in a spirit of holiness or purity, the Divine presence is with them.

—Nachmanides, thirteenth-century C.E. biblical scholar

Jewish comedy is the essence of Judaism to me, in a cultural sense, at least. Humor, provided by the likes of Mel Brooks, Bette Midler, Barbra Streisand, Alan King, Woody Allen, and too many others to mention, is one of the most meaningful things in life.

—Harley Diamond, attorney,
Housing Authority of New York City

God hath made me to laugh, so that all that hear will laugh with me.

—Genesis, 21. 6

The Jewish spirit, the Jewish soul, is the most important thing we have. I'm sure it is all we have, all that is worth having and living and struggling for.

—Rabbi Judah Magnes, educator, community and religious
leader in the early 1900s, and cofounder
of the American Jewish Committee

For Jews, the love of their life must be life itself, since life includes all of the precious people, moments, and *simchas* that we tend to cherish individually.

—Lyle Shemer, student, Jewish Student Union,
Syracuse University

Oh may your breasts be like clusters of the vine and the scent of your breath like apples and your kisses like the best wine.
                                        —Song of Songs 7:8–9

Bagels are doughnuts with a college education—and the college is probably Yeshiva.
                                        —Leo Roston, in *The Joys of Yiddish*

Man will be called to account in the hereafter for each pleasure he denied himself without sufficient cause.
                                        —Rav, Third-century C.E. Babylonian scholar

The beauty of Judaism is that it is a religion based on real world living, not pie in the sky living. Judaism encourages us to question. It even allows us to question the existence of God. Questioning allows thinking, and thinking is what the real world is all about. As far as I know, Judaism is the only major religion that allows us the privilege of questioning.
                                        —Micah Engbar, radio personality and producer, Maine

Judaism sees sexual relations as a legitimate source of pleasure and not only as a means of making babies....Our tradition also recognizes the legitimacy of our need for intimacy, for feeling loved and cherished, and for loving and cherishing in return.
                                        —Rabbi Harold Kushner, in *To Life:*
                                        A Celebration of Being Jewish and Thinking Jewish

Jews have devoted lots of time to investigating the world and seeking to acquire wisdom. Wisdom is a preoccupation, an ideal, an objective. It brings out the best of each individual. It says man is free to become whatever he wishes.
                                        —Moses Maimonides, Jewish philosopher

Food is like sex to a Jew. Do it first and think about it later.
                                        —Ilene Springer, health editor and columnist,
                                        Jewish Family and Life

Fill thy mouth with laughing, and thy lips with rejoicing.
                                        —Job, 8:21

Some societies seem as if they live to kill. By quite a distinctive contrast, Jews more or less kill to live. We do so figuratively, because of how wonderful a gift life is to us, and literally, when fear, jealousy, and ignorance require it for self-defense.

—Alan J. Berg, writer, Westbury, New York

I believe that within the majority of American Jews, Judaism does not have so much to do with a belief in God as it does a way of life. Jews share many values and ethics not found so universally among non-Jews. By virtue of the fact that we have survived so long, I feel it is incumbent upon each one of us to preserve our Jewish heritage and identity.

—Rick Dronsky, founder and executive director, Mosaic Outdoor Clubs of America, Miami Beach, Florida

A man has no better thing under the sun than to eat, drink and be merry.

—Ecclesiastes 8:15

One has only to read history to see that because of Judaism the world has become a more perfect and holy place. Through its teachings on life and the right to individual freedom, Judaism has done more good for the world than any other religion or philosophy.

—John David Scalamonti, former Catholic priest, author of *Ordained to Be a Jew.*

There is, it seems to me, something at the core of Judaism that causes and nourishes a deep sense of kinship, simply through *being* Jewish. There seem to be many levels on which Jews can connect. I have never met a Jew who I couldn't connect with on some level. Even the most secular Jews possess characteristics of camaraderie and belonging.

—Elizabeth Szaluta, Jewish Student Union, Syracuse University

The first time I visited Israel I was twenty years old. I remember climbing the dusty road to the Old City, wending my way throught he crowded and narrow streets. I remember standing in awe and thinking, I am here where Jews have stood for three thousand years. I closed my eyes, tilted my head back, touched the wall, and let the sun warm my face.

Herbert Ascherman Jr., professional photographer, Cleveland, Ohio

What Ten U.S. Presidents Said About the Jews

- *George Washington (1789–1797)*

May the children of the stock of Abraham, who swell in this land, continue to merit and enjoy the good will of the other inhabitants, while every one shall sit in safety under his own vine and fig tree, and there shall be none to make him afraid.

- *John Adams (1797–1801)*

The Hebrews have done more to civilize men than any other nation.

- *Thomas Jefferson (1801–1809)*

Moses had bound the Jews to many idle ceremonies, mummeries, and observances of no effect towards producing the social utilities which constitute the essence of virtue.

- *Ulysses S. Grant (1869–1877)*

I have long since believed that in spite of all the vigilance that can be infused in Post Commanders, that the Specie regulations of the Treasury Department have been violated, and that mostly by Jews and other unprincipled traders....The Jews seem to be a privileged class that can travel anywhere.

- *Benjamin Harrison (1889–1893)*

The Hebrew is never a beggar; he has always kept the law—life by toil—often under severe and oppressive civil restrictions.

- *Woodrow Wilson (1913–1921)*

Here is a great body of our Jewish Citizens from whom have sprung men of genius in every walk of our varied life; men who have conceived of its ideals with singular clearness; and led enterprises with spirit and sagacity....They are not Jews in America, they are American citizens.

- *Franklin Delano Roosevelt (1933–1945)*

This is a Protestant country, and the Catholics and the Jews are here on sufferance.

- *Harry S Truman (1945–1953)*

I am not Jewish, but if I were I would not be ashamed of it.

- *Dwight D. Eisenhower (1953–1961)*

I grew up believing that the Jews were the chosen people, that they gave us the high ethical and moral principles of our civilization.

- *Richard M. Nixon (1969–1974)*

Christ, if it weren't for me, there wouldn't be any Israel. They know that in Israel, Golda Meir knows that, even though they may not know it over here.

Conclusion

What Do All the Names Mean, Anyway?

Judaism, in certain ways, has been a series of chapters in an endless book. An epic, really. An epic so large that nobody would be able to keep it in their locker because it would be the size of a Hyundai. Why is it so large? Because is has over five thousand chapters, one for each year, and each chapter is divided into separate sections devoted to passion, terror, comedy, tragedy, farce, peace, mayhem....

The epic began, more or less, with a curious and wily little boy who knew that the ominous stone idols his father carved for a living could not control our destiny, as everyone, including the father, had thought. So the boy knocked down the idols one night to prove his point, and when his father asked the next morning what had happened, little Abraham said that one of the big idols got angry and broke all the little idols with a giant stick. That's when his father realized something was rotten in the land of Ur.

Among the many chapters that have been written since that big event are several starring other curious, wily little boys and girls. Not all of them have been Abrahams, but their courage and curiosity have been integral to the growth and strength of our faith. And while no one involved in the conception or production of this book is an Abraham of biblical proportions, we have tried to be a little curious and a little wily in the hope of building and strengthening pride in, or respect for, Judiasm among our readers. We have listed many people, some of whom have not been listed in other books of this nature, and we have covered many topics, some of which have not appeared in other similarly themed manuscripts. Collectively, and in the final analysis, this book may be light-years away from being one of the most important chapters in American Jewry, but it is a chapter nonetheless, and we are proud to have had the opportunity to contribute. We hope we have given our readers further license to *kvell.*

Even if we wanted to list every Jew in America, we could not. A large percentage are not even listed in temple membership logs, which would be the only way of creating such a list since the U.S. Census regards religion as a strictly optional category.

But that was never our intention anyway. Doing something like that would only pose more questions than we have the time or resources to try to answer. What if we were to list Fiorello La Guardia, for instance, the popular Mayor of New York City from 1933 to 1945, whose mother was Jewish? That would have required a discussion of who is and who is not really Jewish—and according to whom—a discussion we feel would contribute little to the major theme of this book. (La Guardia was raised as an Episcopalian, anyway.) How about Abbie Hoffman and Jerry Rubin? Had they been included, would we then not be prompted to probe the Jewish role in radical politics—a subject that would require a book if its own?

In any event, we did steer clear of most of the La Guardias and Hoffmans, and even people like Harrison Ford, who rarely if ever make mention of their religious upbringing or current beliefs. (Ford's mother was Jewish.) We concentrated instead (with some infamous exceptions) on those who have made significant contributions to American society and culture and have not necessarily kept their Jewishness a secret.

Indeed, there are some who say that American Judaism is the Judaism of the twenty-first century. If we have succeeded in producing a book that helps usher Judaism successfully into the next millennium, we will be more than gratified. There is a lot of cautious optimism out there about that. Noted sociologist J. Alan Winter, author of *Jewish Choices* and professor of sociology at Connecticut College, predicts there will be a relatively stable total Jewish population size, a growth in Jewish day schools, little if any further decline in observance of major Jewish holidays, more women rabbis, a continued hasidic presence but less modern Orthodoxy, a growing of Reform Judaism and a relative decline of Conservativism. Rabbi Jack Moline of the Agudas Achim Congregation in Alexandria, Virginia, says that while there will be a dwindling American-Jewish community, there will be new expressions of faith in American society. He also thinks that Israel's economy and technology will soar if war is avoided, that if it does, Jewish creativity will be breathtaking, and that many people will be attracted to Judaism as a result.

So where does that leave me? After all, as I've already shown in the Introduction, I have certain reservations with the organized portion of American Jewry. But despite that, as I have also explained earlier, I have never been one to need a shot of Jewish pride. I was born with it. Here's how I know. I was driving home from Walt Disney World with my family, where we did everything from Pirates of the Caribbean in the Magic Kingdom to Raiders of the Lost Ark at Disney/MGM. Halfway home my wife and I toyed with the idea of relocating to the Orlando area. We weighed the pros and cons. The kids in the back seat listened with growing interest. They could not believe that we might actually one day live in a place where they could swim all year long. Celia wanted to know if we could have a built-in pool. Kate wanted to know if friends from New Jersey could visit monthly. Dan wanted to know if he could go on Tower of Terror every day of his life. My wife, Bonnie, wanted to know if she could have a screened-in porch and a greenhouse. But what *I* wanted to know was if there'd be enough Jews around.

Other than Indiana Jones, that is.

BIBLIOGRAPHY

Allen, Steve. *Schmock-Schmock! The Inimitable Wit and Humor of Steve Allen.* Garden City: Doubleday, 1962.

The American Jewish Yearbook 1997. New York: The American Jewish Committee, 1997.

Anson, Robert Sam. *Exiles: The Unquiet Oblivion of Richard M. Nixon.* New York: Simon & Schuster, 1984.

Ausubal, Nathan. *Pictorial History of the Jewish People.* New York: Crown, 1954.

Bamberger, Bernard J. *The Story Of Judaism.* New York: The Union of American Hebrew Congregations, 1957.

Berger, Phil. *The Last Laugh: The World of the Stand-Up Comics.* New York: William Morrow, 1975.

Birmingham, Stephen. *The Rest of Us: The Rise of America's Eastern European Jews.* Boston: Little, Brown, 1984.

Bridger, David. *The New Jewish Encyclopedia.* West Orange, New Jersey: Behrman House, 1976.

Contemporary Authors. Detroit: Gale Research.

Cowan, Paul. *An Orphan in History.* Garden City: Doubleday, 1982.

Current Biography. New York: The H. W. Wilson Company, 1997.

Dimant, Max. *The Jews in America: The Roots and Destiny of American Jews.* New York: Simon & Schuster, 1978.

Epstein, Lawrence J. *Conversion to Judaism: A Guidebook.* Northvale, New Jersey: Jason Aronson, 1994.

Fischel, Jack and Sanford Pinker, eds. *Jewish-American History and Culture: An Encyclopedia.* New York: Garland Publishing, 1992.

Fleming, Thomas. *Liberty: The American Revolution.* New York: Penguin Group, 1977.

Furnas, J. C. *The Americas: A Social History of the United States, 1587–1914.* New York: G. P. Putnam's Sons, 1969.

Gellman, Marc. *Does God Have a Big Toe?* New York: Harper & Row, 1989.

Gould, Allan, ed. *What Did They Think of the Jews?* Northvale, New Jersey: Jason Aronson, 1997.

Greenberg, Hank. *Hank Greenberg: The Story of My Life.* New York: Times Books, 1989.

Greenberg, Reuben. *Let's Take Back Our Streets!* Chicago: Contemporary Books, 1989.

Gross, David. *The Jewish People's Almanac.* New York: Hippocrene Books, 1994.

Gross, David. *1,001 Questions and Answers About Judaism*. New York: Hippocrene Books, 1990.

Hadda, Janet. *Isaac Bashevis Singer: A Life*. New York: Oxford University Press, 1977.

Halberstam, Joshua. *Schmoozing: The Private Conversations of American Jews*. New York: Berkeley Publishing Group, 1997.

Hamby, Alonzo L. *Man of the People: A Life of Harry S Truman*. New York: Oxford University Press, 1995.

Hart, James D. *The Concise Companion to American Literature*. New York: Oxford University Press, 1986.

Howe, Irving. *World of Our Fathers*. New York: Harcourt Brace Jovanovich, 1976.

Jacobs, Louis. *The Book of Jewish Belief*. West Orange, New Jersey: Behrman House, 1984.

Jacobs, Sidney J. *The Jewish Word Book*. Middle Village, New York: Jonathan David Publishers, 1982.

Kanfer, Stefan. *A Summer World*. New York: Farrar Straus Giroux, 1989.

King, Alan and Chris Chase. *Name-Dropping: The Life and Lies of Alan King*. New York: Scribner, 1996.

Kushner, Harold. *To Life! A Celebration of Jewish Being and Thinking*. Boston: Little, Brown and Company, 1993.

Lester, Julius. *Lovesong: Becoming a Jew*. New York: Henry Holt and Company, 1988.

Malka, Victor, ed. *The Wisdom of Judaism*. New York: Abbeville Press, 1996.

Marcus, Jacob Rader. *The Jew in the American World*. Detroit: Wayne State University Press, 1996.

Mason, Jackie and Ken Gross. *Jackie, OY. Jackie Mason From Birth to Rebirth*. Boston: Little, Brown, 1988.

McBride, Joseph. *Steven Spielberg: A Biography*. New York: Simon & Schuster, 1997.

Miller, Merle. *Ike the Soldier: As They Knew Him*. New York: G P. Putnam's Sons, 1978.

Miller, Ruth. *Saul Bellow: A Biography of the Imagination*. New York: St. Martin's Press, 1991.

Monti, Ralph. *I Remember Brooklyn: Memories From Famous Sons and Daughters*. Secaucus, New Jersey: Birch Lane Press, 1991.

Morgan, Ted. *FDR: A Biography*. New York: Simon & Schuster, 1985.

Novak, William, and Moshe Waldoks, eds. *The Big Book of Jewish Humor*. New York: HarperPerennial, 1982.

Press, David P., and Elizabeth Kaplan. *Culture of America: Jewish Americans*. New York: Marshall Cavendish, 1995.

Rivers, Joan, and Richard Meryman. *Enter Talking*. New York: Delacorte Press, 1986.

Rosenberg, Roy A. *Everything You Need to Know About American Jews and Their History*. New York: Penguin, 1997.

Rossel, Seymour. *Let Freedom Ring: A History of the Jews in the United States*. West Orange, New Jersey: Behrman House, 1995.

Rosten, Leo. *The Joys of Yinglish*. New York: McGraw-Hill, 1989.

Scalamonti, John David. *Ordained to Be a Jew*. Hoboken, New Jersey: KTAV, 1992.

Schappes, Morris U. *The Jews in the United States*. Secaucus, New Jersey: Citadel Press, 1958.

Seltzer, Robert M. *Jewish People, Jewish Thought: The Jewish Experience in History*. New York: Macmillan, 1980.

Shenker, Israel. *Coat of Many Colors: Pages From Jewish Life*. Garden City, New York: Doubleday, 1985.

Silberman, Charles. *A Certain People*. New York: Summit Books, 1985.

Sloan, Irving J., ed. *The Jews in America 1621–1970*. Dobbs Ferry, New York: Oceana, 1978.

Smith, Bill. *The Vaudevillians*. New York: Macmillan, 1976.

Strassfield, Sharon, and Michael Strassfield. *The Third Jewish Catalog*. Philadelphia: The Jewish Publication Society of America, 1980.

Suhl, Yuri. *The Jews in America*. Danbury, Connecticut: Franklin Watts, 1972.

Suskin, Steven. *Opening Night on Broadway*. New York: Shirmer Books, 1990.

Werblowsky, R. J. Zwi, and Geoffrey Wigoder, eds. *The Oxford Dictionary of the Jewish Religion*. New York: Oxford University Press, 1997.

Wigoder, Geoffrey, ed. *The New Standard Jewish Encyclopedia*. New York: Facts on File, 1992.

Wouk, Herman. *This Is My God*. Garden City, New York: Doubleday, 1959.

FOR ADDITIONAL READING

In addition to the books in the bibliography there are literally hundreds of others that provide illuminating and thought-provoking lessons, ideas, and debates about Judaism and the Jewish people, in America and abroad, today and throughout history, both in highly entertaining and intellectually profound ways. Those mentioned below represent a small but intriguing and worthwhile sampling.

Celebration: The Book of Jewish Festivals, consulting editor Naomi Black (Middle Village, New York: Jonathan David Publishers, 1987). A source book, reference guide, and picture book of the history, rituals, practices, foods, and activities of the major Jewish holidays.

The Complete Book of Jewish Observance, by Leo Trepp (New York: Behrman House, Inc., 1980). A complete guide both for the practicing Jew seeking deeper understanding and newcomers to the faith seeking general understanding.

Jewish Literacy: The Most Important Things to Know About the Jewish Religion, Its People, and Its History, by Rabbi Joseph Telushkin (New York: William Morrow, 1991). Trends, concepts, and personalities of religious history, told in an entertaining narrative.

Messengers of God, by Elie Wiesel (New York: Random House, 1976). Biblical portraits and legends brought to life with great imagination and perceptive interpretations.

The Nine Questions People Ask About Judaism, by Dennis Prager and Joseph Telushkin (New York: Simon & Schuster, 1975). Straightforward answers for the intelligent Jewish skeptic.

Our Crowd: The Great Jewish Families of New York, by Stephen Birmingham (New York: Harper and Row, 1967). An insider's view of the rich Jewish upper class in New York of yesteryear.

Wanderings, by Chaim Potok (New York: Ballantine Books, 1978). A panoramic review of four thousand years of Jewish history, told in the style of a master storyteller.

Who Needs God?, by Harold Kushner (New York: Summit Books, 1981). A discussion of how religious commitment can make a difference in our lives.

ABOUT THE AUTHOR

Joel Samberg has written for *The New York Times, The Daily News, New Jersey Monthly, The New Manhattan Review, The Young Judaean,* and many other publications and has been a humor and opinion columnist for several newspapers. A native Long Islander, he is a graduate of Hofstra University, where he studied drama and journalism, and has also been involved in community theater and corporate communications. Joel now lives in Verona, New Jersey, with his wife and three children, and has just completed a novel in addition to a play called *Assorted Nuts at Passover, or the Night I Felt Like I Became the Last Real Jew Left in America.*